LifeScripts

LifeScripts

A Collection of Prose and Poetry

The Joslyn Center Writers

Thunderbird PRESS

LifeScripts
A Collection of Prose and Poetry
©2020 by The Joslyn Center Writers

Cover Design by Mark Gaulding
Background Cover Photo courtesy of Bruce Feagle
Book Layout and Design by Jean Giunta Denning
Feather pen clipart courtesy of netclipart.com

Published for The Joslyn Center Writers by
Thunderbird Press
P.O. Box 524
Rancho Mirage, CA 92270
thunderbirdpress@dc.rr.com

Library of Congress Control Number: 2020940980

The Joslyn Center Writers
    LifeScripts
    A Collection of Prose and Poetry
    ISBN: 978-0-9860149-9-4

Printed in the United States of America

With thanks
to our encouraging instructors,
Frances Noble
and
the late Dr. Joyce Wade Maltais

With love,

Linda Hemmingh

Foreword

September, 2020

AS I WRITE THIS, The Joslyn Center is in its 40th year serving seniors and older adults in the central Coachella Valley. As a community we are also facing one of the most challenging times in our history with a virus changing how we live our daily lives. The Joslyn Center is here to provide a space for seniors to socialize, make new friends, learn new things and build new lives. For many, after a lifetime of work and raising a family, The Joslyn Center offers the opportunity to relax, remain healthy, and do that "something I have always wanted to do." That's why this collection of writings from our Creative Writing and Writing Your Memoirs class is so special. The writings are an expression of newly discovered creativity for some, or the opportunity to enjoy an almost forgotten or long neglected talent. This collection represents the essence of why The Joslyn Center exists.

The class participants have come together, even in these unprecedented times, to share their stories, collaborate on this book, and deliver that kind of support that only a shared history and common interest can provide. Their talent is nurtured and a special community is built through this class and thought-shared inspiration among the members. Many of the writers have been working together in this class for over fifteen years with this book representing the third anthology of their work. The writers come from a varied background, yet have found community together.

I am honored to have gotten to know some of the authors and look forward to enjoying their work for years to come. I know you will enjoy their work as well, and will feel the sense of community, creativity, and support that has made this collection of writings possible.

—Jack Newby
Executive Director
The Joslyn Center

Preface

IT IS MY SINCERE PRIVILEGE to present *LifeScripts*, the newest collection of prose (short fiction and nonfiction) and poetry expressing experiences, imagination, hopes and dreams written from real life and fictional "life scripts" by The Joslyn Center Writers. *LifeScripts* follows on the footsteps of *SandScripts*, The Joslyn Center Writers' latest anthology published in 2012.

The authors represented in this collection are participants in the creative writing and memoir writing class at The Joslyn Center, Palm Desert, California. This diverse group of writers ranges in age from the fifties to the nineties. In retirement, their various backgrounds inspire their prose and poetry. Some have been writing all their lives; others have taken writing up as a new challenge. Several members of the group are completing their first novels and stories for publication, of which The Joslyn Center should be very proud. During the three years I was honored to lead the class, I was able to experience the excitement, growth and enthusiasm demonstrated each week as the class members shared and encouraged one another. The group is very close knit; some have been writing and meeting together at the Center for over fifteen years. To learn a little about the authors, please see their short biographies at the end of the anthology.

I would like to personally acknowledge the following persons for their roles in bringing *LifeScripts* to publication. Thank you, **Linda Hennrick**, for co-editing the book, for coming up with our chosen title . . . and especially for taking over the reins in leading the class. I look forward to hearing about the writers' future accomplishments; **Mark Gaulding**, for converting the manuscript into InDesign and for designing the cover; **Bruce Feagle**, for your beautiful cover photograph (see details below)* **Karoline Kessler**, for your graphic design expierence and your help in getting the finished product ready for print.

My thanks also go to members of The Joslyn Center staff . . . **Abel Becerra**, for arranging our meeting room each week, always with a smile; **Rebecca Ruffing**, Programs Chairman, for being so cooperative and encouraging to the creative writing/memoir class at the Center; and **Jack Newby**, Executive Director of The Joslyn Center, for your leadership providing this wonderful venue available to seniors in our community.

The Joslyn Center Writers hope you enjoy the excerpts in *LifeScripts* as much as we enjoyed creating them.

—Jean Giunta Denning
Coordinator and Co-Editor

* About the Cover: The cover background photo of the comet NEOWISE was taken on July 22, 2020 at Yucca Mesa, near Joshua Tree, about 45 miles north of the Coachella Valley in Southern California, by photographer Bruce Feagle, a noted photographer for both his film and print work (bruce.feagle@ thecreativemonster.com). Bruce photographed NEOWISE over several days and locations throughout Southern California. This comet is named after NASA's Near-Earth Object Wide-field Infrared Survey Explorer (NEOWISE) mission in March 2020 when it was first discovered. NEOWISE is considered the brightest comet visible from the Northern Hemisphere since 1997's Hale-Bopp. It is headed beyond the outer solar system, now traveling at a speed of 144,000 miles per hour, and will not return to the Sun for another nearly 7,000 years.

Contents

Nonfiction/Essays / 45

Nonfiction/Memoirs / 93

Continued ...

Nonfiction/Memoirs, Continued

Continued ...

Nonfiction/Memoirs, Continued

Continued ...

Nonfiction/Memoirs, Continued

Poetry / 277

Continued ...

Poetry, Continued

Fiction

A Little Ole Lady or a Little Ole Girl

—June Gaulding

MY DADDY MARK ASKS ME, "Are you a little ole lady or a little ole girl?" Well, sometimes I feel like both. Of course, I want to be a little ole girl. I am going to be fifteen years old in May. I am a typical Jack Russell Terrier with white hair and some light brown trim on my face and ears. Now I have grey hair on my face and ears. They say that goes with my age.

My name is Wallis. Let me tell you a little about myself. I remember back when I was about six weeks old in 2000, and I was in a cage in a San Diego pet store with other dogs, cats, mice, etc. At night it was pretty quiet with strange sounds from the different animals all around me. I tried to be brave because I am a terrier and not supposed to be scared. During the day there was a lot of action going on with people walking around looking at animals and talking a lot. Sometimes they came back and looked at me, but would walk away.

One day two men and an older woman walked up to me and said, "What a cute little Jack Russell Terrier puppy you are." I wagged my little tail as fast as I could. They talked to me for a while, but I didn't understand a word they were saying. Finally a boy who worked there took me out of the cage and put me into someone's arms. I was passed around to each one with a lot of "cooing and petting."

Upon going to the front of the store I began to get excited, as I had dreamed that maybe I would be going to a nice home as others have done. Yes, my dream came true. We left there with arms full of toys, food, collar, leash, and a puppy bed softer than mine here.

I was excited on the drive to my new home. One of the big decisions when arriving there was to give me a name. It seems that my family would be Daddy Mark, Daddy Steve, and Grandma. I have since changed her name to "Gammaw" because she has two grandchildren that call her Grandma Bug, and I have to be different. I understand the family takes turns naming their pets, and it was time for Daddy Mark to christen me with a name. Daddy Mark had studied the history of England's Duke and Duchess of Windsor (former King Edward VIII and wife, Wallis Simpson). He liked the Duchess' name, so he christened me Wallis. Maybe this means I am from a royal background. I can wish, can't I?

We lived in the San Diego house for a few years, and then I moved to Palm Desert with the family and had a big fenced-in yard and pool that I loved to run and, yes, swim in. I just loved doing this and could stay in the water chasing a ball for hours. Of course, I wasn't allowed, as I might get tired. You wanna bet?

In a few years I learned to share the yard with a little male street mutt they brought home from the pound to live in our home. They named him Chips. He was about five years younger, probably a combination of beagle hound and corgi mix. He was really cute, but I had to show him I was the "Alpha Dog" in this home. He learned to abide by this and stayed clear of me most of the time. They did bring another little stray black and white terrier (not a "JRT") named Spencer to live for a few months. He was cute but jumped on Chips and nearly killed him. I guess he felt threatened by another boy dog. They had to find another home for him.

We are living at my Gammaw's condo now, and I don't have a big yard to run around in like I did. Of course in my old age, as the family says, I have learned how to control this household. By now I know that "JRT" dogs have to be loud and act wild. I bark loudly when it is time for my meals twice a day. I even sit at the feet of whoever is eating at the table and look sad in hopes they will drop me a crumb. It doesn't hurt to beg! If there is an animal showing on the television I run up to the screen and start barking. I really get yelled at for this.

Yes, I still feel young at heart and love to run out the doggy door to the fenced-in patio and bark at any sound in my territory. I also run like crazy through the house when I feel like it and jump on the sofa or chairs. However, I do one thing that I am not proud of. Sometimes I do things that I get scolded for, and I go off and pout. I find a spot on the floor close by and leave a little messy pile. I don't know why I do it, except it lets them know I am still in charge. Yet, I get told at that time that I am a bad dog and shamed. I can't win!

Chips and I ate from bowls close to each other, sat on the sofa or slept in the bed on different sides. I didn't want to give in one bit. With age, though, I found myself sometimes inching up next to him while lying on the floor to keep warm. He wasn't that bad, and I am sorry I was mean to him sometimes. He is in "doggy heaven" now, after he became real sick. We still can't talk much about him, because it is so sad.

As a Jack Russell Terrier, I will always be proud of my heritage and act crazy like a little ole girl at times, but I do enjoy lying around and acting the age of a little ole lady most of the time.

Born Again

— Larry Ballard

JACK DEFIANTLY SHOVED THE FLOODED BOWL of cereal back across the table toward his mother. A small wave of sugar-drenched milk broke its confines and washed over colorful, neatly placed linens. Jack knew what was coming and screwed his pliable four-year-old face into a stubborn scowl.

"No." His scowl deepened.

His mother, dark hair tightly bound in prickly red curlers, eyes black with anger, flew out of her chair and raced around the end of the table, almost falling as her feet slid on the slick, spotless linoleum.

"I'll teach you," she screamed. "I'll teach you a lesson you'll never ..." She scooped up the refused meal and slammed it, upside down, on Jack's head.

Stiff, unrepentant Jack pushed back his tears. A hot, deep, demanding impulse filled his body.

"*Don't cry, Jack,*" new voices murmured.

"*Don't let her know,*" they whispered.

"*Ah, something new, something tasty,*" said a more ancient voice.

Jack could still feel the bowl pressing the rim of his scalp, could still feel the warm trickle of blood trailing down the side of his face. He traced the smooth ridge of scar tissue forming a half circle across his forehead. He tried to open his eyes, but the dream had too firm a hold on him and dragged him deeper into its world of blood and violence. Familiars of this dominion stomped through gore, splashing savage messages on thin,

6

barely containing walls. Voices urged him on into the next room. Their will became his will, and he followed them, landing blow after blow, feeling relieved as he felt life leave broken body after broken body.

He felt a sharp pain in his right upper arm; a rush of icy cold washed over him. The voices diminished to faint, interwoven whispers, their bodies reduced to indistinguishable shadows. Something covered his face, damp from his sweat, clinging, making it hard to breathe.

Why was it so dark?

A familiar voice gently parted the fog.

"Jack—can you hear me? Do you know where you are?" A hand pressed his shoulder, gentle, reassuring. "It's time, Jack."

It was time. It was time to go. Yes, time to go.

"Goodbye, Jack. May God's mercy go with you."

Cricket

— Irene Knudsen

I AM A CAT. I was born in Athens, Greece, year 2012, on Valentine's Day. That does not make me feel special, as I am not a romantic. I remember my mother being kind, taking good care of my siblings and me. I was the only one that looked like her with my long, smooth white hair. I am pretty — no gorgeous — a real head turner. One of my eyes has a stain of blue, which makes me believe I might have some noble Turkish Angora in my genes. My father was one of those multi-colored Greek alley cats that think they are God's gift to catkind. Many females fall for those bad boys. Obviously, my mother did, and got in trouble. I am said to have a streak of Father's feral instincts in me.

I would not be one of those loose females, as I was adopted by a couple. *Big A* is American, and *Big N* is Greek, like me. I got fixed right away, and do not have to deal with messy childbirth, and I kept my lean figure. Not long after settling in my new environment I developed a severe case of ringworms — itchy things, all over my body, which I shared with my new family. For weeks we were all covered in a smelly substance. Once a day I was rinsed clean by *Big N* under the faucet in the bathtub. Didn't he know that cats hate water? Luckily, it took care of the problem.

Big A served me homemade cat food. I did not like it that much, but ate it to make her happy. I dreamt about that Greek stuff I could smell from the stove. Sometimes when they were busy they fed me from a can, which *Big A* pointed out was not very good for me. But I like fast foods.

For the first two years I lived peacefully in an apartment on the fourth floor in Piraeus. My favorite place was the balcony outside the living room. I liked to sit on the railing and watch the ships go by and spy on the hanky-panky going on with the cats down below. I am glad I did not have to compete with those tramps.

One day my life drastically changed. I do not like change. I am a cat. *Big A* suddenly disappeared with two big suitcases. *Big N* was still around, but I was alone a lot. One morning *Big N* left me, by mistake, on the balcony. That meant I would miss my lunch. Looking to check if the bedroom door was ajar, I had to jump to another balcony a few feet away. Collecting my feral instinct I jumped and missed, and fell through some branches of a tree, slowing me down before hitting the pavement. I was terrified and had a hard time focusing, but managed to drag myself to safety to the corner of a doorway. I tried to calm down and started licking my hurts.

After what seemed like an eternity *Big N* appeared and put me in a small cage and drove me to a pet hospital. A man, a veterinarian, poked and pressed on my tender body, assuring us nothing was broken and sent me home to rest. That's what I did for days, not giving the balcony even a glance. I am glad a cat comes with nine built-in life insurances, and I still have eight left.

Suddenly one day my second life became threatened when *Big N* put me in a very, very large cage and drove me to a strange, noisy place. I was handed to a man who decorated my cage with lots of stickers and carried me to a dark, cold, lonely place. He closed the door, and after bumping around for a short time, I was being lifted up in the sky. I am not supposed to be flying. I am a cat. What had I done to be uprooted like that? I started feeling sleepy. *Big N* must have given me something for my nerves. I woke up when somebody opened the door.

"Wilcommen in Frankfurt. Was für eine schöne Katze du bist!"

I had no clue what that meant, and I did not care. I had to keep worrying about myself, as I was now being transferred to a similar place together with two other miserable-sounding creatures. My sharp feline intuition told me we would be flying again, and of course I was right. This time I flew for a very long time with some unstable instances that made me hold on tight. Still woozy, I thought back on my last life on the balcony with the nice breeze from the Mediterranean Sea. My account now holds only seven lives.

"Welcome to L.A. Oh, you are such a beautiful cat."

That I understood. But I was not looking for compliments; I needed to get out of the cage. Instead, another stranger picked me up and carried me to a car. She gave me fresh (questionable) water and some dry food, which I did not eat. At least this time I would stay on the ground. When I was just about to give up and withdraw another life, we stopped. I was put inside a house, and finally released. The first one I saw was *Big A*. She bent down to pet me. I showed no emotion, not after what she had put me through. I had a new territory to explore on my wobbly legs. *Big A* was holding a little person, a *Little e*. I was also introduced to *Big I*. I learned that she would be my new caretaker. I see her as *IK*. I am the only *I* here. She is older, which could be favorable when you have to train someone. They are usually slower, and more confused. After awhile, *Big A* left with her *Little e,* and I was alone with *IK*.

IK has a nice big house with a lovely garden full of birds and lizards. I do not miss the balcony a bit. The problem was I liked the next-door garden better, and then discovered another one, and in a short time I was garden hopping over the whole neighborhood. I got multiple complaints, especially from dog and cat owners, as I liked to tease their pets by sitting on the fence, cleaning my silky fur or taking naps. The dogs never shut up, and sometimes I stay extra long to get them more riled up. I became classified as a "neighborhood nuisance." *IK* had to keep me inside the house, and I could only watch the garden life through a screen — the same kind of life as the pets I had teased. Bummer! If I had been a sneaky non-descriptive alley cat, I could probably have gotten away with it; but I understand it is not always easy to go unnoticed being so beautiful. I made do. *IK* and I get along.

My name is Cricket, but I rarely listen when *IK* calls me ... only when she shouts "gotte gotte," which means my food is being served. She spoils me with fast foods every day, canned fish or chicken. I think the American turkey is overrated. I do not touch it.

Last spring *Big A* came to visit with *Little e* and another little person, *Little k*. *Little e* chased me around a lot. I did not like that, and l lost my patience and hissed at her. I got scolded and was called a "bad girl." Who cares? I have to protect myself. *Little k* kept my interest; she just sat there on a fuzzy, claw-itching blanket playing with fun stuff. I could spy on her for hours.

I have a big complaint about authority, like Vets and Groomers. *IK* tried three places before she found somebody to take me on. When I get my nails done, the whole crew is called for. They roll me in a carpet, hold me down and cut my nails in super speed. I protest fiercely. My father would have been proud. When I show up, there is a deep sigh by everyone. Last time they doubled the price. Well, I am not asking for it. My nails are my pride. I am a "feline femme fatale."

At night I am locked out of the bedroom. I am "a midnight-to-early-morning runner," and *IK* did not like me running on her bed playing tag. That's fine. I like doing my exercises unsupervised, and in the morning I wait on a small carpet outside the door. I do not dare to wake her up. Then all hell breaks loose. I want to savor my breakfast in peace, and when *IK* has her first cup of coffee, I like to keep her company by snuggling up on her lap. There is always a give and take in a relationship. Although, I like take, more.

At times *IK* takes trips to her family in a place not far from my homeland. I stay behind at a pet hotel renting a three-cage condo. I do not like that a bit, and am not welcome there either. We will see how long that lasts.

I listen very carefully when *IK* makes her plans for those trips, as I know by experience that she will be flying. If she mentions Lufthansa, I will go ballistic. I like her, we are a team, and I do not want her to sit forever in that dark place crammed inside a cage with a bowl of water and her suitcase. I have no clue why on earth they always have to carry that around. Fortunately she has better choices. I want her rested and happy when she comes back so she can spend a lot of time with me. I know I am selfish.

I am a cat.

Cutie the Cucumber

— Linda Hennrick

ONCE UPON A TIME, there was a cucumber named Cutie.

Cutie and her brothers and sisters were born in Grams' garden. Together they hung on the Mother Vine all day basking in the warm sun, soaking up the water, growing longer and stronger and greener each day.

When they'd all grown into fine young cucumbers, Cutie's brothers and sisters began to disappear. Day after day, Grams would find them one by one and snip! Off they would go.

But day after day, Grams passed Cutie by.

"Take me too! Take me too!" Cutie said in her little cucumber voice. "I don't want to be alone!"

But no matter how loudly Cutie cried, Grams didn't hear her.

And so, Cutie remained on the Mother Vine and continued to grow and grow. She grew so large that she became five times the size of most cucumbers. She even outgrew her green color and turned white.

"What are you?" asked a bee buzzing by.

"I'm a cucumber," Cutie replied.

"No, you aren't!" said the bee. "Cucumbers are green, but you're white! And you're much larger than any cucumber I've ever seen. You look more like a daikon radish."

Just then a butterfly fluttered by.

"What have we here?" asked the butterfly.

"I'm a cucumber," Cutie replied.

The butterfly flew up and down Cutie's length for a better look.

"No, you aren't!" huffed the butterfly. "Cucumbers are green, but you're white! And you're much too large to be a cucumber."

Cutie was confused and sad. She missed her brothers and sisters. She didn't want to be alone anymore.

And so she hung on the Mother Vine and wished with all her might that someone would find her.

Then one day, Cutie heard voices in the garden.

"Grams, what's this?" a little girl with red hair asked pointing directly at Cutie.

Cutie held her breath.

"Why, it's a cucumber. It should have been snipped from the Mother Vine a long time ago. Look how big it's become. Too big for eating," Grams said.

"May I have it, Grams?" the little girl asked. "Please?"

And with that, Grams cut the cord that held Cutie to the Mother Vine, and Cutie dropped into the little red-haired girl's arms.

That night, the little girl wrapped Cutie in a blanket, cuddled her, and sang her a lullaby, as if she were a doll. Cutie was happy she no longer had to be alone. But she knew that once a cucumber left the Mother Vine, it didn't have long to live.

After the little girl had gone to sleep, Cutie lay awake for a long time. "I wish I may, I wish I might, have the wish I wish tonight," she whispered into the dark.

Suddenly, a tiny light appeared and hovered over Cutie. Cutie gasped. It was the Cucumber Fairy!

"What is your wish, my child?" the Cucumber Fairy asked.

"Oh Cucumber Fairy! I wish I could stay with the red-haired girl who loves me," Cutie replied.

"That's an unusual request," the Cucumber Fairy said, "but you're an unusual cucumber. I will grant your wish."

The Cucumber Fairy waved a magic wand over her, and before Cutie knew it, she was green again and had been transformed into the cutest cucumber doll in the world.

"Oh thank you, Cucumber Fairy, thank you!" Cutie said.

And Cutie lived happily ever after.

Goosebumps

— Linda Hennrick

MY EYES FLEW OPEN in the dark. Something was wrong. Straining my senses through the deep still night, I heard a noise downstairs. Someone was in the house.

I tossed off the bed covers and tiptoed toward the sound. Peering down from the landing at the top of the stairs, I spied the figure of a man dressed in black, his face hidden by a yellow baseball cap, moving furtively about below.

The thought of someone violating my personal space made me angry. Unmindful of my own safety, I shouted down at him, "Get out of here, or I'll call the police!" At least, I thought I shouted.

I've heard that one shouldn't wake a person in the midst of a nightmare, but my husband shook me gently awake, as he sometimes does when I cry out in my sleep, saving me from what might otherwise have been a horrible fate. Turning over in bed to face him, I found his hand near my pillow, held it in mine, and tried to go back to sleep.

I'm not a good sleeper. Even with the Melatonin I take regularly, I don't fall asleep easily and often wake to imaginary bumps in the night.

My husband, on the other hand, can fall asleep at the drop of a hat anywhere, anytime, and wake up refreshed. Lying next to him night after night, waiting for the Melatonin to kick in, I listen as his breathing deepens into snores in a matter of minutes after the lights go out, sometimes before. I've always envied him this — for me — uncanny ability.

That night was no different. After waking me from my dream, my husband slipped easily into the arms of Morpheus while I lay awake next to him wondering why I couldn't enjoy the same embrace. Only a few minutes had passed when he squeezed my hand rapidly several times and mumbled some gibberish aloud, lost in a nightmare of his own. Returning his earlier favor, I squeezed his hand to rouse him. He stirred and sighed and went immediately back to sleep, this time peacefully.

I must have finally drifted off as well — the next thing I knew it was morning. I rose first and brewed the coffee, as I always do, and was at my computer checking emails when my husband joined me.

"Did you know you were talking in your sleep?" I asked. "What were you dreaming about?"

Cup of coffee in hand, he sat down beside me. "I dreamt that someone had broken into the house," he said. "I held a gun at him, but he laughed in my face. So I pulled the trigger, but the gun wouldn't fire. So I pulled it again. And again. Nothing."

I was about to tell him that I'd also dreamt about an intruder when he added, "I didn't get a good look at him, but something struck me as odd. He was wearing a yellow baseball cap."

[First Place Winner in a Palm Springs
Writers Guild Monthly Writing Challenge]

Hummingbird Playmates

— June Gaulding

ABOVE THE TINY MOUNTAIN VILLAGE of Red River, New Mexico, about twenty-five miles from Taos, there were two families of Rufous Hummingbirds that lived in their nests high up in the pine tree branches. The Jones' and the Edwards' families were neighbors in the same pine tree. Mr. and Mrs. Rufous Jones had a little girl named Susie, and Mr. and Mrs. Rufous Edwards had a little boy named Eddie.

Of course, anyone could recognize a tiny, tiny Rufous Hummingbird with its bright orange-red back and tail feathers. The wings sported a combination of orange-red and green feathers with light yellow breast feathers. The head was a light green color. The parents were about three inches long with a very slender beak to get nectar from the colorful flowers that grew everywhere. Susie and Eddie were smaller but a spitting image of their parents. They had to learn to flit and whir their little wings about moving their little bodies real fast so other big birds in the air wouldn't try to chase them.

On a really nice warm summer morning Momma Jones wanted to get nest cleaning done and said, "Susie, it is so nice outside. Why don't you go out and exercise your little wings."

Susie exclaimed, "Oh, that sounds like fun," and off she flew with her momma yelling, "Susie, look out for any rowdy playmates."

Every summer there were visitors coming to the cabins below the pine trees, and they would place pretty red hanging bottle feeders outside their windows with yummy red sweet liquid to sip on. This was to invite the hummingbirds to enjoy the treat so they could watch them. Susie cautiously flew close by one cabin and spotted the treat but waited until it was safe to get a taste of the sweet treat.

About this time Eddie's mom told him to go fly around a bit to rid himself of the high energy that she noticed during breakfast. "Can I, can I really go out and fly high and maybe do some quick dives for the fun of it?" he asked.

She knew she wanted to do some baking, and if she didn't have the nest to herself, the baking would be a failure. She answered, "Of course, Eddie, enjoy yourself, but watch out for rowdy playmates."

He started out with a fast, high-flying pass over the red feeders when he saw Susie eyeing the treat, too. He thought, *I'll see if I can beat her to it*, and so he flew by her with a whirring of his wings and dived in for a sip. He almost knocked Susie over, so she held back and whirred her little wings to get out of the way. Eddie backed off, and Susie thought, *now I can have my sip*. When she flew up to the feeder for her sip, Eddie yelled, "Move over. I am coming in." And he did, while almost knocking her over, not even thinking he was a rowdy playmate.

Susie decided to go home. She flew in quietly and sat on the edge of the nest and said to her momma, "I thought Eddie was my friend, but he is one of those rowdy playmates, and I don't like him." After Susie flew away, Eddie knew he would be in trouble at home for being mean to his friend. He flew into his nest with a buzz of wings and landed with a thud on the nest floor. Mom was busy baking cookies, but knew something was wrong when Eddie came in like he did. "How was your play time?" she asked Eddie.

He hesitated but finally answered her. "I thought it would be fun to scare Susie away from enjoying the red treat that was placed in the feeders, and she went home. I know I hurt her feelings."

Mom answered, "Don't you want to be her friend?"

"Yes, I do, but what can I do now?" questioned Eddie.

"Maybe you could think about what you did and go talk to her. Even an apology to her would be a good gesture of friendship."

Eddie thought for a minute and said, "Mom, that is a good idea, and I am going to fly over to see her right now." He was really happy that Mom hadn't punished him, but helped him learn a lesson on friendship.

Susie felt much better after talking to Momma about Eddie. She would try to think about what she could do to be Eddie's friend. About that time there was a whirring of wings on the edge of the nest, and she looked up and saw Eddie. She didn't know what to do, but Eddie blurted out to her, "I am so sorry, Susie, that I scared you and hurt your feelings. I want us to be friends. Would you like to go with me to get a red treat?"

"Of course." She shook her head up and down and smiled at Eddie.

They were hummingbird playmates now, and they would enjoy the summer being friends.

Malaga Cove

— Linda Hennrick

WE LOVED TO CRUISE the winding coastal road of the Palos Verdes Peninsula, car windows lowered, sunlight and salt air on our faces.

Cruising at night was even better. Sometimes we'd stop to gaze upon the sparkling lights of the South Bay below, a treasure chest of jewels.

But most nights, my boyfriend Dale and I were more interested in finding a dark, secluded place to neck. Our favorite place in Malaga Cove next to an old church with red Spanish-tiled roof was so quiet we could hear waves crashing against the cliff far below.

Friends at West High often talked about the Blue Ghost, a sea captain from a bygone era with a hook for a hand said to haunt the cove; the tale added spice to our late-night explorations. Tendrils of low fog creeping across the church graveyard made it easy to imagine a phantom roamed the night. The scene lacked only a hooting owl.

One night in late autumn found us parked in our usual spot. Dale slid over on the front seat to crush me against the passenger side door. We were soon oblivious to everything except each other.

Suddenly the wind rose and hurled a handful of dry leaves clattering across the roof and windshield. We came abruptly to our senses, the mood broken.

Something had changed since we'd arrived earlier, and it wasn't the wind. Dale sat up and looked around; his body stiffened.

Far across the graveyard near the cliff's edge, a pale blue glow emanated from a figure near a headstone. Dressed like a sea captain of yore, the figure raised a ghostly arm; blue light glinted off the hook at its end. An icy chill went through me.

Dale moved first. Scooting behind the steering wheel, he turned the key. The engine wouldn't start. He tried again. Nothing.

"Lock the door," Dale commanded and tried the ignition yet again. Still nothing. He gripped the steering wheel and swore.

I could no longer see the blue-lit figure in the graveyard. I wasn't sure I'd seen anything, but the panic I felt was real.

The wind blew stronger. Clouds played hide-and-seek with the moonlight. Leaves swirled as the car rocked slightly. Above the wind, another sound — the screech of metal on metal.

I slid over next to Dale, my eyes glued to his profile. "Try again," I squeaked, fear strangling my voice.

Dale turned the key. The engine caught and started with a roar to wake the dead. Dale threw the car in gear, and we squealed down the street as though the hounds of hell were snapping at our tires.

As we sped further from the church, we finally relaxed. Safely parked in front of my house, we laughed aloud. What would our friends say if we told them we'd seen a ghost?

Always the gentleman, Dale walked around the car to open my door — and stopped in his tracks.

Dangling from the car door handle was a metal hook.

Mexican Flowers

— Richard A. Vasquez

The world changed in 1914 in a way that had never come before. A way that many may have thought impossible. There was war. But that in itself was not new, but this was war on the earth as a whole.

World War I had begun.

On April 6, 1917 America entered the fight with a declaration of war against Germany. Boston became a busy hub, with troops leaving to be shipped off to Europe and other places. Then in time they started returning back to America, back to Boston, where hospitals and medical help awaited them.

IT WAS EARLY MAY 1917 when Virginia came running down the stairs in her nurse's uniform.

"Where do think you're going?" Virginia's father asked.

"Father, you see me wearing my uniform. Where else would I be going but to the hospital for more training?"

Virginia was telling the truth. There would be some nurses' training at the hospital, but it would be later that day. At this moment Virginia was hoping she would to run into Lieutenant Murphy before he left his post at the newly conscripted hospital in Boston. She had volunteered as a nurse to support the American war effort, something that young rich socialites like her had started to do. It was deemed appropriate behavior — patriotic and compassionate.

The war still was a romantic concept in her mind ... brave young men defending their country and the American way of life. And then there was Lieutenant Murphy, a handsome dark-haired Adonis in his uniform.

"It seems to me you're spending far more time at the hospital than you are at home," Mr. Flowers continued.

"Really, Father, have you forgotten there is a war on? I have to prepare for the worst, Head Nurse Agatha told us."

"I hope you never see the worst, my darling. War is a ghastly thing."

"Brave men are putting their lives at risk to protect us. The least I can do is be there to ease their suffering when they come home."

"I don't know if I approve of this any longer—young ladies out of their homes among strange men, at all hours."

"You, Mother and I have discussed this, and Mother agrees that I should contribute. She thinks it will be socially advantageous after the war. We'll be able to say we supported America's victory."

"I'm going to have a talk with your mother."

"All right, fine, but I am going," Virginia said as she left.

Virginia was in love. And there was not much that could have held her back this day. The young lieutenant had told her he would be shipping out soon. She wanted to spend as much time as she could with him before they were thousands of miles apart.

As she walked down the street to the hospital, military trucks full of men in uniform moved everywhere. Soldiers walked past her and took long appreciative looks. She didn't think she liked this. Boston had been a quiet place before where gentlemen didn't look at women in that fashion. It was rude, she thought.

When she walked into the hospital she looked for the lieutenant at his post, behind the glass office windows, near the entrance. She did not see him. She felt deeply disappointed. She stood there for a while wondering what she would do, until her training session began.

"Miss Flowers," a voice from behind said. It was her lieutenant.

"I suppose you're on your way to your training?" he said.

"Actually, I've arrived an hour early by some mistake. It's quite silly of me. I must have looked at the clock at home incorrectly."

"Well, I was hoping that you would join me at the café across the street. Maybe you can wait out the hour there, and we can have a chance to talk."

Virginia felt like she was weightless, like some other power had taken over the gravity of the earth.

"I would love to," she said.

The days went by quickly. Too soon they had to say goodbye to each other. The lieutenant promised to write her often and to return to Boston to find her.

As war waged on and her father's words came true, Virginia's romantic notion of war turned to horror. She saw the utter ugliness of it. The maimed and mutilated bodies began to arrive. Too often there was nothing anyone could do but watch the poor unfortunates die. She thought she could take no more of death all around her. Then, something came back with the war weary and broken men who had already seen horrors beyond description. It was something worse that they had to face now — worse than the enemy, the guns, cannons, and bombs. At least those things you could see. This was an invisible monster, an insidious killer, with no qualms about killing the young, old, women and children … the Spanish flu made its presence known.

The lieutenant's letters stopped coming. She felt like she was dying herself — of a broken heart. She feared that every soldier that was brought in wrapped in bandages close to death might be him.

[Excerpt from the novel
Mexican Flowers]

One Enchanted Onomatopoeia Evening

— Linda Hennrick

GATA-GATA. GATA-GATA. Sliding wooden doors rattle as the wind blows *gō-gō* and shakes the old wooden Japanese house from top to bottom. Keiko gazes out a window at the late evening sky. A handful of stars sparkle *kira-kira* directly overhead, but dark clouds roil and bloom on the horizon—a storm heading her way.

A bolt of lightning flashes *pikkato*, and thunder rolls *goro-goro*. Keiko hurries *bata-bata* here and there through the house making sure all the windows and doors are locked up tight, ready to wait out the storm. *Pikkato! Goro-goro.* The storm is almost overhead, rain already pouring down *zā-zā*. As she closes the kitchen window, Keiko spies her Japanese bobtail cat running through the garden past the koi pond toward the back door.

"*Nyā, nyā!*" Tama complains as she opens the door to let him in. Poor thing is *bisho-bisho*—wet all over.

"*Gomen, gomen*—sorry, Tama," Keiko says as she dries him off with a *fuwa-fuwa* fluffy towel and tickles him under the chin. He blinks his eyes slowly in pleasure and purrs *goro-goro* deep in his throat, a small rumble that imitates the thunder outside. She feeds Tama his dinner, and when he's finished cleaning his dish, he licks his face *bero-bero* with great relish.

Suddenly Keiko feels *peko-peko* hungry too. Her stomach growls *gū-gū*, and her throat is *kara-kara* dry. She sits down on the tatami straw mat floor at the low table in the living room. "*Itadakimasu,*" she says as she reaches for her chopsticks and helps herself to the simple meal she made earlier, washing it all down with a *hiya-hiya* cold glass of beer. The thinly sliced cucumber pickles are fresh and *shaki-shaki* crispy. A small fish—grilled whole—stares *jiro-jiro* up at her with one eye. White rice, perfectly cooked, sticks *neba-neba* to her chopsticks, but the *nuru-nuru* slimy *wakame* seaweed in the miso soup is hard to grasp. She eats *paku-paku*, much too fast, and soon feels *pan-pan* — very full. "*Gochisōsamadeshita*," she sighs. "It was a feast."

The dinner dishes washed and put away, Keiko settles in for the rest of the evening. While the storm continues to rage outside, she reads a magazine flipping the pages *gasa-gasa*. The grandfather clock in the hall keeps a steady *kotsu-kotsu* rhythm, and the room is *pokka-pokka* warm and cozy. She soon catches herself nodding off *kokkuri-kokkuri*. Time for bed.

Tama watches as she spreads her futon out on the tatami floor. Before she's finished, Tama leaps atop it and turns in circles several times before curling up *kuru-kuru* at its foot. "*Oyasumi* — good night, Tama." He's fast asleep long before Keiko drifts off.

She dreams she's wearing a red kimono, its sleek silk *sara-sara* against her skin. She's in a grand room lit by *gira-gira* dazzling chandeliers, speaking English *pera-pera* fluently to a tall good looking young man with blond hair and blue eyes. An unseen orchestra plays a waltz. The young man smiles at her *niko-niko*, his straight teeth as white as his dinner jacket. Her heart beats *doki-doki*, and her head feels *kura-kura* dizzy as she gazes adoringly up at him. She closes her eyes as he leans in for a kiss.

Choki-choki. Choki-choki. Keiko's eyes fly open. Something must have woken her. The storm has blown itself out, but in the silence, she thought she heard another sound. Was it the creak of a floorboard? Is someone — a mouse, a thief — sneaking *koso-koso* though the house? The hair on her arms stands *biri-biri* on end. Tama is no longer at the foot of her futon.

Choki-choki. Choki-choki. There it is. That snipping sound like scissors is what woke her. Still *fura-fura* woozy with sleep, Keiko reaches for some *dabu-dabu* baggy pants and a sweatshirt to put on over her pajamas to go and investigate. But her legs feel *yobo-yobo* wobbly, and she falls back onto her futon. Shivering, she pulls the covers up over her head and closes her eyes tight, hoping whatever or whoever is there will just go away and leave her alone.

"Kokekokko!" The rooster crows in the yard next door. Keiko sits up and stretches her arms *nobi-nobi* above her head. Fully awake now, she realizes she must have dreamed everything. She shakes her head and grins *niya-niya* at herself as she opens the shutters on the big sliding doors. It's a beautiful day, the sky washed clean by the storm. The sun shines *pika-pika* brightly. Tama greets her in the kitchen, *"Nyā, nyā!"* as though telling her not to linger *guzu-guzu*. He's hungry for breakfast.

"Gomen, gomen — sorry, Tama," Keiko says and busies herself with his food and water dishes. As she sets them down, she feels a cold chill run *zoku-zoku* up her spine.

A red silk kimono lies *bara-bara* scattered in pieces on the floor.

NOTE: Just as in English, the Japanese language is full of words that imitate sounds that animals make as well as sounds found in nature. But there are also words that describe things that don't make sounds, like appearances, conditions, emotions, feelings, and even textures. I have included several in this short piece, but there are dozens more. I hope the reader not only enjoys the story but can also grasp the sense of these onomatopoetic words.

One More Christmas, Please

— Mary Kirk

HERE I AM SITTING on a bottom shelf amid the leftovers and throwaways. I know my box has wrinkles at the corners, and there's a crease across my picture on the front. But if someone would just open the lid, they'd find me waiting, ready to warm their heart at holiday time.

For years I sat on the counter, shiny, round and white, with my bright red sweater and glistening black buttons. Everyone always loved my wide smile, those rosy cheeks, and that pointy carrot of a nose. But best of all, they loved my jaunty top hat, tilted just so, as if urging everyone to lift it and peek underneath.

Sometimes the children tried to sneak just one more treat. Then, as they slowly lifted my hat, the cheerful notes of jingle bells would signal everyone a cookie theft was in progress.

But the children grew up and moved away, and no one wanted to bake the special cookies any more.

So here I am, alone in my box on the thrift store shelf, just waiting for someone to look inside—hoping they'll take me home for another Christmas.

Sig Gets the Blues

— Richard Vasquez

I WAS SURPRISED WHEN I SAW Atlee's house. I drove past the gates and down the circular driveway to the front. I picked up my clipboard and the manila file with the paperwork on Atlee's case. I walked up to the entrance. It didn't look like a place where a crazy person would live. But, that was the unanimous consensus. Frank Atlee was two screws short of a tight hinge. Cuckoo. I knocked on his door. I heard a gruff voice through a speaker near the door say, "Who's there?"

"It's Detective Jonah Hunch, sir, from the Police Department." *I didn't mention that I was there more in the realm of psychology rather than crime investigation. I thought that I would save that fact for later.*

"For heaven's sakes, are you another one of those dimwits coming here to ask me stupid questions again?"

"Mr. Atlee, would you please open the door. I need to sit down and talk to you, sir."

"What is wrong with you damned people? I've told you the truth about everything I know." I heard the lock click—then the door opened slowly.

"Come in … don't suppose I can get rid of you any other way."

When I came in, once again I was surprised. The inside of the house was well arranged, orderly. I could tell that there had been a woman's touch when it had come to the decorating of the home. Nevertheless, I knew that Atlee now lived alone because of the passing of his wife six months ago. I sat on the couch, and Atlee sat in a stuffed chair facing me.

"I got beer. Do you want a beer?"

"No thank you, sir. I just want to get started."

"Okay, ask the questions again — as if I haven't heard them, and answered them already."

"Mr. Atlee, I understand that your wife died six months ago."

"Yes, it's been six months and three days that Margie has been gone. I can't believe that it went by that fast. We were married for fifty years, you know."

"Mr. Atlee, three months ago you were at the police department's headquarters, and you claimed to be responsible for her death ... is that correct?"

"Yes, but later I explained to what's-his-face, Homely, Horny, whatever his name was."

"Detective Hornsby?"

"Yeah, him."

"And, recently you've recanted your confession. You at this time state that you were not responsible for her death in any way."

"Yes, and that's really the truth. I'm not responsible."

"Maybe you can explain to me why the two different stories."

"There's only one story to tell, and I told you that I explained all of it to what's-his-name."

"Detective Hornsby?"

"Yeah, that guy. Didn't he write it all down? He was doing a lot of writing."

"Why don't you tell me the story now, Mr. Atlee. Let's start with why you initially claimed responsibility for your wife's death."

"Regis."

"Regis — do you mean the television personality?"

"Hell no! Not that moron ... I guess she didn't think I'd remember when she named him that."

"Who's Regis then? And who is 'she'? Do you mean Mrs. Atlee?"

"He's a sniveling mama's boy ... that's who he is. I can still hear her now."

"Hear who? Who do you mean, Mr. Atlee?"

"She was a witch, a spawn of Satan, that one."

"Are you referring to Mrs. Atlee?"

"No!"

He stared at me for a moment seeming to be taking stock of what was going on and maybe wondering who I really might be.

"'I told you not to marry Frank,' she would say. 'You would be so much better off with Regis.' Every damned Thanksgiving, every time we were around her I would hear that crap. I would take her daughter all the way to Connecticut, just to listen to that."

"I'm sorry to hear that, Mr. Atlee. But can we get back to the reason why you first claimed to be responsible for her demise?"

"Where do you think she would have wound up, then?"

I shrugged, concluding that asking a question was not exactly working.

"I'll tell you where, living with his mother, that's where. He's still there. She's 101 years old, and he's still there."

Regis, I surmised.

"Take a look at this place—I worked my ass off to get her this house."

"Yes, it is a very impressive place, Mr. Atlee."

"And she would have been living in a spare bedroom with that mama's boy at his mother's house if she had taken that old battle-axe's advice."

"So, this former acquaintance of your wife somehow caused you to confess responsibility for her death?"

"What? No! That namby-pamby? I would kick his ass if I ever heard him mention Margie's name. Or if I knew that he even thought about her! I would throttle him and send him home to his mommy."

"Then can you please tell me what this person has to do with the initial statement you made to the police officers who interviewed you."

"Nothing."

"Why did you claim responsibility?"

"I told you — Regis."

My head was spinning. Maybe I would take him up on that offer of a beer. On the other hand, maybe something a little harder if he had it.

"Mr. Atlee ..." I felt myself losing my professional decorum. "What the hell does this person Regis have to do with any of this?"

"Person? What person?"

"Regis!"

"I told you. She named him Regis."

"She named who Regis?"

"He's not a person. Although he thinks he is."

I sat stunned for a few seconds — I rubbed my aching forehead.

"Mr. Atlee, for the last time, who or what is Regis!"

"The dog," he said, looking at me as if I hadn't been paying attention.

I began to realize that my trip down the rabbit hole had just begun. I paused for a moment and surveyed my notes — the last entry: Regis is the Dog. I clicked my pen several times, fastened it to the clipboard, and then tossed the clipboard beside me on the couch. I rubbed my eyes with both hands and began to ponder on what to ask Atlee next. *Dare I step off the precipice and continue no matter how nuts it all sounds,* I asked myself ... Then — *it's your job to figure this out. Hornsby wants to hang him, and like the captain said, you may be the only guy in the department that can help him —* shot back.

"Damn," I muttered.

"What's that?" Atlee asked.

I shook my head and said, "Never mind."

Two hours earlier: I had walked into the department, and Blue greeted me with, "Captain wants you in his office ASAP, Sig."

This is not a good way to start the day, I thought.

Sig is short for Sigmund Freud. It has become my new appellation since the Christmas party, a wry moniker given to me by Hornsby. I made a grave mistake. I decided to psychoanalyze my co-workers spurred on by a considerable amount of Bacardi and Coke.

After years of pursuing one goal, to be a psychiatrist— since the age of seventeen—I graduated from college with a psychology major. Then ... I became a cop. It made no sense to people who knew me. But there were reasons that made sense to me.

My thought at that time was—it would be a job, a source of income while I continued to pursue my real goal to be a shrink. The evening of the Christmas party, the cop part of my being became obscure with the booze. I played the psychiatrist that night. I came up with the diagnosis of Narcissistic Personality Disorder for Hornsby—true, but still a stupid thing to say aloud.

Now, after a number of years on the force, I am beginning to realize my mistake. No one becomes a cop to pass the time, until they get to some other place. Once a cop—you become someone else. Your former life becomes a foreign place, where your love, dreams, and hopes are left behind like abandoned children—a place, too far to visit very often.

It was somewhat disturbing to hear Blue use my newly-imposed moniker of "Sig." We have a close working relationship, and we tend to be respectful to each other. Why was it bothering me? I'm sure she was just being playful. Then it occurred to me that what she thought of me was important.

One would think that Blue was her own nickname because of her striking blue eyes. However, that's really her name. Officer Elisa Blue. I love that name.

"What do the blinds look like?" I asked Blue after she gave me the unhappy greeting of *Captain wants to see you ASAP*. I was referring to the horizontal blinds that were on the glass windows that separated the captain's office from us mere mortals.

"Didn't notice," she said. "Good luck," she added, with an amused expression on her face. I walked toward the captain's office giving the blinds a review before I knocked. The general rule of thumb is: if the blinds are completely shut thus sealing the captain off from the world and us, it's a dangerous time to knock. But if the blinds are open to the point that one could look in, then it's safe. My examination, however, brought me to a quandary. The blinds were open in a manner that he could see out, but we could not look in. *What does it mean,* I wondered. I decided since it was neither a 'leave me alone,' nor a 'come on in' signal, that it must mean 'take your chances.' I knocked. My theory that he could see out was proven right.

"Get in here, Hunch," the captain said. At least he was still calling me Hunch.

"Good morning, sir."

"Yeah, yeah. Hunch, I've got a case for you that's right up your alley," he said, as he tossed a file across his desk towards me.

"What is it, sir?"

"The case on Frank Atlee. Personally, I think that he's Looney Tunes, but basically harmless. He gave us some rambling confession about possibly being responsible for his wife's death. I think he's confused, but Hornsby's theory is that he's a cunning murderer. He thinks he can get the goods on him and get an indictment for us. Familiarize yourself with the file and look into it … let me know."

"Captain, I have all my other cases, and I don't know that I'm experienced enough."

"Look … you might be the only one here that can help this crazy bastard. I think Hornsby had a good idea when he suggested you join the investigation, with your psych background and all."

"Hornsby?" — *what is he up to* — ran through my head.

"Get Blue to help with your other stuff. Now get the hell out of here and bring me a report — the Chief is asking questions."

I took the file to my desk and started looking through it. I was trying to see who all the players were. There was Atlee and Atlee's wife, of course. But then there was Carlyle Manchester, Margie Atlee's half-brother, same father different mothers — a little tryst gone awry for Margie's father. He later married his mistress, Carlyle's mother, and then there were two Mrs. Manchesters, the former Mrs. Manchester being Margie's mother and Frank Atlee's mother-in-law — his hated nemesis. Carlyle was playing the grieving brother. However, according to various statements, he and his sister hadn't spoken in two decades. He was asking for the coroner's inquest to be reviewed. What was his game?

I looked through the file with an open mind. I had been a detective long enough to know nothing is what it seems. Hornsby had dug up some dirt all right. A friend of Margie's stated that Frank was an unkind and uncaring person. Then a business partner claimed that Frank had cheated him. But the worst of all, Hornsby found a life insurance policy for two hundred and fifty thousand dollars. Margie and Frank were both insured for the same amount. It seems like peanuts nowadays, but it still could be construed as motive.

"So, what's up, Sig?" Blue said walking up a little bit later. This was often meant to translate to — do you want my help — without her having to come right out and ask. This was the game we played. We had been partnering up on cases a lot. And she didn't want to have to admit that she preferred it that way. This way, if I asked for help, it was my idea.

"Captain wants me to work on the Atlee case, Blue."

"Isn't that Hornsby's case?"

"Yeah, but he requested I join in."

"What's he up to?"

"That's the same thing I asked myself."

Hornsby was not the type to ask for help. In his mind, he was much smarter, and a much better cop, than anybody else could be.

So now here I was in the middle of, who knows what, talking to Atlee. For some reason I had been chosen. I know that the captain had said it was because of my psychology background and all of that, but with the knowledge of Hornsby being involved, I wasn't buying it.

"Mr. Atlee, why don't you tell me more about your dog, Regis."

"What do you want to know?"

"Tell me how he figures into everything that's going on. What could he possibly have to do with you claiming culpability for Mrs. Atlee's demise?"

"I don't know that I did anything that has to do with that word, whatever it means, but that damned dog is crazy. And he's probably listening to everything we're saying."

"The *dog* is crazy?

"Yeah, and he wasn't my dog; he was her dog — even though I was the one who rescued him from the dog pound and brought him home. She kept saying, 'I don't want a dog.' I think it was the cheese puffs."

"Cheese puffs?"

"Yeah, they used to sit around here together watching soap operas and eating cheese puffs. They became very attached to each other — do you like those?"

"No, I've never watched them."

"I mean the puffs. I like the crispy ones, not the puffies."

"As a matter of fact, I like the crispy ones, too, Mr. Atlee. But let's get back to the dog. How or why did Regis have anything to do with your confession?"

Atlee seemed to think for a while and then said, "I guess it was just a desperate and stupid move on my part. He blames me for Margie not being here, you know. He thinks it's my fault."

"Regis blames you?" … *here we go again,* I thought. "How do you know this? How did you figure out that Regis blames you?" I couldn't believe that I had just asked that question.

"It started first with him growling at me every time he saw me, after Margie stopped being here. Then, after that, he was snarling and nipping at me. I think somehow he's figured out that Margie is d-e-a-d."

I'm not sure, but I think Atlee was hoping that if the dog was listening, he couldn't spell.

"Regis blames me," he added.

"He does?" I said, going along with his theory to see where it landed me.

"Now that crazy dog has decided to try and kill me," Atlee continued. "Maybe it's all those damned soap operas that he's watched."

"Regis has attempted to kill you?"

"Yes!"

I didn't think I could be hearing it right, so I decided to regress a bit.

"Mr. Atlee, what kind of dog is Regis?"

"He's sneaky, spiteful, and ungrateful, that's what he is."

"No, I mean his pedigree, what type of dog is he?"

"He's a pedigreed mutt, a small, black and white, crazy mutt."

"Mr. Atlee, you think the dog is trying to kill you?" I finally asked again, just to see if I had heard him right.

"I don't *think* he's trying to kill me, I *know* he's trying to kill me!"

It started becoming clearer — why Hornsby involved me in this case. Oh, the laugh he must be getting out of it.

"Okay, Mr. Atlee, could you then describe the attempts by Regis — to kill you?"

Good grief, how am I going to keep from busting out laughing myself?

"Well, he stabbed me right here," Atlee said, pulling his shirt sleeve up and showing me a wound on his upper arm.

I sat up straight — goggle-eyed. The man was showing me a wound on his arm — a wound that looked like a stab wound.

"Mr. Atlee, are you trying to tell me that your dog — Regis — picked up a knife and stabbed you in the arm?"

"Think about it … what kind of cop are you anyway?" Atlee said sounding annoyed.

"What do you mean, sir?"

"Dogs got paws — how are they going to pick up a knife?" he said, demonstrating by closing his fingers and thumbs on both hands, and forming them into the shape of paws and continued by trying to pick up an imaginary knife. "It doesn't work," he concluded.

This gave me hope that he wasn't completely delusional.

"So, Regis didn't stab you with a knife?" *We're making progress.*

"I didn't say that."

Oh God, what now?

"He threw it from up there," Atlee said, pointing to a balcony with a balustrade that hung over the living room.

I looked up and paused to think, *I guess the dog could have picked up a knife with his mouth and dropped it through the balusters. Maybe the old boy isn't completely delusion. What are you thinking? How can you believe that a dog could have murderous intents?* I tried to rein in my run-away mind.

"Do you think that I might be able to take a look?" I asked, pointing to the staircase that led up.

"Yeah, I want to take you upstairs to show you the bullet hole anyway."

"Ah, what? … Bullet hole?"

"The bullet hole through my closet door. I told you the damn dog is trying to kill me."

He now pulled up his shirt on the right side and showed me a wound that looked like a bullet had grazed the upper side of his torso. I sat speechless staring at the wound. *Grab hold of yourself; don't you get carried away — there's a rational explanation somewhere — yeah good luck finding it, Sig. God I'm not only talking to myself — I'm calling myself Sig.*

We climbed the staircase that took us upstairs. Atlee led, and I followed. We arrived at the balcony area. I saw an inset room that wasn't visible from the living room. There was a chaise lounge, a stuffed chair, some tables and lamps — minimal furnishings. But the walls were lined with books — bookcases full of books.

On the furthest wall, opposite the balustrade, there was a window. You could see blue skies and white fluffy clouds. Birds were flying. I could envision Margie reclining, reading a book, and looking out the window occasionally. She did have it pretty good with Frank.

"Yep, that's all mine," Atlee said, noticing me admiring the situation.

"I thought you said this was Mrs. Atlee's reading area?"

"I don't mean *this*—I mean *that*, all the way to those buildings," he said, pointing out the window. I squinted and could just make out the building outlines past all the treetops, about a half a mile away. Ole Frank was sitting on beaucoup prime Atlanta acreage.

"Some property development company was trying to buy it from me to build a golf course, but I told them to stick it. I worked too damned hard to buy it for my Margie."

"Mrs. Atlee was still alive when this happened?"

"When what happened?"

"When you turned down the deal."

"Yes. Why does that matter?"

"No reason," I said.

I was going to go look at a bullet hole. But I still had no idea how it might fit into Frank Atlee's confession. It was all a disturbing puzzle so far.

I walked into the master bedroom following Atlee. He then pointed to louvered closet doors, the kind one could see through if you were behind them.

"There you are," he said.

I'll be damned if there wasn't a hole about three feet off the ground as if a bullet may have torn through the bottom of one of the louvers. Even more telling, there was a hole directly across the room in the lower part of the wall. One might conclude that the trajectory of a bullet that would have gone through the hole in the door would have put a hole in the wall exactly where it was.

I no longer made any pretense of being in control of the situation.

"Mr. Atlee, do you know where Regis may have gotten the gun," I asked matter-of-factly.

"It's my gun — I kept it on a shelf in that closet."

"Where's the gun now?"

"After Regis shot me, I found it on the floor in the closet, and I put it in my safe."

Then something dawned on me. Something I was surprised I hadn't asked already. Throughout the entire time I had been there, I had not seen, or even heard, a dog around.

"Mr. Atlee, where is Regis? I haven't seen Regis anywhere."

"No, and you won't either, but he's here — that sneaky, conniving, mongrel is here lurking somewhere. He's probably peering at me from some dark place, waiting for you to leave, so he can exact his revenge on me."

The idea that there was a dog on a murderous rampage, doing reconnaissance, and waiting for an opportunity to kill — made me a bit uneasy.

"Mr. Atlee, did Detective Hornsby or any of the other police officers see Regis?"

"No, they didn't. Nobody has seen Regis for months."

"So, no one besides you has ever seen Regis?"

"Of course other people have seen Regis, just not lately. He doesn't want to be seen, I tell you. He wants to be alone to plot his revenge."

Okay Detective Jonah Hunch, all you have to do now is find a knife-wielding, gun-toting, invisible dog and arrest him.

[Excerpt from the novel
Sig Gets the Blues]

The Big Fish

— Larry Ballard

MARY WAS FED UP WITH BOB and moving rapidly toward outright anger.

"Advance the line out," Bob yelled, as the great fish broke the surface in an explosion of foam and water.

"Give him some slack, for crying out loud. You're going to lose him. Bring him around those rocks. Christ, you're going to lose him."

She trembled, not from the excitement of the struggle with the big bass on the end of her line, but from the rage she felt toward Bob's ranting from the back of the boat. His face was as red as the flaring gills of the fish as it thrashed across the water trying to disgorge the lure from its mouth.

"You win," she muttered. She yanked with all her might. The metal lure came free and whistled through the air past Bob's ear, nearly ripping it off. Arms flailing, he slung the landing net far out into the lake, as he tumbled off the back of the boat. He came to the surface sputtering, arms churning in the brackish water, struggling to stay afloat against the weight of his waterlogged clothing. Susan scrambled over the seats, tackle boxes and white foam cooler, grabbed the steering arm on the small electric trolling motor and turned the boat back toward him.

"What's wrong with you? You idiot!" he screamed.

Mary hesitated for just a second, then reached under the seat and pulled out an old cork-filled life jacket and tossed it to him. She twisted the throttle full open, swung the boat around and headed toward the barely visible public docks on the far side of the lake. She took one look back at Bob who was futilely waving his arms in the air, and turned back toward the boat dock.

"Boy, I hate first dates!"

The Resolution

—Linda Hennrick

A STYGIAN NIGHT. A winding mountain road. The giddy thrill of speed. The sudden glare of headlights too bright, too close. A tremendous impact. A stomach-lurching plunge. A jolting, bone rattling stop.

An echoing silence. The plaintive cry of a deer. Then, silence profound. Peace. Nothing.

But something. Gradual awareness.

Eyes open wide, staring into the thick velvet darkness, I can but sense the carnage around me. The twisted metal. The brittle shards of glass. The broken tree limbs scattered on the forest floor. The deep scars gouged in the rich autumn earth.

The acrid smell of gasoline fills my nose, bringing me fully alert. What if the gasoline ignites?

Suddenly afraid, I try to move. To flee. To escape. But I can't feel my legs. Are they pinned by the wreckage? Do I still have legs?

I try to scream, but my voice fails me. Is anyone there? Can anyone hear me? Help! Help! My mouth gapes open and closed. Fish out of water.

I clench my hands in frustration. At least I can still feel my hands, although they tingle in the cold, a cold as sharp as knives.

I imagine I hear voices around me.

"This is what comes from your gallivanting around. You're a grown-up now. You should act like one. Take on some responsibility," my father's voice complains.

"He's just sowing his wild oats," my mother's voice answers. "Let him be young while he still can. He'll settle down soon enough."

"Shame about the car. That Maserati was one sweet ride," one of my school chums says.

"It was a beauty all right," says another.

The voices fade. Was I hallucinating?

But I think about what I heard. I'm sorry for not living up to my father's expectations. Sorry that my mother has such low expectations of me. Sorry that my friends think more of my possessions than of me. Have I always been so shallow? I resolve to live a better life. To live up to my potential. To be more compassionate, more caring. To be somebody.

But now I only feel cold. All over. Colder than I've ever been. Icy fingers insinuate deep into my being. My teeth chatter in a macabre rhythm, and my whole body joins the torturous dance. It seems endless. How can I endure?

Just when I think I'll surely go insane, I sense a warm glow emanating out of the darkness, pulsing with hope and promise. I want to cry with relief, but no tears come. I want to laugh, but an old man's wheezing fills my chest. I reach out to embrace the welcoming light.

The first snow of winter softly falls, erasing all signs of the accident in a cloak of white.

[First Place Winner in a Palm Springs
Writers Guild Monthly Writing Challenge]

Nonfiction/
Essays

DNA Testing for Genetic Genealogy

—Jean Giunta Denning

AS PART OF MY GENEALOGY QUEST, I had my DNA tested through Family Tree DNA, and more recently with Ancestry DNA™. This was another facet of genealogy research introduced at one of our Italian genealogy club conferences. I was fascinated with the whole idea. I had my mtDNA tested (my mother's side) and asked my cousin John to test his Y-DNA for me (my father's side). After meeting Bennett Greenspan, head of Family Tree DNA, at our Italian genealogy club conference, he asked if I would head a "Sicily Geographic Project." I agreed to help launch the project, and attended the next Family Tree DNA International Conference on Genetic Genealogy held in Houston, Texas in November 2006. The group grew very fast, and I was fortunate that a fellow genealogy buddy Mike Maddi came forward to co-manage the project with me and then offered to take over. At the end of 2006, we had twenty members in our Sicily group. At the beginning of 2020, we had over sixteen hundred.

As of this writing, Family Tree DNA has expanded to 10,793 surname, lineage, and geographic groups, and has approximately two million people in its data base. Family Tree DNA also does the testing for the National Geographic Genographic Project. Persons in the FT DNA data base are asked to include their results in the National Genographic Project to combine data.

So, what exactly is DNA, and how does it relate to genealogy?

Scientific atDNA, Y-DNA and mtDNA

DNA (Deoxyribonucleic Acid) is essentially our genetic fingerprint—often called the molecule of life—which is present in our cells. There are about three billion base pairs of

DNA found in the nucleus of human cells which are grouped in 23 pairs of chromosomes. Twenty-two pairs are non-sex chromosomes called autosomes that determine our uniqueness (atDNA). The 23rd pair of chromosomes is what determines the sex of a child (XX = female; XY = male). A female child inherits an X chromosome from each parent, but a male child inherits an X chromosome from his mother *and* a Y chromosome from his father.

Autosomal DNA (atDNA) is inherited from all lines, including both parents, as well as their parents, grandparents, etc., as far back as eight to ten generations. The further back in generations, the smaller the fragment of shared autosomal DNA.

Y Chromosome DNA (Y-DNA) is found only in males, and is passed on exclusively from father to son without change. The original traceable Y-DNA is known as Y-Chromosomal Adam, or Scientific Adam.

Mitochondrial DNA (mtDNA) is non-nuclear DNA, located outside the cell's nucleus and has its own DNA. MtDNA is the powerhouse, battery back, or energy of each cell in our body. The X-chromosome is passed on from mother to daughter, female to female, consistently from one to the other. It is also passed on from mother to son, then son to daughter, but stops there. The original traceable mtDNA is known as Mitochondrial Eve, or Scientific Eve.

Autosomal DNA testing is best done by the oldest generations wherever possible — parents, grandparents, aunts and uncles. Siblings tested may have inherited parts of parents' DNA that you may not carry. Unfortunately for me, my siblings, parents, and all my aunts and uncles have passed away. I have only four living first cousins, two on my father's side and two on my mother's side (one in Canada and one in Sicily). The number of markers decreases by about half each generation. Therefore, inheritance is more random and unequal from more distant ancestors. AtDNA is the genealogical test done by Ancestry DNA™ and the "Family Finder" test done by Family Tree DNA. Both give matches to genetic cousins, as well as ethnic percentages. As of this writing, Ancestry DNA™ does not yet test for Y-DNA or mtDNA. The Y-DNA and mtDNA testing goes far beyond the eight to ten generations resulting from atDNA. Another company that does genealogical testing is 23 and Me, which also provides a test for health traits.

DNA testing for genealogy can:

- provide migration patterns for your ancestry.
- provide a list of your ancestors' countries.
- provide links to genetic cousins who may have vital records and photos of family members.
- prove paternity if you have a doubt.
- provide new countries to search for additional ancestral records.
- correct records that may have been wrong.
- prove or disprove a family story.
- provide ethnic origins you might not know you had.
- provide an opportunity to break through your brick walls.

Genetic genealogy is all about matching. The higher the number of markers tested, the higher probability of matching. E.g., with 12 markers, you may have a 50% probability of a match; with 37 or 67 markers, you will have a 90% to 95% probability of a match. If you want a 90% probability of matching someone within 600-700 years, then you increase the number of markers tested. How many markers should you order? FT DNA recommends 12 to start with; you can always upgrade later if you find a match and want a more definitive period. You do not have to retest to upgrade. Samples are held for twenty-five years. Results are released to matching individuals only with your permission.

Markers and Haplogroups

Markers are random, naturally-occurring mutations in the DNA which can be mapped through generations, revealing our lineage. Populations are organized into branches called haplogroups, using Y-DNA and mtDNA, both of which can be used to define genetic populations.

Classifications of human haplogroups based on genetic markers have been rapidly evolving over the past several years as new markers are found. Within Y-DNA and mtDNA, haplogroups are lettered, and further subdivided using numbers and lower case letters. The more markers you test, the more definitive your haplogroup becomes.

My father's Y-DNA is Haplogroup R1b1cU ... or most recently, R-Z36 (a subgroup of R-M269). According to Family Tree DNA, "Haplogroup R1b is the most common haplogroup in European populations. It is believed to have expanded throughout Europe as humans re-colonized after the last glacial maximum 10–12 thousand years ago. This lineage is also the haplogroup containing the Atlantic modal haplotype."* In my case a simple DNA swab by my B&B manager and/or the Giuntas in Pozzallo would tell me immediately if I am, indeed, related to the Pozzallo Giuntas.

My mother's mt-DNA is Haplogroup H7c6. According to Family Tree DNA, "Haplogroup H7 is an uncommon branch of haplogroup H and is found at low frequencies in both Europe and the Near East. Its age is estimated to be around 15,000 years. Further research will better resolve the distribution and historical characteristics of this haplogroup."* According to the National Genographic Project, the highest percentage of this line in Europe is in Ireland, where it makes up 61% of the population.

* Courtesy of Family Tree DNA, Gene by Gene, Ltd., Houston, Texas.

My Ethnic Test Results

My Family Tree DNA autosomal test revealed the following ethnic make-up: 76% European (61% Southeast Europe and 15% Iberia); 20% Middle Eastern (10% Asia Minor and 10% West Middle East); and 4% Jewish Diaspora (Ashkenazi).

If I am interpreting my origin maps correctly, the European and Middle Eastern Concentrations are in the following locations and levels.

European Concentration – High to Low

Level 1   S. Italy, Sardinia (not Sicily)
Level 2   Central Italy, S. Spain, Portugal
Level 3   N. Sicily, Central Italy, W. Greece, Albania, W. Republic of Macedonia, Montenegro, Central Spain, N. Morocco
Level 4   Sicily, N. Italy, E. Greece, Republic of Macedonia, Kosovo, N. Morocco, N. Algeria, Switzerland, Liechtenstein, Eastern France, NE. Spain, rest of Morocco
Level 5   W. Austria, Central Germany, E. Belgium, Central France
Level 6   E. Austria, Slovenia, W. Hungary, W. Slovakia, Czech Republic, E. Germany, Netherlands

Middle Eastern Concentration – High to Low

Level 1   Turkey
Level 2   Armenia
Level 3   Azerbaijan, N. Syria, Egypt, Jordan
Level 4   Cyprus, Georgia, Israel, Lebanon, Syria
Level 5   Iraq, Saudi Arabia, E. Libya

My Ancestry DNA™ autosomal test revealed slightly different ethnic origins: 75% Southern European (Italy/Greece); 11% Middle Eastern; 7% European Jewish; 3% North African, and less than 1% each for Ireland, Scandinavia, Caucasus, and Southern Asia. Other areas tested with zero percentages were Eastern Europe; Western Europe; Britain; the Iberian Peninsula; East Asia; Finland; NW Russia; Southeast, South-Central and Central Africa.

This will undoubtedly be an ongoing project for me as I have more markers tested and investigate my "matches."

Eyes First

— Jane Ruona

OUR SOCIETY IS AGING. The fastest growing age group is over sixty-five. This is due to an increase in longevity and a lower birthrate in the United States and throughout the world. As an R.N. and Geriatric Nurse Practitioner for fifty-nine years, I have studied preventive health. Finally my profession and age have come together. It is humbling to see mistakes when experiencing aging myself. Many theories and practices in medicine have changed over the years. It is a challenge to be able to be flexible and change when good research indicates the necessity.

My mother and grandmother had very positive attitudes about aging. To quote my mom: "I am just along for the ride." Now that I have the opportunity to experience aging like an aware guinea pig, I would like to pass on my personal reactions starting with vision changes.

My first hint of aging was vision change. I was about forty-five when small print was blurry to my eyes. I could not read the small print on the conditioner container, so I used it for shampoo. I thought why doesn't the manufacturer use large legible print? I decided to change containers so I could differentiate with my hands. I felt foolish and did not admit this to anyone. These early changes in vision are normal and gradual. The lens becomes less flexible to focus on nearby objects; the condition is called presbyopia. This vision change is easily corrected by reading glasses.

I also noticed I needed more light to read the labels on vitamins and medicines. This could result in an overdose or the wrong medication.

The other problem I noticed was that my cholesterol medicine was the same shape and color as my blood pressure medicine. No wonder patients experience side effects such as dizziness or falling.

One should have routine eye exams at least every two years to check for diabetes, hypertension, and macular degeneration. Next the provider should check eye pressure for glaucoma. Good nutrition, lutein and omega-3 acids are useful in prevention of eye disease. More serious signs that need follow-up by ophthalmology are:

1. Fluctuating vision may be a sign of hypertension or diabetes.
2. Increase in floaters and flashing lights may be a tear or detached retina and needs immediate follow-up.
3. Loss of side vision is a sign of glaucoma.
4. Distorted vision (wavy lines on a grid) may be macular degeneration.
5. Double vision, loss of vision on one side, or a double image may be a stroke or temporal arteritis.
6. Sudden eye pain and redness may damage the optic nerve due to acute glaucoma.
7. Cloudy vision or halo around lights at night may be cataracts.

Seniors are very sensitive to vision changes because of their fear of loss of driving privileges. This could lead to radical life changes.

My husband, Bill, is sixteen months older than I. One day he began tilting lampshades to get more light. He was also using a flashlight and magnifying glass. I am now following his lead. Also a lighted magnifying glass on a stand can be helpful for close work. Put glasses in the same place so you can find them easily. Wouldn't it be a bonus if glasses had computer chips so you could "find my glasses?" Last, it is important to remove scatter rugs, any pillows you may have tossed on the floor, and other things that may impede your path to the bathroom at night.

Using hiking sticks while walking on trails can prevent falls. In my senior community there is group called "pole walkers."

It is important not to rub the eyes. To rest your eyes, use the 20/20 rule when using the computer. After twenty minutes of reading, look in the distance for twenty seconds.

Smoking damages blood vessels to the optic nerve as does uncontrolled diabetes.

Hydration is important. If you have dry eyes, use a humidifier and drink more water. Glasses can keep eyes moist.

Avoid excess coffee; substitute green tea.

My hope is that you can tiptoe into your senior years with a positive attitude, good health, and "just go along for the ride." You will understand when you are my age!

María Valentina

—Elia Vasquez Fuller

THE HOT SUN BEAT DOWN on the green cornfields where María and her brother, José, were hiding. Between the cornstalks they could hear the woman cursing.

"Desgraciados!" the woman yelled. "Worthless!" She pushed the tall cornstalks aside, trying to find them.

Shadows of dark clouds and a strong wind suddenly swept over the fields, forcing the woman to turn around and walk back to the house, seeking shelter from the brewing storm. Between loud crashes of thunder and lightning, the two children could hear her spewing threats about what she would do to them when she found them.

Peering through the corn stalks, the children could see the woman taking things out of their house and loading them into a cart.

"She's stealing all our things!" María gasped. "When Papá gets back, there won't be anything left." They saw the woman pushing the loaded cart to the road until she was out of sight. Quickly, María ran back into the house to see what the woman had taken.

Suddenly, she heard the wheels of the old cart coming back, grinding loudly as they got closer and closer to the house. María ran back into the cornfield with an iron and some pots and pans that she had managed to grab. She prayed that she and her brother would not be discovered.

They continued to watch as the woman came back to the house, again and again, loading the wagon with their things. There was nothing they could do now but wait for their father's return.

The first night they spent in the cornfield was the hardest. They were hungry and cold. The sound of howling coyotes frightened María. She thought she heard footsteps coming towards them. She shook José awake.

"Listen!" she whispered. "I hear her. She's coming to get us."

José sat up quickly and listened, intently.

"No, it's not her." He put his arm around María's shoulder. "It's just the mice climbing up the stalks eating the corn. Don't be afraid. I won't let her hurt you. Go to sleep."

"If she finds us I'll hit her on the head with this iron," María said, but her courage wavered when she heard an owl's long high screech over her head.

She's turned herself into an owl! She's a witch, she thought. María knew that witches, like owls, can see in the dark. She started reciting the prayers that her mother had recited whenever witches whistled around their house, at night. José was asleep. Her trembling hand reached for her mother's rosary which she always wore around her neck.

She remembered when the woman had arrived at their doorstep after their mother, Narcisa Cortez, had died. Their father, Luciano Maya, needing a woman to care for María, and José had taken her in. Their father left them often to sell vegetables from his small plot of land in Zaragosa, Mexico. It was during his absence that María and José suffered from the woman's unpredictable behavior.

After many hours, María fell asleep clutching the rosary. She awoke to the sound of raindrops falling on cornstalks. The morning light found her and her brother soaking wet.

They sat up and crawled on their hands and knees to the edge of the cornfield where they could see their house. Everything was quiet. The cart was gone. They watched and waited a few more hours. When they thought it was safe, they slowly ventured to their house and peered inside a window. There was nothing and no one inside the house. The woman had taken everything. She was gone. Two days later, their father returned to find the children alone and starving, sleeping on the bare floor.

When the children told him what happened he blamed himself for allowing the woman to live with them. "Hay pobrecitos! Mijitos, my poor children ...," he cried as he took them in his arms.

The long trip had taken a toll on him. He had made no profit from his sales. And seeing his children like this, he knew they needed him more than ever, but his weariness overcame him, and he fell into a deep sleep. In his dreams, he was being chased by a pack of snarling dogs. He was trying to run as fast as he could, but his legs felt numb and he couldn't move. The wild dogs were catching up to him. He woke up — his heart beating fast. In a daze, he heard María's voice.

"Papá, José is sick."

He could hear José coughing on the other side of the room.

"My head hurts," moaned José.

He touched José's forehead and felt him burning up with fever.

The red rash on José's face gripped him with a fear worse than his nightmare of the snarling dogs. *Maybe I'm wrong*, he thought. *Maybe it's not scarlet fever.* He looked closer at José and saw that the rash had spread to his stomach, and his arms. There was no doubt about it. He had seen other children with scarlet fever; most of them had died. He knew what had to be done.

"What's wrong with him, Papá?" asked María.

"It's nothing to worry about. He will get well soon. Today is Sunday, mija. Remember that I promised your abuelitos that you and José would go to church with them to light a candle for your mother today."

"But, I want to stay here and help you take care of José," María pleaded.

"Well, now that José is sick you must go with them and light his candle, too. Your abuelitos will be here soon, so go get dressed for church."

Sad that she would be leaving José behind, unable to even light his own candle, she started walking towards the blanket where José was lying. She wanted to comfort him, to tell him that she would be back soon. But her father quickly stopped her. He pulled her away and said softly, "He's sleeping. It's better if we don't disturb him."

Matilda

— Corinne Lee Murphy

SHE WOULD HAVE DIED in the home in which she was born, but she was not afforded that small mercy. Her oldest grandchild, one of only two, had called for an ambulance. He was a grown man with a family of his own, a lawyer. He watched from the porch as the ambulance mistakenly rushed past, unsure of the location of the ranch house on the Old River Road. He jumped in his car and sped away to chase the ambulance down. And, so, the ambulance returned and took her away from the home in which she had lived for her 94 years, and she would never return.

Matilda's oldest great-grandchild, only four, had watched the scurrying in and out of her bedroom adjacent to the large farmhouse dining room by the girl's father and grandmother and then the ambulance crew. The girl was not surprised when she was told a few days later that Matilda would not return, that she had died. After all, she understood that her other grandmother had died already, and the small little woman was so very old. She had been so slight of frame with her shoulders narrow; bird-like, with eyes small and darting. Her grey hair was gathered into a knot on the top of her head. She wore old-fashioned dresses with small patterns and broaches at her neck and, almost always, aprons. And that is how the girl would always remember her, and the girl would later have Matilda's rocking chair in her home, never refinished to obliterate where Matilda's arms had worn smooth the original stain down to the wood. The girl remembered Matilda sitting in the chair in front of the wood stove in the dining room, where almost all family gatherings took place, most around the large farmhouse table.

The girl was the only one of her great-grandchildren who would remember her.

Matilda was born in 1865 into a secure life. Her parents owned the land they farmed. She loved being outside and active, playing and working the animals that fed them and brought in more money. There were heads of cattle for meat and milk, chickens for eggs and Sunday dinners, sheep, hogs and horses. There was an orchard of walnuts. They grew grain for feed and sale. There were large barns, often filled with bales of hay, and a smaller shed-like building with a huge anvil for metalwork and a visiting blacksmith.

The home was spacious, with two stories. The kitchen was very large with a separate room for the fancy blue kerosene stove. There was an icebox for perishables. Spacious enclosed porches extended on both sides of the home, and one was situated over a well so that an iron hand pump brought water directly into a big metal sink.

On Matilda's twelfth birthday, she was presented with an ornate organ which had been manufactured in the Midwest and transported all the way to California. The organ was too precious to reside in the parlor downstairs because the Sacramento Valley did not yet have the extensive network of dams and weirs and causeways and was subject to flooding in exceptionally rainy winters. So the organ was put upstairs into "Annie's room," the small bedroom which had been set aside for the Irish maid they would import when the funds accumulated sufficiently, but who never came. When the ranch was sold, the organ finally came down the stairs, making the turn at the landing with the dusty window, and would eventually find its way into the care of the girl.

Matilda learned a few tunes on the organ, but the lessons never really took. She was trained in cooking but didn't particularly like it. She learned to sew and had a treadle sewing machine that was decorative as well as useful. She accomplished tatting, knitting and crocheting. She prepared to be a wife, and so she eventually was.

Matilda married a man considerably older, whose family had emigrated from England and whose own brother had fought in the Civil War for the Union before Matilda had even been born. Her husband had come on his own to California, and so they met and found each other acceptable. They married and began having children. The first two were boys, Edward and Charles, but then came Elsie and, a few years later, Emma. The children were fortunate that the schoolhouse was on a piece of land around a bend in the road that had been donated by the adjacent ranch and the walk to school was not arduous.

The boys helped with chores, but Matilda was very pleased when sweet, compliant Elsie was old enough to cook for the work crews and family. Matilda preferred being outside working with the men. Emma, the baby, was spoiled and headstrong. She detested her name which she thought sounded like a cow and insisted that she be addressed as Elizabeth, the middle name she shared with Matilda. She was an attractive girl and, although the boys boarded in Chico for high school, she had drawn the interest of distant cousins in Eldora, Iowa. The father of that family was the town banker, and they invited Elizabeth to live with them and attend high school there, a "finishing school." The finishing took to a point, and she became engaged to a young doctor in Iowa. But Elizabeth was prone to willfulness, and they quarreled. The engagement was broken, and Elizabeth returned to California with a barrel filled with Limoges china in tow for her hope chest. She began to attend college, Chico Normal School, a teacher's college that would become California State University at Chico. Elizabeth graduated and began teaching nearby.

Matilda's girls were now home with her, but her boys had left to seek their fortunes, Charles in Alaska and Ed in Woodland, near Sacramento. But Charles returned to California and joined the Army during WWI, and Matilda, by now a young widow, received word that he was dying of the Spanish flu and she should find her way to him in Ventura if she wanted to see him again. She took the train and found him, helping to nurse him to health. And Ed returned home to run the ranch.

The family was Presbyterian by way of Scottish ancestors, and the men were Masons. The girl had heard of their rectitude and law-abiding nature many times, and a prime example held up was the fact that during Prohibition they had a bottle of whiskey for medicinal purposes, but it was never opened during Prohibition, from 1920-1933, because abstinence was the law of the land. In the 1980s an old chest from the ranch, undisturbed for decades, was finally pried open. In it was the fabled bottle. And the girl has it now, still filled with whiskey.

Although life was, in fact, lived with a certain rectitude, Matilda was not completely without vanity. She had decorative hats with long bejeweled pins, small pieces of jewelry, a compact with a drawing of Paris on its face and a fur with minks biting each other's tails that she draped over her shoulders. There were social events beyond the ranch.

In the meantime, Elizabeth had observed that none of her older siblings had married. She was concerned that she had slipped into spinsterhood, and she set her eye on the older brother of some of her students, a redhead of limited education but hardworking and manageable. He was twenty and she twenty-five, and they got on a train and eloped to Stockton, with an evening before the wedding unaccounted for in any decorous fashion. (This began the fiction that she was five years younger than her actual age, a situation that was only straightened out when she was seventy, and she had blithely continued teaching past the mandatory retirement age of sixty-five. A reckoning was had with both social security and the State of California.)

Apparently influenced by Elizabeth, Elsie had accepted courtship by a much older rancher from a nearby property, near Durham, and they married, and she moved into a handsome farmhouse on his ranch. Charlie had struck out again for faraway places, and now it was just Matilda and Ed running the ranch.

The Great Depression was not the struggle for the family that it was for so many because the land belonged to them, and they were essentially self-sufficient with food. It came and went. As did WWII, although not without suffering. Her grandson was shipped to Europe for the Battle of the Bulge, was shot and grievously wounded. But he recovered with scars and a limp, and he returned to California to finish his education and then graduate from law school.

Matilda presided over her growing family at holidays and such. But the family was not growing very fast. Her two sons never married. Her daughters only managed a child apiece, the boy for Elizabeth and, then, a girl for Elsie. And the grandchildren only produced four great-grandchildren between them, and Matilda only held three of them, two of them still infants on that day she left her home for the last time.

Ed lived alone on the ranch for two more years, lonely, but caring for his animals and seeing to the harvest of the crops. The girl remembers him outfitted in a slicker on a cold and rainy night, tenderly bringing a baby lamb into the kitchen for warmth. But at age seventy-two, his heart stopped in the field where he fell, and he was buried next to his mother with whom he had spent almost his entire life. It was as if he had had a premonition. He had sold the hogs years before for the reason that hogs eat anything, and he did not want to be pig fodder in the event he died in their pen.

Elizabeth and her husband took over the ranching for a few years until it just became too much, and the ranch that had been in the family for more than one hundred years, was sold. It is gone and not yet forgotten, but soon it will be.

My Life-Long Love Affair

— Anita Sharf

MY LOVE AFFAIR WITH WORDS probably started shortly after my learning to read, which included the sounding out of each letter and of syllables. That learning was and is music to my eyes and to my ears.

Writing is very important to me. First, it was the excitement I felt, and still feel, to write about things that I knew—some happy, some sad. As I became braver, I found the joy of writing fiction, as well as fact, and the ability to blend the two. It was, at times, an escape to another world. I found it is easier to write pathos and sadness than to write humor. It is difficult to find a reader's funny bone. My excitement about writing and finding the words that make that writing come alive on a page has not abated.

I compose in long hand on lined, yellow pads. The flow of words, that not only tell, but when the right ones are written, create—with very little effort on my part—a poem, a story, or even just an expression. I become surrounded by an aura. The words actually seem to write their own entire story. They take over and guide and move my pen.

MAY IT CONTINUE!

Petey the Poltergeist

— Mark Gaulding

IN 1984 I LIVED IN DALLAS in the Oak Lawn area. My new girlfriend and I lived in a small group of two-story town homes on Gilbert Avenue. The units were divided by a long walkway. Our neighbor across the way was a friend. Her name was Annie. She was an interesting middle-aged woman who suffered from a disability and did not work. She lived with her two canine "children." I think she was once attractive.

Frequently she would invite my girlfriend, Stella, and me over for wine. Stella had already established a friendship with Annie before I moved in. We enjoyed our Annie visits. But we also sensed that we were doing something that brought Annie joy.

Stella and I would leave these periodic Annie "happy hours" and walk across to our townhouse. And then we would analyze and recount the remarkable experience of that evening. One particular evening, I shall never forget. Annie talked about a poltergeist that haunted her townhouse. His name was Petey. I think their "friendship" was intense. Annie told us of the naughty things that Petey would do throughout each day. Petey the Poltergeist's antics were mostly childish hijinks. And then Annie became very sad and talked about the night that Petey pushed her down her townhouse staircase. She was very upset and angry. Stella and I were mutually horrified. But I do remember thinking at the time that Petey was Annie's best and worst friend.

Jump forward to 2018. My mother and I were rescued by a sweet little Chihuahua mix, "Bella Bobble Head" as we named her. She was very frightened and skittish. It made me remember my neighbor Annie all those years ago in Dallas. Shortly before Bella rescued us, we had our kitchen appliances replaced. Our new refrigerator with the front door ice and water dispenser was convenient. But it occasionally dispensed ice by itself, unprovoked. My mother and I would laugh at the unprovoked ice dispensing, and I told her about Annie and her Petey the Poltergeist. And we decided that Petey had come to live with us.

One time, Petey's antic ice cube throwing left a melting puddle on the kitchen tile. I was in the kitchen preparing dinner and I slid on the water and made quite an epic fall. I ended up in the ER, via ambulance, with a fractured femur and knee.

Since then, I have talked to Petey the Poltergeist who resides in our refrigerator door ice dispenser. Bella is always enthralled. We will all be sitting watching television in the living room, and Petey in the attached kitchen, for no reason, will spit out two pieces of ice. Bella always looks at me quizzically, but knowingly. As if to say: "There goes Petey."

And so, Petey the Poltergeist has become a member of our small family. Like me, Petey must be ancient. I speak loudly to him now as I imagine he has grown hard of hearing. Every day Bella's water bowl needs to be refreshed. I pick it up, and Bella eagerly waddles behind me to the refrigerator. I knock on the ice dispenser and yell: "Petey wake up. Bella needs fresh water and ice." Bella believes this totally. Usually she is frightened by loud noises. She bobbles her head from side to side. She knows that our friend Petey is giving her fresh water and ice. And she loves it and is appreciative of Petey's faithful contribution to her care.

This watering has become a beloved ritual in our little household. And I like to think that somehow wonderful Annie from Dallas still lives on. And her poltergeist migrated to Palm Desert to retire. And the more I age, the more I am sure that we are not alone. It took a lifetime for Petey to visit me. And I am thankful for the memory. And the experience. And I will never forget Annie.

Stupidity vs. Us

— Larry Kueneman

GIVEN THE EXPERIENCES OF THOSE who first left England to come to North America, to Australia, and to India, the terrible fear of fire they held had been well earned. Starting simply as fears based on the limited means of protection they experienced, these fears made sense. However, over the following centuries, conditions and firefighting equipment has changed much for the better. Yet even with new understanding of both fire and of forests becoming far more controllable, the original fears and resultant understandings have failed to change one bit. Yes, four hundred years ago, given the environment and the low level of technology, as well as other conditions, these fears were protective and made sense. However, these seriously mistaken original understandings of fire conditions still permeate environmental thinking to the extent that most refuse to modify their beliefs. This is for the simple reason that people today still find comfort with their original fears; this, unfortunately, is comfort bordering on stupidity. However, it was not—and is not today, stupidity; it is just nature.

We know the first Colonists, the same ones who saw the devastation of their European villages from wildfires, panicked when they discovered Native Americans teaching some of them how to initiate ground fires when nature had failed to do so in forests for too many years. They banned such action immediately because they simply had no understanding of the role natural fire plays in maintaining forest density. They could not have known these same Native American tribes had been helping nature keep the forests of North America natural for upwards of 14,000 years.

Without fires, three centuries was plenty of time for forests to explode in density. Following a major fire that burned in several states and a province of Canada in 1910, the head of the then five-year-old U.S. Forest Service, Gifford Pinchot, ordered that henceforth, all fires were to be extinguished by 10 a.m. of the morning following their discovery. This has been both the rule and the way of thinking now for more than a century. We have thousands of firefighters who do battle every year, sometimes losing their lives. With both lightning initiated and other fires put out quickly, there is nothing now to control the density of a forested area, but the rule remains in place.

A secondary problem exists with that severely increasing forest density. Back when the Native Americans were in charge, habitat was perfect. This means habitat for birds and animals, but it also means habitat for trees. The first fire we call a wildfire likely occurred around 1850. With the absence of Native American-introduced fires, and the elimination of lightning-initiated fires as quickly as possible, the forests continued to become more and more dense. Sadly, the problem has now been with us for so many years, and habitat has become so poor, very few people ever mention habitat anymore. However, this forest home for birds and animals continues to diminish as each year passes and governments do nothing except increase the problem by putting fires out.

Okay, realistically, the problem could have far more easily been dealt with two hundred years ago when the density was far lower, but we have become so adept at putting out fires, natural densities simply do not exist.

The remedy for this problem is simple, but will entail a huge project—and that project must be accomplished in stages. First, it must be declared that clear-cut forestry in any forested area is permanently banned. The reason for this will become apparent. Second, the ground must be prepared by severely thinning out the undergrowth in preparation for timber removal. And some young trees should be left in place. Third, with the strict guidance of a certified forester, mature trees must be carefully thinned to recover a reasonable density. This will allow maturing trees to gain thickness. <u>Fourth</u>, after cleaning up the ground of debris, ground fires should be introduced where the work was accomplished. This removes the last debris. (This burning also converts plants to carbon, which is fertilizer for plant and tree growth.) And <u>fifth</u>, the area so thinned must be understood to be natural, not damaged. No, at the moment it is not pretty; but we, today, forget what forest control looks like, for the simple reason no one alive today has ever seen it. Once this point has been reached, and the area has been watched, we will usually see natural fires recurring—about four to twenty years after the cleanup. It was when the Native Americans saw no natural fires after that roughly twenty years, that they initiated their own cleanup fires. This means observing the area not only for fires, but unusual increases in undergrowth that could, with lightning, initiate another fire. This is the natural process that was stopped four hundred years ago. And it was stopped wherever the British and the Spanish landed, be that anywhere in the Western Hemisphere, or Australia, or India. These nations were all victims of that ignorance.

In an area treated to recover natural forests and eliminate wildfires, the timber removal will help pay for the work. In addition, under these new conditions, while lightning and ground fires may take place, because of this new density, it is impossible for what we came to know as a wildfire to occur, and if fires need to be moderated, that effort will be easy and safe for people and nearby structures.

I mentioned above that stupidity is not the cause of the problem.

No, that responsibility lies with the nature of being a human being. Our ancient ancestors felt fear when people-eating animals were about. But to take this question to its base, fear is the first, and most prominent emotion, of every creature of every type ever born on this planet. The recognized presence of fear sets up for the seeking of comfort, and if two answers show up to a question, and one is not comfortable, it will be rejected.

And that is the case even when the uncomfortable answer was a hundred percent right on the money. We want comfort, and mankind feels the answers they came up with regarding fire were correct, for the simple reason it is comfortable. Sorry, the U.S. Forest Service is not the culprit; it's the fact we are human beings, and are prone to error.

The Replacement Wife

— Mary Kirk

HOW HAD IT ALL COME TO THIS?

Mary looked around at the barren landscape as she clung to the bench seat of the wagon. Choking red dust was continually kicked up by the team, nearly blocking the view of the forbidding cliffs on either side, the scattered sage brush and the occasional scrub trees along the trail. The valley was as lonely and forbidding as the life that lay ahead.

She was the replacement wife for her lifelong friend Sara. Sara was dead. Sara, whom she played with in the streets of Hemyock in Devon, traveled with to France where they worked as governesses, then back to England and on to Zion. This was to have been the adventure of a lifetime.

How had it all come to this?

Mary's papa, Samuel, was a stonemason, but jobs had been scarce. He never had the money to join the mason's guild and instead was apprenticed to the local parish. Only guild members were hired to work on the big manor houses. But what few jobs he did find at least kept him out of the nearby quarries. During the frequent strikes, he would sometimes go days and weeks without a single job. To help the family, everyone was expected to work, from the youngest brother, to the oldest sister.

Devon, and its surrounds, was a desperately poor area of tin mines. Most of the boys could only find work in the dangerous diggings, working long hours as they breathed in the foul air underground. Many of the young girls labored on the surface handpicking the best ores and breaking rocks too large for the crushers. Although Papa and Mama had tried hard to keep their children out of the mines, they weren't always successful.

Mama, beautiful Mama, couldn't bear to think of her precious young children growing up to spend the rest of their lives struggling amid the heart wrenching poverty she saw around them. She taught them all to read and write, just as her mother had done for her. And the girls learned to sew and keep house — the hope was to find them a position in one of the nearby manor houses. And there was music — always there was music.

They were friends, the three of them, and they had promised to be friends for life — Mary Ware, the youngest; Sara Meredith; and Matilda Price, whom they called Tilly. On those rare occasions when they weren't hard at work, they would sneak off to Hemyock Castle and play among the ruins. They danced with holly wreaths on their heads and climbed to the top of the walls to look out over their kingdom — playing at being queen or lady of the manor. They had such wonderful dreams it caused them to forget how cold and hungry they were most days. Queens and Ladies were never cold and hungry.

Then one day life as Mary knew it changed. Mama had been getting thinner each day, and rarely was strong enough to see to the family. Mary would always remember crawling out of bed that cold damp morning — the bed she shared with her older sisters. She found her father kneeling beside Mama's cot which he'd pulled close to the fire. Papa was beside himself with grief and fear. Grief for the loss of Mama, and fear over what was to become of them. They tried to carry on, but Papa seemed lost, and the music was gone.

In the months that followed, the three friends found only a few precious moments when they could return to the castle — but when they did, they still dreamt of the future. It was all fantasy, and they knew it, but it was a bright spot in those dreary days.

"I will find a handsome knight to take me to a new country," Sara declared.

"And I shall have a beautiful home and lots of wonderful children," was Tilly's dream.

Mary paused looking out over the countryside, and thinking about her life, she quietly added, "And there will be food, more than we can ever imagine." She always seemed to be hungry these days. Papa was often too tired or weary to look for work, and so what little food there was had to be carefully parceled out so that it would last—sometimes for days.

Not long after Mama died, Mary's older brothers, William and Richard, were apprenticed to the building trades. William was just twelve.

"They won't get paid," Papa told the children that first evening after the boys left. Looking around at the young faces silently accusing him, he added, "But just think, there will be two less mouths to feed. More left for each of you." He thought this would cheer them, but instead they turned silently and walked away.

One day, unexpectedly, Papa brought home Caroline, his new wife. Things didn't start well. This new mother had no intention of continuing to train the girls and, in short order, sent Harriet and Sarah Almeda out to work as domestics in a nearby manor house.

"Please don't make them go," Mary pleaded with Caroline. But it was to no avail. Mary was barely eight years old, and was to remain at home to help with the cooking, cleaning and taking care of the younger ones. And she knew there would one day be more babies to care for. Mary was lost—Mama was gone, her sisters Harriet and Sarah Almeda were leaving, the older boys had been sent away, and Papa, he just wasn't like Papa anymore.

One spring day not long after, the three friends, Mary, Sara and Tilly, were talking together excitedly as they perched atop one of the broken walls at the castle, their feet dangling over the edge. Sara had heard there were recruiters looking for young girls to travel to France as live-in nannies. France sounded like one of those far-off lands they'd been dreaming about.

"We will be in service as nannies for several years," Sara explained, "after which we can return to England, and they'll even pay our way back home." The friends agreed they were going to do it — all three of them, but for now they would tell no one what they planned.

Tilly, always the practical one, asked, "How do we find these recruiters?"

"I'm not sure," came the reply. "I heard two girls our age talking about it at the market yesterday."

"Why don't we try to find some other girls to talk to," Mary suggested. "Let's see if anyone else knows more about it."

"We're probably too young to go anyway," Tilly added.

"Well then, we'll just have to go as apprentice nannies." Sara stood abruptly, stomped her foot and turned away, determined to stop Tilly from trying to discourage them.

"You're right," Mary agreed, as she jumped up to join Sara. "We will be nannies, and we will travel to Paris. And you're going too, Tilly."

The heat of the day was causing Mary to doze off just as a wagon wheel suddenly hit a rock. She was startled and looked around to see where she was. She had been remembering Hemyock and the fantasies she had shared with Sara and Tilly. Quickly she lowered her head so Jacob wouldn't catch her smiling to herself. What dreams they had been.

As she rode along through the desolation, her thoughts drifted again back to those days when they longed for far-off places and a magical life with their knights.

Samuel had moved the family from Hemyock to Barnstaple in the hopes of finding more work. Mary was not much more than a child, but her childhood dreams were left far behind her at the castle. All but one — France — and she clung to that one with all her might.

The three friends were now scattered far and wide across England. Tilly's father had lost everything, and the entire family was forced to move to Birmingham where they opened a millinery shop. Tilly worked there alongside her mother and father as they tried to save enough money to move to America. Her parents had heard a missionary talk and had joined the Mormon church. They were determined to make the pilgrimage like so many others — to Zion, the Great Salt Lake Valley.

And Sara was in Kensington outside of London. She was living with a family as one of their domestic servants.

The friends wrote scraps of notes to one another over the next few years, but they never talked again about the time when they were once Queens and Ladies of the Manor.

Barnstaple was disagreeable. It was close to the coast, and the wind never stopped — not for a moment. The chill seemed to have seeped into their bones and their souls, as well. Mary would always remember that house. It was dark and cold, without a touch of life in it. Caroline, her stepmother, was expecting her first child and stayed in bed most days. Mary was left with the task of caring for the younger children and running the house. She would climb into bed at the end of the day too tired to even think about what would come tomorrow. There was only a flicker of her dream left.

Word came about better stonemason jobs in Bristol, and once again Mary found herself bundled into a cart. But it no longer mattered. One bleak day followed closely upon another. For her, the darkness left by all the changes never seemed to brighten, except for those rare times when she heard from Tilly, Sara or her sister Harriet.

The new baby came shortly after they arrived in Bristol—
Caroline Jane. Just a baby—for some reason Mary never really
thought of her as her sister. She already had three sisters. But
she did her best for the baby and longed to remember the songs
Mama had shared with her, but it seemed so long ago. The weeks
and months drifted by in a fog. Soon Baby James was born, but
he barely lived a week, and after a time, little Eliza May arrived,
only to die within hours.

The cloud of sorrow and grief never seemed to lift from the
house. "I've no one to talk to," Mary wrote her sister one day.
"I work and do chores in the house all day long, and yet Papa
seems to have forgotten I'm even here. And since the loss of the
babies, Caroline never comes out of her room."

Then one day she penned a reminder to her friends. It would
soon be time to find those recruiters they had talked about so
many years before.

At long last it was time. Mary was thirteen years old. Old enough
to travel to France, but not as a nanny. Instead they wanted her
to be a governess to teach English to the young children of a
wealthy Parisian family. They would pay her a few francs, and
she would live in their house. It all sounded so exciting. The
agency would send a chaperone to accompany several girls on
the journey. Letters were exchanged among the three friends,
but, sadly, Tilly would have to stay in Birmingham. Sara was
going with her, and Mary dreamt again of Queens and Ladies
of the Manor.

She had to tell the children she was leaving. Grace, just a year
younger, would be left to care for the others—Will, barely five,
and Charles, who would turn five just after she left. And there
was baby Caroline to look after. Mary's older sisters and brothers
were miles away—no chance to say goodbye. She wondered if
she'd ever see them again. Her father and stepmother were only
too glad to see her go, as if her leaving would dispel the gloom

in their lives. The train had recently come to Bristol and with it more jobs. But even with the additional work, Papa seemed locked in his misery, seldom smiling. He had little time for Mary and the others.

Mary packed the small carpet bag with her few possessions: clothes, a bible given to Papa at her Christening, and the precious rag doll her Mama had sewn. Each child was hugged in turn and kissed goodbye; then she went with Papa to the train station. The chaperone, tall and unsmiling, was there to meet them, and Papa handed her over and walked away without ever looking back. He had said he would write, but she wasn't sure. Little did she know she would never see her father again.

The train thundered into the station with clouds of steam billowing from its sides. This was the Great Western Railway, GWR, but most people called it God's Wonderful Railway, since it brought so many new jobs to Bristol. As it ground and screeched to a stop, Mary stood as tall as she could, determined to look like she belonged there. After all, she was leaving on the adventure of a lifetime. But having to be boosted up to the steps of the second-class car reminded her of just how young she was, and she was heading into a world she knew nothing about. She wanted to press her nose against the window as the train rushed through the countryside, but that was childish, and she wouldn't give in to it. After all, Mary was going to be a Lady of the Manor one day, and Ladies don't make nose prints on the glass. The train flew onward towards London. And a trip that would have taken several days by cart, took just under three hours.

The steam rushed from beneath the car and blocked the view as they pulled into Paddington Station. When it cleared, there was Sara, small bag in hand, scanning the windows for a first glimpse of her friend. She clambered up the stairs, not caring how she looked, and rushed into Mary's arms, only to be turned around by the chaperone, and ushered abruptly off the train. Everyone was hurried into a waiting carriage. They were in a rush to get to the London Bridge Station and the South Eastern train leaving soon for Dover. Over the years to come she would look back on that day, happily remembering the thrill of the train ride, but more than that was the joy of reuniting with Sara.

It took just two hours to get to Dover, where they would spend the night before boarding the ferry for Calais. Thoughts of acting grown up were forgotten as the two young girls huddled on the high-backed train seat sharing stories. Tears mingled with laughter. More than anything else, it was the wonderful happiness at being together again. Just before they arrived, they passed Dover Castle, and elbowing each other in the ribs they burst into giggles — their Queens and Ladies dreams alive again.

The next morning they had their first look at the imposing white cliffs and far below, the Admiralty Pier. At least they wouldn't have to wait for the tide to change now that the new harbor was finished. A horse-drawn stagecoach took them slowly down the narrow road carved in the face of the cliff. Waiting below was their boat, a small paddle steamer, equipped with sails just in case the engine broke down. The captain said it was faster than the larger sailboats, but the chaperone told them a boat that little was more likely to be unmercifully tossed around on the waves as it made its way across the channel.

It was late November, 1857. The families wanted them to arrive before December to take care of the children during the Paris holiday season which lasted all month long. But the channel didn't reflect the gaiety of the season; instead, it was gray and menacing. The girls decided to bundle up with all the extra clothing from their bags and stay outside for the crossing. They clung to the railings, the wind blowing their hair, scarcely noticing the cold as the boat made its way across the waves. It was an adventure … one they greeted with smiles and laughter. It took only three hours to make the crossing, but most of those who had stayed inside were sick the whole time, including the chaperone.

On the other side of the channel, there was a train waiting at the pier-side station in Calais. Once more they climbed on board and were soon fast asleep with their cheeks pressed against the corduroy fabric of the seats. They awoke, what seemed a short time later, and laughed as they saw the marks the seat material had left imbedded in their cheeks. It didn't matter. They were in Paris — their new home.

After a short ride from the station, the chaperone deposited each of them at a different house along the main streets of the city. Sara and Mary would be with different families, but they vowed to stay in touch. At last it was Mary's turn, and she was taken to the door of a tall narrow building with a shop on the ground floor. Looking up, it seemed to go on forever. Inside the gas lamps were lit, and from the porch it looked warm and welcoming. The door was answered by a woman in uniform who waved Mary into the house. As she entered the doorway, Mary turned to say goodbye to the chaperone who was already climbing back into the carriage. Years later she would wonder if she had ever known her name. She was just "the Chaperone."

Mary followed the woman in uniform up a narrow set of stairs. At the top was a room almost as large as her entire home in Bristol. The ceilings were high, and gas lamps lit every corner. She slowly turned, gaping at the tall windows, walls covered in fabric, chairs like nothing she had seen before and a huge fireplace with a crackling fire warding off the chilled air that followed her in from the street. She found herself staring up at a man and woman. As they gazed back at her, she couldn't help but compare them to the father and mother she had left behind. It wasn't their clothes; it was their faces. Everyone in Bristol looked so weary — almost too tired to go on, but knowing they must. There was a calmness here, a warmth that didn't just come from the fireplace.

In halting English, they introduced themselves and briefly explained her duties. Mary would live upstairs and work in the nursery with the Nanny, helping to care for the children and teaching them English. Each month she would earn two francs and have one day off when she could spend time with Sara exploring the streets of Paris. Mary had barely spoken a word — she just nodded and continued to look around in awe.

With bag in hand, she walked past the entry stairs and slowly climbed another steep flight to an oversized bedroom and sitting room, then up again to a floor with more bedrooms and a playroom. Above that was the nursery and the Nanny's room, and finally, high up under the roof, rooms for the servants. One of them, a small room, not much bigger than a closet, was just for her. Mary set down her suitcase and peered through the window. This was the faraway land she had dreamt of.

The next morning she met Nanny Claire and the children. The Nanny was from a poor village not far from Paris. Her husband had died, and her newborn baby was sent to an orphanage. The Paris family had hired her to be a wet nurse for their infant son, and to care for the older boy and girl. Mary immediately liked Nanny Claire. She helped her with English, and Nanny in turn helped Mary learn a few words in French so she could be understood when she was out exploring the city.

Over the next three years, Mary and Sara watched in amazement as the city changed around them. Slums were torn down and streets widened. There were new parks and rail stations. And buildings, covered with white stone, were being constructed all along the broad boulevards — buildings that glowed with the reflected light of the new gas street lamps. On their days off, in the evening, the girls would often follow behind the uniformed *allumeurs* as they stretched long poles topped with tiny lanterns high in the air to light the lamps. It instantly turned night to day.

In her attic room, Mary wrote to Tilly and her sister Harriet trying to share all that she was experiencing. Her stepmother and father had joined the Mormon Church before she left home, and Harriet wrote to say they had decided to go to America. The Church would give them free passage, and in exchange they had agreed to settle in the Salt Lake Valley. The family would be gone before she returned home. They hadn't even told her they were going.

Not long after her sixteenth birthday, Mary (and Sara) agreed it was time to go back to England. Both had saved most of their earnings and had enough for the ferry and train rides that would take them to Birmingham. There, they would stay with Tilly until they could find a room to rent.

And so their time in France came to an end as they retraced their journey across the channel — another adventure just around the corner.

We've Made a Terrible Mistake

— Larry Kueneman

A COUPLE OF CLARIFICATIONS HERE before we get started.

When we ask a question today, we usually understand what we are asking. This is because we generally have at least a partial understanding of what the subject is about, and the answer we receive is hopefully designed to increase our understanding. This was not the case with our very ancient ancestors, who had no concept of what they were asking questions about. The second thing is that the primary emotion of virtually every creature that has ever been born is fear, and with most creatures (including us), fear is a major controller of our responses to everything around us. That should not distress you, because fear is also what can guide us to the right answers. The primary cause of what I call active fear is simply ignorance. If you don't understand what is going on, it can be fearful. Fear seeks answers, and our acceptance of an answer depends on how comfortable we are with the answer we arrive at. This means that throughout our lives we adopt answers that are comfortable, but which only might be correct, or might be in our best interest.

Imagine you could travel back in time to when the first thinking humans lived. This would be around five million years ago, long before they developed to the point of becoming our species — homo sapiens. These people had no concept of what they were witnessing, or even an understanding of why they saw what they did in the world around them; or even if there was any meaning to why it occurred. They saw the sun come up in one place and go down in another. They were aware that part of the time the sky was bright, while another time the sky was dark, yet they could not have related the brightness or darkness to that fiery thing they saw in the sky. They saw water drop from above, they saw lightning, and often experienced a shock to their chest when thunder rocked the sky. They saw a tiny, screaming creature come from the body of a woman, and they saw people stop moving while their bodies simply rotted. In short, they had absolutely no concept of science, of nature, or of life and death. When they witnessed an act of nature, all they knew was they had not caused it, so who could have? Over time they developed the idea that some powerful super being had done what they experienced — at this point, their thought would not be one super being for all they did not understand; rather, it was a single super being for each question nature brought to their minds.

At first they could not even discuss their observations and thoughts with others, because man had not yet developed the ability to speak or to understand the sounds of others that did not simply imply anger. But mankind eventually developed the ability to speak as grunting itself developed into our ability to speak in words, and languages came into being. At this point, as speech and the ability to discuss their thoughts became the norm, they came to identify the super beings they believed in as gods. Over many thousands of years, ancient man invented more than four thousand gods they felt responsible for some act of nature, and each was given a name. Each was both honored and feared, which means a great deal of time was spent in thinking about the imagined gods they had invited to dominate their lives.

This was the case until about 1450 B.C. when a leader of a nation tried to reduce the amount of time people thought about gods. It was then that Egyptian Pharaoh Amenhotep IV, who had changed his name to Akenaten, ordered his people to primarily honor Ra, the sun god, as the new chief god, and to consider all other gods subservient to Ra. This change didn't even last until the death of Akenaten, when the people of Egypt went back to belief in (and fear of) the more than 4,000 gods.

Also born in Egypt about one hundred years later, Moses (yep, that Moses) as an adult, moved to live with the Israelites, who later renamed themselves the Jews. Moses took Akenaten's concept of a chief god with him, introducing it to the Israelites.

Now, we all know the game of telephone, where within a group of people, the first person whispers a couple of sentences to the next person, who then whispers what he thinks he heard to the next person. It only takes a few minutes for the message to make its way across the entire group, but from the beginning to the end, the message is almost never quite the same. We easily see how this plays out in a few minutes of conversation. Imagine discussing a subject for fifteen hundred years and have the end result come to sound anything like that of the beginning; it's simply not possible.

From the time of Moses to the time of Jesus was about fifteen hundred years. While Moses had introduced the idea of honoring a chief god to the Israelites, by the time of Jesus, fifteen hundred years and many thousands of conversations had transformed the idea of a chief god to an all-powerful God, which was one of the concepts Jesus pushed. The belief in a single, all-powerful God was formally accepted by the Jews around the year 70 A.D., long after Jesus was gone. Many people led the way of honoring Jesus, along with what was now simply called God, and these folks were called bishops. Around the year 312 A.D., the Roman Emperor Constantine himself adopted a belief in and the following of the teachings of Jesus, and in 325 A.D. he called together what came to be known as the Council of Nicea (a town now in the nation of Turkey). It was at this initial main gathering that the Roman Catholic Church was formed to focus on believing in and honoring one God, and following the humanitarian teaching of Jesus.

Seen through the light of today's understandings, that founding would have been considered also to be the formation of the world's first corporation. The reason I say this is this new organization, the Roman Catholic Church, introduced several mechanisms to force people to become members of this new church, including the use of torture and death to get their message across. The tragedy here was that such action was the complete opposite of the humanitarian message Jesus had taught.

Another interesting thing happened at the Council of Nicea few people are aware of. At the time, no one knew what year it was. Virtually all documents up to that point were dated, for example, "In the third year of the reign of King So-and-So." The Council assigned a group of people to look at what would have been many hundreds of documents to determine when Jesus was born, with the idea of using that year as year one. Then they used the same documents, of course, to move forward in time, assigning the year to events up to their own time. They did a remarkably good job for the time, because with today's level of science, we now know Jesus was actually born at some point in the year we call 4 B.C.

What am I talking about? The primal emotion of every creature ever born is fear. Fear introduces questions, and questions demand answers. However, this presents a real problem in that we have a strong tendency to accept only those answers that make us comfortable. For example, if a question attracts two possible answers, and one makes us uncomfortable, it is the more comfortable answer that likely will be accepted, adopted, and defended. This is the case even when the comfortable answer is dead wrong, and the uncomfortable answer is correct. This is not just a weakness in some people, it is the way you and I were born, and how we live our lives. Although they are rarely aware of it taking place, this is a challenge every child works to overcome. It is the way the first thinking being on earth was born. It is simply human nature. It is a real problem we all must live with. It is sometimes also the cause of huge errors.

I stated that the presence of fear invites questions, and that we tend to adopt only comfortable answers. This is why mankind initially came up with more than four thousand gods. I also mentioned it was an effort by Akenaten to reduce the tensions brought to his culture by the honoring and fear of more than four thousand gods that brought about the introduction of honoring Ra instead. And it was this thinking that eventually led people to develop the concept we live with today.

Who Ruineд the Forests

— Larry Kueneman

THE GOVERNMENT'S CAMPAIGN TO TAME wildfire in the United States has actually made the problem dramatically worse. The reason is when natural fires in what were then natural forests were prevented or stopped as a regular practice, nature did what it does best: everything continued to grow. Where an average of forty trees covered an acre of land 400 years ago in a western mixed-conifer forest, today we often find densities so high they don't allow trees to mature. From forty trees per acre (tpa), forests today can easily be more than two thousand tpa.

In considering the above, I am reminded of a visit I made to an ancient site. I was looking at the solidly built remains of Pueblo Bonito in Chaco Canyon of New Mexico. This beautiful little community of rock homes was built centuries ago by the Anasazi Indians, but is now "maintained" by the federal government. On one side of this small community, there was a cliff around fifty feet high backing up to the ruins. A large portion of the cliff had separated with a large vertical split running from side to side. In recent years both the left and right edges (small areas of the cliff separation) had fallen, harmlessly leaving a noticeable protrusion of perhaps forty feet long with a width of twelve feet from the face to the vertical crack. And that crack was almost ten feet wide. Over the years, the government took special efforts to periodically measure the width of the split, reporting several times that it was growing wider. However, regardless of the monitoring, the government took no efforts to either tie the separated portion to the more solid rock, nor make an effort to remove that which was to eventually crash to the lower ground, virtually destroying about twenty percent of the ruins below. They simply watched it happen. This was not an act of nature; this was bureaucratic stupidity, and reminds me of the television advertisement where a security "monitor" informs those present that a robbery is taking place, but no preventative or protective action is taken.

The reason I include this story is that the same thinking permeates bureaucracies everywhere. Going back to the tribal members teaching those colonists who ventured westward from the Boston area how to control areas by burning off the undergrowth when nature failed to do so for an unusually long time, the scientists on the scene today write the reports; then the isolated bureaucrats who never see the potential or what's happening on the ground make the decisions.

Of course, there are exceptions to the above, but this is the norm.

As citizens, we simply assume that the agencies of the federal government generally act with transparency and good intentions in the decisions they make and in the directions of their efforts. This turns out to be a terrible error. The agencies of the federal government whose responsibilities include protection of the environment, employ a few who are like religious zealots when it comes to their work. Rather than making decisions based on the scientific findings of themselves and others, these folks ascribe to a belief that man should not take pains to alleviate problems, rather just report on what takes place. And we are not accommodating nature when we stop natural fires. Rather, we are in fact, slowly destroying nature.

Certainly, our stopping of natural fires is not a new action. This means the forest conditions we see today are far beyond natural. We cannot simply re-introduce fires today to a forest area made over-thick by generations of fire exclusion. Great care must be taken to thin and to clean up an area prior to very carefully setting a natural ground fire. At that point, what the fire does will let us know if our preparatory work was correct; and if not, we can see what else needs to be done only if we both look and report, and then act.

Toward the typical end, these individuals make certain that testimony on any subject before congress or other agency with decision-making power, is provided that only supports their narrow, and self-serving view. When this happens decisions are made by representatives who may have honesty at heart, but are not provided with honest information. Their decisions cannot be in the public's best interest.

Enough said.

On February 22, 2007, in the *Christian Science Monitor*, Amanda Paulson wrote of the mountain pine beetle laying waste to vast swaths of the lodgepole pine forests in an area around Silverthorne, Colorado.

Alexis Madrigal from *Wired Magazine* wrote on the 27th of November, 2007 of the natural pine beetle ecosystem going off the rails with the loss of great numbers of the lodgepole pines, a loss that had begun in 1997. The trees were all of the same age and size in areas that had been clear-cut years before, thickly replanted, and were prime for the beetle attack.

Then on July 26, 2010, a non-attributed editorial in the *New York Times* told of the white bark pine forests of Wyoming, Idaho and Montana, where perhaps sixty percent of the forests had been decimated by the bark pine beetle, and that the greatest loss here will be habitat for the grizzly bears of the area — and we know unhappy grizzlies can be a real problem.

This also was a problem that showed itself up front. Efforts could have been made to thin the trees that were stressed because there were simply too many for the available water. But wood volume was the only consideration of the timber companies — and our agencies know what happens to stressed conifers: beetles attack. Again, what started out as an act of nature, ended up the result of an inept government frozen to inaction because of wrong thinking by aggressive preservationists who call themselves environmentalists.

Although it was touted as the act that was going to save nature, like so many congressional efforts that are mis-sold to the American people, the passage of the Endangered Species Act (ESA) may have, in fact, been the final nail in the coffin of nature, and it will remain so unless the ESA is severely modified by Congress. The ESA is a major source of millions of dollars every year for law firms masquerading as environmental organizations, and it has been a tremendous success. As a means of saving creatures or plants, it has been an abject failure.

Michael S. Coffman, Ph.D., as President of Environmental Perspectives, Inc., submitted an article entitled "The Problem With The Endangered Species Act" to *NewsWithViews.com*. Dr. Coffman's article describes one of hundreds of such tragically misguided efforts by the federal government to protect endangered species. The following are excerpts:

> "Fourteen hundred farmers owning 200,000 acres in the Klamath River Basin of southern Oregon and northern California were denied their water rights during the summer of 2001 citing the Endangered Species Act of 1973 (ESA). Nearly $200 million of life savings and hard work were wiped out instantly as the farmers were left with essentially worthless land.
>
> "They are not alone. This has been the legacy of the ESA from its inception. It has confiscated billions of dollars of private property, harmed or destroyed the lives of hundreds of thousands of Americans and has not saved one species. Not one.
>
> "[The National Wilderness Institute] conducted a study in which they found that over 306 of the 976 recovery plans for species [then] listed as endangered 'had no hard information about the status of listed species.' For instance, the plan for the endangered Cave Crayfish cites 'Sufficient data to estimate the population size or trends is lacking.'
>
> "If there is not even sufficient data to estimate the population size, let alone trends, then how could [the US Fish and Wildlife Service] even know it was endangered in the first place? How could it write a recovery plan? The agency could not have. But it did anyway."

The bottom line here, is that the passage of the ESA made us feel good, and it has created thousands of jobs. It has also made hundreds of millions of dollars for law firms who file suits. But in the meanwhile, the aspects of nature that it is purported to protect are not only not being protected in any way, they are in fact dying. The real tragedy, as far as change is concerned, is our representatives in Congress are terrified of saying anything negative about a program most Americans were fooled about.

It is important to remember that the stated intent of this work, this aspect of the ESA, is to describe conditions in and about forests, not desert, or prairies, or swamps, or oceans. But the results of the ESA have been without bias in their failure. And we must be aware, that if somehow we were able to change the conditions in our mixed-conifer forests so they were healthy and productive, the way the ESA exists today, we would one day, see someone from an environmental organization law firm proposing the pine bark beetle and the gold-spotted oak borer as endangered species.

A forest of even eight hundred tpa might have one or two larger snags (dead, bare trees) per acre. These snags are often used as homes by certain species of birds, and just a couple of snags per acre is sufficient. If a wildfire or crown fire comes through killing all the trees, the sensible thing to do would be to remove the now dead trees so replanting can take place to redevelop the tree stand. However, what often takes place is a lawsuit filed in the name of the ESA to prevent the removal of any trees with the argument that these now dead trees can become homes for birds, and the vehicles used to aid the removal would kill the new trees that would be coming up following the fire. The environment is not the aim; money is the only goal.

The entire thinking in the presentation of these arguments to a court of law borders on the psychotic. Yet the decisions of the courts are often equally as baseless. Owls do not suddenly need hundreds of dead trees per acre, and the wheels of the vehicles could be stirring up the soil bringing fresh viable soil to the top rather than the sterilized soil that rests on the surface from an intense fire. Now, you might say, this is a silly example, one that would not take place.

Sorry, but that is the norm.

It is critical for the improved health of America's forests, for the continual improvement of habitat, and for a severe reduction in forest wildfires, that laws be enacted that include each of the following interrelated aspects. Examples follow:

- Clear-cutting for timber as a practice be ended and forbidden nationwide.
- All forested areas within the United States and its territories, regardless of ownership or national or state area designation be subject to periodic inspection by certified foresters. And such width to be determined by the tree crown-width of the particular species variety that predominates in that area, but such space between crowns generally equals a typical crown width.
- Where logging is the goal, all such areas be subject to individual tree removal requirements, specifically pursuant to the directions only of the certified foresters.
- Once thinning is finalized in a specific area, that a ground fire be initiated in that area (or be allowed to burn if started by nature) to clean the forest floor.

Nonfiction/
Memoirs

Adventures With My Sister Mary

— Ruth Gray

MY PARENTS AND I WERE LIVING in Portland when I first met my sister Mary. My father had left his job as a bank clerk and was selling real estate on the northeast side. I was three years old, and my father and mother left our little home on Alameda Street late at night to take me to my great-grandmother Reed's home on NE 82nd.

All I remember is being taken upstairs to one of the big iron beds, being left alone, and watching a bare lightbulb in the hall swinging back and forth on a cord.

The next day others gathered to take care of me, and there seemed to be much coming and going. My aunt Nell and uncle Bert, my grandparents Metta and Charles Reed, Uncle Jim, my great-grandmother Samantha and finally my aunt May from Parkdale were no doubt there at various times and probably at the hospital where my mother was. There seemed to be much excitement and discussion, but I had no idea what was coming.

In those days, women who had babies in hospitals were kept in their hospital beds for five to eight days for "recovery." When Mother and baby were released and we returned to the Alameda home, I met my sister Mary. I do not have memory of any specific thoughts or feelings, except that my mother did not seem well, and a few months later, my aunt May started taking me to Parkdale for "visits" at the ranch.

My parents and Mary often visited us in Parkdale, and I became very good at being the older sister and showing Mary my pets, especially my lamb. By this time, Mary was a toddler and walking. The lamb, "Lammy" followed us around in our play and explorations. Next to Aunt May's home was a cabin. Mary and I sometimes slept in the cabin, and I would let the lamb inside who would sleep on the floor by our bed. Mary let me boss her around in those days.

A few months later we were having Sunday dinner at my aunt Barbara's (my father's sister), who lived on the ranch next door. About ten of us were sitting around the round oak table in the dining room. My uncle Glen started joking, winking to the others, and laughing. All of a sudden I realized he was talking about Lammy. It dawned on me that Lammy was our dinner! I started crying and left the table. My mother always said I was "dramatic" by nature, but I still to this day feel teasing of any kind is cruel.

One June, when Mary was four years old Aunt Ida and Uncle Joe Ingram (my great aunt and uncle) came from Salisbury, Missouri to visit Great-Grandmother Reed who was Ida's mother. Mary was cute and winsome, and they decided to take her back to Salisbury with them on the train. Mary had been born on their anniversary, and they had no children, so they considered her their "gift" child. I must have been happy that summer to have my parents all to myself.

My uncle and aunt were wealthy, as he was President of two banks and owned many farms and homes he had acquired during the Great Depression due to foreclosure. My mother had been raised with her sister Rayberta in their large yellow brick Craftsman home with a surround porch during their school years. In those days, the Ingrams had chauffeurs, maids, a cook and other servants. By the time Mary visited, the household staff had been reduced. Nevertheless, those three months of Mary's visit were pivotal. She returned to us "spoiled"!

She insisted on having TWO silver spoons at her plate or she would not eat. Other expectations and demands were persistent, and I discovered I could no longer "boss" my little sister. I was indignant, as I had loved being in the role of a big sister. We fought. Mother could not cope with the two of us, so soon I was off to Parkdale with my great aunt May again.

A year later, the attack on Pearl Harbor occurred, and we entered World War II. Dad was recruited by the Bechtal-

McCone Corporation to develop property in Downey, California for housing for the growing Army Air Force Base near there. Mother, Dad, Mary, and new baby Rachel moved to Downey, but I stayed with Aunt May.

The following year Aunt May and I made the trip to join the family in Downey, as the Bechtal-McCone Corporation had promoted my father to oversee the rearming of our nation for the war effort. Factories which had previously produced cars, or steel trusses, were now mobilized to produce tanks or bombs. Dad was now a "Government Expediter" in the ship-building effort.

Both Aunt May and my sister Mary developed pneumonia soon after we arrived. Aunt May was immediately hospitalized, taken by ambulance to the local hospital. I was too stunned to say goodbye or hug Aunt May, and that troubled me later. The local hospital did not have an available specialist for Mary, so Father had made arrangements with an Inglewood doctor. Later the same day Aunt May was taken to the local hospital, we crowded into our family car for an emergency trip to a Los Angeles hospital for Mary's treatment. We drove straight to the emergency entrance at the hospital, arriving during a storm in the midst of thunder, rain and darkness. I have written a poem about this traumatic trip, when on our way we received word of Auntie's death. Mary survived, thanks to the hospital care.

Our family never returned to Downey, but flew to New York City where a rental home was awaiting us in Scarsdale.

After that, our family followed Father wherever he was assigned, and most of these places were in the east. One year Mary and I attended six different public schools. I think it made us very adaptable. I thought of it as an adventure, but it may have been harder on Mary. However, Mary is the most "social" of any in my family, so she must have learned to adapt to varying personalities and situations through these many venues.

One of the pleasures for me at this time was my growing love for my mother. I had attached myself to my aunt May as a youngster and still grieved for her. But now Mother seemed to be thriving in our Eastern sojourn and enjoying her three daughters. When we were living in White Plains and Scarsdale, New York, her best friend was the wife of the President of General Electric, Charles Edward Wilson, who was also on the War Production Board. My mother, who was in a philanthropic educational organization called P.E.O., was brought into Margaret's local chapter. One of my memories was that Charlie himself picked Mary and me up for Sunday School on Sunday mornings to take us to class. Mom and Dad would join us for church later with Rachel.

(Mother related a story to me that I have never forgotten: Charlie Wilson was treated cruelly by his grade school teacher when he was just twelve years old. When it happened several times, his mother told him he did not have to go to school any longer, but he would need to work. He got a job sweeping floors for a company, then became an errand boy, then was given more and more responsibility. He worked himself up to a high position and eventually became President of G.E. due to his integrity and trustworthiness.)

Mother took us for wonderful excursions in New York City: museums, Radio City Music Hall, and the Metropolitan Opera. Most of all, we loved visiting Uncle Ed, the retired physician and brother of George Higgins, my grandfather. He lived at a posh country club. He would always order a feast for us, and it was there that we first tasted cherrystone clams in the half-shell. I was eleven or twelve years old, Mary was eight, and Rachel was four by this time. We would be sitting with Uncle Ed around a table with a white starched tablecloth, beautiful silver and bright flowers. He was so proud of Mother and her three daughters. He would compliment us on our good behavior, manners, and comportment, and he was especially charmed by Mary. Mother was beaming and happy.

We lived in other cities in the East in Connecticut, New Hampshire, and Massachusetts, always renting for a few weeks or months. Dad had a Government "priority pass" that allowed him access to short-term furnished rentals which were hard for ordinary folks to find during the war. When we lived in Hyde Park, we were in the Italian section where the homes had once been grand and Victorian but had fallen into disrepair. Most of the families had many children and relatives living under the same roof. I especially remember the big family next door and the wife who taught Mother some delicious Italian dishes. Mary and I first learned to ice skate here, when Daddy flooded our lawn with water which turned to ice. Many neighborhood children joined us.

The home we lived in while in Boston was especially notable. It was a mansion in a neighborhood of elegant estates with landscaped gardens, fountains, trellises and gazebos. We had a huge grand piano with uplifted lid in the dark, wood-paneled library, and on the third floor was a ballroom with a billiard table and a small stage with blue velvet curtains.

One day our father brought home to us a darling little Boston Bull puppy we named Bully Boy. We only had him for a few days and were playing with him in the front yard when he suddenly ran into the street and was instantly killed by a car. When we realized what had happened Mother gave me a shoebox to place his little body in. But Mary had disappeared. When we found her she was hiding in the back of a dark closet. A little later she and Rachel joined me in the backyard where we dug a hole and gave him a proper funeral with songs, prayers, and testimonies similar to the human funerals we had witnessed.

When the war was over, Dad's job ended. We returned to the Hood River Valley in Oregon where our father had completed buying Aunt May's fruit ranch from her estate. However, before we moved into her little green cedar-shingled home, my parents had to make a trip into Portland to buy equipment for the ranch, as well as supplies for the house, so our parents left us with a woman they had known who was willing to take us for a few days. Unfortunately, they did not know her husband very well. It was here that Mary and I had our first traumatic sexual encounter. Things were fine for a couple of days, but then one day, when our caretaker was gone, her husband came home early and opened up the fly of his trousers and brought out his penis! He asked us to touch him. Instead, shocked and scared, I grabbed Mary's hand, and we fled into the bathroom, locking the door. The frightening thing was that he banged on the door demanding that it be opened for what seemed like ages. Finally he gave up and moved away from the door, but I will never forget the fear I had looking to the one window above us to the outside—frightful that we would see his face, and my worry that he would break the window and enter. Our caretaker came home after awhile, and we fled into her arms telling her what had happened. She started crying. Our parents came to pick us up that night, and I never remember seeing him again. Father took care of that.

That fall I entered the 7th grade, Mary the 4th grade and Rachel the 1st grade. We were each in our separate worlds and experiences: Mary found a group of five fast friends that formed a coterie that meets together and sees one another to this day. My world mainly centered around my violin, orchestra, and the Hood River Music Festival and concerts. But when I received my driver's license at the age of sixteen, Mary and I again found adventures together.

The first trip we still enjoy recalling. We loaded Dad's open jeep with sleeping bags, swim suits and our collie Lassie, and headed for Pacific City with a big sign we had made across the back of the jeep that read "Beach or Burst!" The journey was about five hours in those days, and we were headed for "The Black Shack," a one-room wood cabin that Grandfather "Oppa" Reed had mounted on a flat-bed and parked a block or two from the ocean which he maintained as his fishing retreat. When Mettamama and Oppa vacationed from their home in Portland, she resided at her brother's comfortable cottage called "Honeysuckle Lodge" in Cannon Beach a few miles away, but Oppa always headed for his lair where he could clean and prepare the flounder, bass, and crab he would catch.

Oh, the excitement we had stopping along the way to eat and re-gas! Mary was only thirteen, but she felt as independent and as capable as I. After all, growing up on the ranch we were all exposed to hard work and responsibility. Our father adored his three strong daughters and made each of us feel we were capable of anything in life. We had put together wooden fruit boxes with nails and hammer during the winter months, climbed ladders in the springtime to thin the fruit, and moved the irrigation pipes to new locations in the hot summer months. Mary had the unique status of driving the tractor through the orchard when the hired man was not available. I had raised a calf for 4-H and had milked the family cow.

When we arrived we were in our glory, "setting up house" in the black shack, running down to the water, splashing in the ocean and exploring the tide pools.

We had no one to tell us what to do as we shopped at the nearby grocery and fixed our supper. After we watched the sun go down it was dark, and there was nothing to do except slip into our sleeping bags. We were so excited we could not sleep! We talked for hours. Then suddenly there was a noise outside! Our imaginations ran wild. We checked the locked door and just to be sure we were safe, we each took a butcher-knife and placed them under our pillows. Of course it was just the wind and our imaginations, but we loved being dramatic!

Mary and I spent several following summers together at Great-Grandmother Reed's home in Portland when I went to summer school and studied violin. One summer we each took turns holding Grandmother's hand as she lay dying. She could no longer talk but could squeeze our hand if we said something soothing to her, letting us know she had heard us. When she peacefully breathed her last breath, we were by her side and witnessed her daughter's (Great-Aunt Ida) grief, and saw our mother calmly place a damp towel around Grandma's forehead to close her eyes. Grandmother was 103 years old. I think this experience helped us be comfortable and see death as natural and inevitable. All three of us sisters have ministered to many others through these circumstances throughout our lifetimes.

After Mary's husband died and my Wes passed a few months later, we started vacationing together at each other's homes in Washington and California discovering sisterly fun again, and yes, even finding adventure!

A Long Life

— Corinne Lee Murphy

THE WOMAN AND HER TWELVE-YEAR-OLD SON were in London again, their last stop on a trip to Europe, as had become their custom. They had been in France for five weeks, and this would be their final week before returning home. They went to a favorite hotel just off Bayswater as it passes by Hyde Park and Kensington Gardens. It sat one lot in from Bayswater next to a petrol station on the corner. The entrance was on the ground floor and unprepossessing. It only provided a place for the bellman to gather bags and direct guests to the elevator to the next floor where there was an attractive lobby and a more than adequate restaurant. This was a serviceable hotel with lovely views of the parks and filled with personnel of American airlines; pilots and attendants moved through the common rooms in full regalia pulling their rolling cases.

The woman had had enough of "charming" old English hotels, drafty in the winter and stifling on the occasionally warm summer days. They were fine in which to sit in the lobby or wander through, but she was delighted to have all the modern amenities that this hotel provided, especially the climate control. There were two tube stops within a couple of blocks, each serving a different line. It was a block to Queensway and many ethnic restaurants suitable for quick meals. It was a short walk to Portobello Market, which they enjoyed on Saturdays, and the trendy wares in Notting Hill.

The woman and her son had spent much time in the parks because they always traveled with a soccer ball so the boy could burn some energy and, often, meet new friends. If you have a ball, you have a game. It was an area familiar to them, like an old friend.

One day, on a whim, they decided to take a half-day bus tour. It included the Changing of the Guard which they had never gotten around to seeing and a favorite site, Westminster Abbey. They boarded the bus which filled up with tourists, domestic and foreign. After they were counted and seated, the tour guide boarded the bus. She was a small woman of middle age wearing a sensible navy skirted suit and equally sensible walking shoes. A scarf was wrapped around her neck, for a little color perhaps. She introduced herself in a no-nonsense fashion and was clearly British born and bred. She explained where they were going, what they might expect to see and what was expected of the group. She held up an umbrella that she would carry so that they might follow her in the crowds. She said that it was the responsibility of the tourists to keep up with her.

The first stop was Westminster Abbey. The woman had always loved the Abbey, with its history so present, filled with the carved stone coffins of the famous and infamous — a living building, not a museum, with regular church services and coronations still breathing life into the vast space. She had been drawn to attend a church service in a small room to the side of the main church once and attended evensong there. The Abbey never failed to stir something in her.

The woman and her son had met two elderly women on the bus, traveling together from the Midwest, excited to be on a trip of a lifetime. The tour guide walked briskly ahead of the group, stopping here and there to enlighten them about what they were seeing. The woman kept an eye out for the women from the Midwest because the Abbey was so crowded with other groups and individuals that it would be easy to be overwhelmed with all there was to see and lose sight of the group to which one belongs. She watched for them and beckoned to them when they straggled too far behind.

And they, too, loved the Abbey and were effusive when they returned to the bus. As the bus readied to leave, one of the tourists called out to the guide that a member of the tour, a young Asian man, had not returned to his seat, had been left behind. The tour guide simply laughed and said that she had told them that they must keep up with her. With that she indicated to the bus driver that he should move on, and the bus pulled out leaving the young man behind. The woman was offended by the attitude of the tour guide and angered that she would be so cavalier about the well-being of one of her charges, who had paid for her services. Strike one.

Having now taken responsibility for the Midwestern travelers, the woman stayed vigilant at all the ensuing stops. But it was almost impossible at the Changing of the Guard. The bus dropped the tourists off blocks away from the viewing area. The elderly women could not walk quickly themselves and soon fell behind. The woman had to keep the guide in view or none of them would arrive at the appointed place, and soon it became impossible to keep both the guide and the stragglers in view. So, the woman's son was tasked with keeping the women behind him in view and his mother in sight to the front … as she kept both him, as well as the tour guide who was striding ahead, in view. Finally, the tour guide stopped, and the tourists began gathering around her for the guard changing. The woman arrived first and then her son, and then they gathered their new friends in like hens with their chicks. The woman said to the guide that the elderly women were having trouble keeping up, but the guide seemed unconcerned. Strike two.

Then it was time to see the actual Changing of the Guard. The guards who marched in were Gurkhas. The guide exclaimed with apparent disgust, "Oh, it's just the Ghurkas." She apologized for the fact more than once and seemed perturbed by the presence of the Ghurkas rather than English soldiers. The woman, herself, found seeing the Ghurkas more interesting. She was aware of their reputation as fierce warriors on behalf of the Empire and the Crown. The woman formed the impression that the guide was a bigot. Strike three.

The woman and her son had only booked the morning tour, but the Midwestern ladies were staying on the bus for the full day. She spoke with them and explained that they would have to be vigilant to stay up with the guide as she would not be watching for them. She said that they would probably lose her at some point but not to panic, just hail a cab back to the hotel. That it would be all right, just part of the adventure. And then she and her son left the bus.

The guide stood on the sidewalk next to the bus as the half-day ticket holders exited, greeting them pleasantly in hopes of a tip. The woman stopped directly in front of her and said neutrally, "I hope you have a long, long life."

The guide replied with a genuine and obviously pleased, "Why thank you so much!"

And then the woman continued, "So that you know what it's like to be lost, confused and afraid."

With that she turned on her heels with the last vision of the guide, standing silent but with her mouth agape. And that vision lingers with her still.

A Moment of Déjà Vu

— June Gaulding

A WEEK AGO I WAS READING my email when a Trip Trivia popped up. It read: Can you guess this location? Below the picture it read: Where can you find this lake-front castle? I recognized the castle, so I read the description of the castle as Chateau de Chillon that sits on Lake Geneva in Switzerland.

Let me take you back to the 1970s when my husband and I visited Switzerland on a General Electric tour from Lubbock, Texas. We had some apartments where we used G.E. products when refurbishing them, so we were invited to travel with the group. There were about twenty-eight people, as well as the leader and his wife. Several of the group were personal friends, so we were destined to have a great vacation on this trip to Switzerland.

Upon arriving at the Geneva Airport, we took a tour bus on a long ride through the mountains to get to Lausanne on Lake Geneva. We would be staying at a hotel on the lake. The mountains were beautiful. It was May, and the mountains were covered with wildflowers and new green grasses. In addition, there were sheep, goats and cows roaming among the spring blooms and grasses. It reminded me of *The Sound of Music* movie.

We enjoyed our stay on Lake Geneva and toured the southern part of Switzerland. One of the tours was to the Chateau de Chillon castle at Montreux. The Chillon Castle sits on a rock along Lake Geneva's banks, surrounded by stunning mountains. The twelfth century fortress was owned by the Counts of Savoy. It was used to control trade on the lake's shipping routes and an essential land route from Italy. In 1536 the Bernese took the castle by force and kept it until the Vaud Revolution (1798). By then, the castle had lost strategic importance and served as storage space and a jail before becoming the most popular historic monument in Switzerland.

The castle had four courtyards and about fifty rooms, including dungeons cut into the rock, the Duke of Savoy's chambers, three formal great halls, a chapel, and a weapons room. Also, there was an 82-foot-high inner tower.

On our guided tour through the castle, we toured a courtyard and several of the rooms along with a couple of the formal great halls. We didn't go see the dungeons or the inner tower. After the guided tour, our group was released to tour on our own with instructions to not go behind ropes and closed doors. I don't think anyone wanted to do this, since the castle was so big. If you got lost, I don't think you could find your way back to the front door. I certainly didn't want to try it.

Several of my friends and I walked to one of the formal great halls. Yes, it was a GREAT hall with a 32-foot-high ceiling. On one side was a large fireplace. I guess this was the only warmth they had in the room when it was cold. On the other side was a stairway about 10 feet wide that went up to a balcony/landing. There was a railing on the front of it overlooking the great hall below. The landing led to a hallway on the right that showed several doors of which I presumed were bedrooms. We didn't go down the hallway.

I was drawn to the landing and looked out over the great hall. For a moment I was watching many couples dressed in formal wear dancing the evening away. I could hear the waltz music playing and see the ladies' dresses moving to the rhythm of their waltzing with their partners. I knew I had been a part of one of those evenings of dancing long ago.

In a moment I was back to reality. My friend Joan Slocum was standing beside me. I turned to her, and I told her I could see the people dancing and hear the waltz music. Also, that I knew I had been a part of the dancing in the great hall at some time in my past. She didn't laugh at me, but she understood that I was serious. I don't believe I shared that experience with anyone else at that time.

Joan and I talked by telephone about it a couple of nights ago. She remembers my telling her about the feeling of my having been in that ballroom before. This gave us a chance to talk about our wonderful trip to Switzerland.

I cannot recall having had a recollection of the past so vividly. I do remember many moments of past trips or other events in my life over the years. This time, I do remember feeling I was living in the moment. Yes, this was a déjà vu moment for me!

A Patɧ Towarᴆ a New Future

— Ruth Gray

WHEN DID MY FAITH JOURNEY BEGIN? Was it when as a nine-year-old I heard the invitation of a Quaker minister inside a worship tent at Twin Rocks, Oregon to come forward to pray about "giving my heart to Jesus"? I do remember kneeling, being very intentional, and rising with the sure conviction that now that He was living within me, I would never be alone, that He could help me be all I was meant to become.

Or was it prior to that time, when I was lazing on my back in our pasture at the ranch, watching clouds moving above and changing shapes, then wondering what life was all about? Or the time I was walking in our woods and suddenly came upon a young doe ten feet from me, both of us startled and eyes deeply locked creature-to-creature for what seemed an eternity? Or was it the shining face of my aunt Grace, blind since birth, singing hymns at home and in church, her voice proclaiming a loving God?

Yes, each a spiritual encounter, a sense that there was more to life than appeared, but more than this, a purpose. That we could know and be known. Yet more than this — beauty: an awareness of unfolding such as a rose unfolds!

As I entered adolescence, I was shaped by my religious relatives in dogma. An uncle who baptized me imprinted on me the belief that God never forgets His own, even when we have strayed far from His design for us, and even if we reject God himself. I felt safe and secure in my belief in a infallible, literal Bible.

In a sense, I now regard my activist adolescence as the time in life I was the most ardent Christian, inviting friends to Youth

For Christ, praying with my girlfriends who became pregnant and were kicked out of school, and for a short time trying to have a Bible study for the high school social "rejects" such as I regarded myself. At graduation I even gave the valedictory speech on "The Four Absolutes." (My father actually wrote my speech, but I preached it with conviction!)

When I left for Whitworth College three months later, I fully intended to someday work in a mission field for the church, but also felt the pull of a music career. But then something changed. I was plunged into the social and religious boiling pot of a small college. I was rushed by the fellows and had a meeting or date almost every weekend night. This was heady stuff for a farmer's daughter from a small town who had not had many boyfriends before. I began noticing that some of the most dogmatic religious guys did not have the characteristics I could admire, and some I discovered I could not trust.

My sophomore year was better. I became active in several social service and music projects, was elected vice-president and social chairperson of our dormitory, was on the staff of *The Whitworthian*, and began to feel my own independence and personhood. That year I was nominated for Snow Queen, and my escort and I won second place. But more importantly, I was dating Dick Gray, the editor of *The Whitworthian* who brought out the best within me: music, art, service, and my spiritual sensitivities and ideals. Yet, he like myself, kept an arm's length from the over-zealous religious types. By the end of the year he was elected student body president. He also asked me to be his wife.

We did not marry until the summer after I graduated. By that time both of us had moved away from our fundamental evangelical roots, and I had been confirmed as an Episcopalian. Yet, Dick and I worshiped together in whatever neighborhood church or denomination we found ourselves as we moved through graduate school in Minneapolis, research for his thesis in Washington, D.C., feature writer on the *St. Louis Post-Dispatch*, associate professor at Northwestern University, full professor at the University of Wisconsin (where I picked up an M.S. in Counseling Psychology), and finally Indiana University where he was dean. We were caught up in raising our sons and developing our careers. Our ideals remained the same, but our religious affiliations and service were loose and negligible.

This abruptly changed for me in 1975 when I was "caught" praying with a nineteen-year-old girl who was dying in our local community hospital.

I had been working as Director of Medical Social Services at Bloomington Hospital for several years when one morning I was paged by a nurse in ICU to visit the bedside of a colostomy patient. Ann had been a student at St. Mary's Academy in southern Indiana, and she had come to Bloomington for surgery. An infection had invaded the site of the operation, and she was having nighttime terrors and a dream that she was dying.

As she related her nightmare to me I realized Ann was truly alone. Tears fell over her pale cheeks onto long brown hair cascading over the thin frame of her shoulders. She told me about her hard working parents in Evansville, her numerous younger brothers and sisters, and why no one could travel that far to see her. Thus I decided to see her every day to talk over her fears and dreams. I also called a local Catholic priest and asked him to visit her.

A few days later the progress notes indicated the infection was worse. So I was not surprised when she asked, "Would you pray that I will get well?" Now I had never prayed with a hospital patient before, but I took her hand in mine, and we prayed together for courage, strength, and healing.

The next day when I came to her bedside she greeted me with a smile. "Oh, Mrs. Gray, I had the same dream, but it did not scare me this time. It had a different ending! I am going to be safe. I told God it was going to be okay." She wanted me to pray with her again.

While we were praying, we heard the curtains surrounding her bed swish open. Her surgeon had seen and heard us and returned abruptly to the nurse's station declaring, "That social worker is going to talk my patient into dying." He then went straightaway to the hospital administrator to report me.

The hospital administrator paged me to his office. He explained that the hospital had previous problems with clergy, and the board of directors had made a deliberate decision not to have a chaplain and to remain a strictly secular institution. Therefore I was not to pray with patients again.

A day or two later, Ann died, and I was grieving for the sweet young girl who had died alone. I related my sadness to my own pastor at First Methodist Church. Dr. Marrs put his head down in his hand thinking and when he looked up said, "Have you considered going to CTS [Christian Theological Seminary] in Indianapolis and learning to counsel theologically? Should you do this you could become a chaplain at Methodist Hospital, or perhaps you could return to this church and start a counseling practice here."

It was a major decision, as it meant a year of seminary plus a year of practicum, then internship at Methodist Hospital. Two years! My husband was willing to support me financially, but our children were teenagers! Did they not need me home when they arrived after school? Indianapolis was an hour away. I agonized.

In seeking to resolve this conflict, I sought the counsel of a respected professor, Dr. Alan Bell with whom I had taken some classes as part of a Ph.D. program at Indiana University. (Before he had become a professor, he had been an Episcopalian priest and had authored a pioneering book on sexuality.) After going over reasons pro and con I argued, "But I am too old! I am 48! I will be ready to retire in twelve years after I receive my M.Div [Master of Divinity]!"

He then asked, "And when the day of your retirement comes, will you be happy you retired as a social worker, or as a chaplain or pastor?"

I left his office, knowing the answer in my heart.

So it was that I began my seminary classes, not realizing that in two years my husband would be dead from a heart attack.

A Sweet Reminder of Christmas Past

—Marilyn McNeill

WE LIVE IN AN OVERLY-CONNECTED WORLD ... too much for those of us in our senior years. The news is often unpleasant and overwhelming. It seems at times there is so little joy or peace in our world. Perhaps we should take a few days and be disconnected.

I have decided to retreat to the warmth and comfort of my kitchen and totally disconnect for the whole day. On my shelf is my old recipe book. I have turned to the dog-eared page that is shortbread cookies. This recipe has been used for at least a century. It is the one that my mother and grandma used. Simple is best—butter, sugar, and flour. I even use the same crockery bowl that has been used by my mother.

I put the butter in the bowl chunk by chunk, add the sugar and then the flour. Next I knead it, then roll and cut the dough into bells and stars, and then sprinkle bits carefully on the tops. My mother used candied cherries on some of her cookies. I thought about my mother and grandma doing the same in much different times.

My great-grandparents were born in Scotland and had come to Canada to homestead, bringing their traditions with them. Butter may have been scarce in those times, and the women likely tried to save this special ingredient for baking those shortbread cookies at Christmas.

Shortbread's origin dates to medieval times. The first printed recipe was dated 1736 from a Scotswoman named Mrs. McLintock. The story of shortbread begins with the medieval "biscuit bread." Any leftover bread was dried out in a low oven until it hardened into a type of rusk. The word biscuit means "twice cooked." Gradually the yeast in the bread was replaced by butter, and biscuit bread developed into shortbread. The butter would create a richer crumbly dough.

Some friends use brown sugar and roll their dough into a round and cut it into wedges before baking. Mother rolled her dough thin and used the top of a small jar to make circles. Some were made into diamond shapes, and cherry bits were put on top.

My mother and grandma only made these at Christmas. Baking shortbread is a deep and emotional tradition that making these at any other time of year seems wrong. Many variations of the recipe can be found, such as adding nuts or orange peel and even some herbs. But the old originals are always eaten first.

The thing about traditional treats is that we eat them through a veil of nostalgia.

What makes shortbread so lovely is not the buttery sugary taste. No, it is special because it is the taste of Christmas Past.

Auntie Zinna

—Gaye V. Borne

PESACH, ALSO KNOWN AS PASSOVER, began this year at sundown on Wednesday, April eighth. Although I was not born Jewish, I consider myself well-blended, having been married to my Jewish husband, Robbie, for forty-two years. Through the years, we always had the Gentile holiday dinners, Christmas and Easter, in addition to Mother's Day, Father's Day and Thanksgiving, etc., at our house in Simi Valley, California. The house would be full of family from both of our family trees. However, every year for Rosh Hashanah and Pesach, Robbie, Michelle and I would drive to Auntie Zinna's house in West Hollywood.

It was always "a push" for us to get to Auntie Zinna's house just before sundown. Michelle and I would wait for Robbie to make it home from his office fifty miles away, and then we would jump in the car and make the trip to Auntie Zinna's house in West Hollywood as fast as we could. Traveling on the Hollywood Freeway with flowers, cards and kosher wine on our laps, it was easy to guess that most of the fellow freeway drivers were also headed to their Seder dinners. Once off the freeway, and into the heart of West Hollywood, the familiar sight of the Orthodox Jews walking to Shul was comforting. After we turned off of Melrose Avenue onto Sierra Bonita, we all breathed a sigh of relief, as we had completed the journey to Auntie Zinna's just before sundown. Her home was always a welcome sight, with the colorful rose-lined walkway that led to her front door.

Once inside, we were always met by the friendly, loving faces of Robbie's second and third cousins, and friends of Auntie Zinna. It was a usual thing for the dinner table to be set for fifteen or more. Auntie Zinna was Robbie's great aunt. Her husband,

Great Uncle Peltiel Nadborny, was the brother of Robbie's grandfather, Benjamin Borne. Together, she and Uncle Peltiel had both survived the horrors and torture of concentration camp and were forever mentally scarred and physically tattooed. Passover was for family, and family was all that mattered to Auntie Zinna.

The Pesach table was always laden with delights of all kinds: gefilte fish, chopped liver, matzoh ball soup, brisket, chicken, salads, tzimmes, etc. Auntie Zinna was the head chef for Cantor's Deli in West Hollywood for twenty-five years. She was presented with many cooking awards and was on a TV cooking show, *Cooking with Zinna*. As you can guess, her food was spectacular both in taste and presentation! One year, a beautiful fish was the serving vessel for her gefilte fish. It was artfully decorated, and the taste was beyond compare! Her matzoh balls were so light and fluffy, a feather would have reached the ground before the matzoh ball! Auntie Zinna was passionate for her Shul. She was well known for her generous gift of self and zeal for fundraising to have trees planted in Israel. She was feisty as well as passionate, her strength of soul enforced by the horrors she had experienced and lived through. She used to walk home from her work at Cantor's Deli, and once was accosted by a thief who attempted to steal her gold necklace. With good old-fashioned guts and chutzpah, she literally demolished the young man by reaching down and grabbing her shoe and bashing him squarely in the nose! You didn't mess with Auntie Zinna!

Auntie Zinna welcomed me with open arms and heart. Her culinary delights were legendary. Her Seder dinners were always joyous, yet reverent events. I felt privileged that she wanted me to participate when she blessed the candles at sundown.

Although Auntie Zinna passed away August 2, 2004, her warmth of heart, soul and spirit remains with me. She was indeed a true matriarch, love for her family being the utmost of her desires. As she always said, "Blood ain't water, honey!" And you know what? It sure isn't.

Badger Brave and Pollyanna Positive

— Jane Ruona

THE ICY WINDS OF WWII were blowing change into my life. We left our perfect picket house and moved to Edison Park which was a suburb of Chicago. Since Dad was spending more time on the war effort, Mom wanted to be closer to family. Between Chicago and Park Ridge were grandparents on both sides, aunts, uncles, and cousins. I now had a real live sister, Nancy. She was almost as good as my doll, Rosebud; however, Nancy cried.

I remember long lines to buy meat and groceries with lots of coupons. Rationing was in full force and required a lot of patience for a four-year-old. I had to raise my hand if I was being naughty. One bright spot was pre-kindergarten. I sat on my "sit upon" and made wonderful new friends. Nancy was two and wanted to go to school with me. One day she just followed me and showed up in my class. The teacher called the police who took Nancy to jail. My grandfather was mayor of Park Ridge. When he found out it was Nancy, he told the police to feed Nancy ice cream and call Mom. My poor mom was frantic!

VE Day finally brought peace in Europe in 1945. The war was ending, and Dad came home. We moved to a big Tudor house in Elm Grove, Wisconsin. We were right next door to a large ice skating pond. That pond became my life. I had skates on every moment I could. Mom even let us keep our skates on (with skate guards) when we came in for lunch. Each November we had to test the ice to see if it was safe to skate. The neighborhood kids formed a human chain with the smallest kid on the end. One step, listen for a crack; second step, "Crack"!! Pull the smallest kid back. Wait another week. Repeat. Parents now would be horrified.

We started on boy's hockey skates, but wanted girl's skates. One day Dad said, "If you learn to skate backwards on hockey skates, I will buy you new white figure skates." We learned in a week. We also learned to 'shoot the duck' (one leg out; the other knee bent), do figure eights, spins, and jumps. Nights were spent dreaming of the Ice Capades. We practiced our shows on the neighbors. Dad lit the pond at night. It was bitter cold, but we hardly noticed it when skating. Minus 30 degrees meant girls could wear pants under their skirts to school.

May brought a hint of spring. We made baskets, filled them with violets, rang doorbells, and ran. I was a born tree climber. No matter how high I went, Dad would say, "I think you can get one branch higher." Wisconsin was the badger state, and we were born brave. Mom never knew we rode our bikes six miles to the nearest lake and swam for hours. I guess I was totally in love with water. My parents said I would run off the pier before I could swim. They would fish me out, and I would do it again. I learned to swim at Brownie Camp and then earned my "Flying Fish." This meant I could swim across the lake.

When I was seven I went to Brownie Day Camp. Before my mom could explain anything about birds and bees, I started my monthly cycle at that camp. It was years before the other girls. I became bonded to the school nurse, Mrs. Winter, and this reinforced my dreams of becoming a nurse. I felt different, but very brave.

I went to Leland Elementary School. It was a small four-room country school supervised by the University of Wisconsin. Our class was studied by their students and given freedom to learn. We read Shakespeare in third grade, played language baseball instead of spelling tests, and did nutrition experiments with white rats. They were trying to instill the love of lifetime learning. They followed us through college, and nineteen out of twenty in my class graduated. I think it took!

When I was almost nine my brother Jim was born. Mom was forty-two. Jim was easy going and loved *Howdy Doody*. My friends liked to practice their "mommy skills" on Jim. That summer we were quarantined to our yard because of the polio epidemic. Several of my friends were very ill. One was in an iron lung. Our local paper *Elm Leaves* had our family picture on the front page, showing how we coped with the epidemic.

The other important characteristics besides being brave were being positive and helpful. The book *Pollyanna* was in vogue. I did lots of chores and tried my best in school. When I finished my work, I went down to a lower grade and taught. My sister, Nancy, expressed middle-child sentiment, "I am not going to ruin my health studying like Jane." I seem to have kept that brave, positive, and helpful attitude, without being naïve.

I did have one incident in my childhood which tested my inner spirit. My dad's best friend worked for my dad and never married. Dad and Doot were very close and hunted and fished together. Doot had a beautiful sailboat on Lake Michigan and would invite Nancy and me to go sailing on weekends. Once we were out on a deep part of this huge lake, he would want Nancy and me to jump off and swim. After several outings he swam very close to me and put his hand down the front of my suit. I was only nine but knew it was wrong. When we arrived home, I never said a thing to my parents, only that I wouldn't go with Doot again. I didn't want to hurt Nancy or my dad. I kept it a secret until now. I do not feel I was injured emotionally or physically, because it made me feel stronger, a real badger.

Bella, Our Little Girl

—June Gaulding

THE FAMILY PETS, Chips, a twelve-year-old Dachshund mix, passed away in 2014, and Wallis, a fourteen-year-old female Jack Russell Terrier, passed away in 2016. They were so much fun to have in the family. After they were gone there was no sound of the little pitter-patter of feet around our house for a couple of years.

In late March of this year my son, Mark, and I decided to get another pet. We wanted to save a pet from being euthanized, so we went to the Desert Hot Springs Animal Shelter. The first day we went out to look at dogs available for adoption the shelter was closing, so Mark went in and quickly walked through the shelter area. We wanted a small dog, and he said they had a few available. So, we went back out the next day, and I went in with Mark to look at them. We found out that most of the small pets were on hold for pick-up. However, this one little female dog was in her cage with another dog, and she looked up at us with little brown eyes. We asked to take her out to the lobby to get acquainted with her. Mark and I held her for a little while, and we could see that she was very scared. She was really a cute little dog, and we knew that she was the one for us. We wanted to help her have a new life and be a suitable pet, so we adopted her. On the way home Mark stopped at Petco and bought a dog bed and other accessories for our new little pet.

Let me describe our new little four-year-old dog. She is a combination Chihuahua and miniature Dachshund. She has short white fur with several little dark brown spots co-mingled among several large dark brown spots on her body. Her little Chihuahua head is dark brown with sparkling brown eyes. She is about nineteen inches long and about six inches wide and weighs eleven pounds—a little stuffed sausage dog, but so cute! We have put her on a diet, as she needs to lose some of her weight to be a healthy dog.

Now that we had adopted her, she had to have a name. They had given her the name Dot—probably because of the big brown spots on her. For a few days we called her Dotty, but it really didn't suit her. We thought for several days and decided on the name Bella. We felt it suited her better. So, Bella was our new little girl's name.

Bella was very afraid of men. Of course, she shied away from Mark. She was okay when around me. In addition, when there was a loud noise she would run and hide under the bed. We had our work cut out for us. Slowly she warmed up to us, but we could see that we had a long way to go to help her overcome her fears. Since she didn't understand commands and was very afraid of her leash, we enrolled her in a Petco dog training class. The instructor, Tony, put her in a puppy class since she didn't understand commands. For two weeks she just sat on Mark's lap and watched the other puppy, Charlie, a female, six-month-old black Labrador, go through her routine. Finally, on the third week we put her down, and she interacted with Charlie and received some treats. Yet, she still was afraid of her leash.

Each week she interacted with the instructor a little more and with Charlie, her puppy friend. At the end of the six-week class, she was friendlier but still a little cautious. She would let us put the leash on her but wouldn't walk with it. Tony felt she did well in the class, so he gave Bella a graduation certificate. We have it posted on the refrigerator door. We are so proud of her to have overcome some of her fears.

Since Bella's training classes, we learned of a thunder jacket or shirt that we could put on her to supposedly make her feel more secure. We now have one for her and put it on her every evening for several hours. When there is a loud noise, or a book drops, she doesn't hide under the bed now. We feel the little gray thunder jacket seems to be helping Bella enjoy life a little more each day.

In the three months since her training classes, she has become friendlier with visitors when they come into our home. She is not as afraid of men as she was. This makes Mark feel better, as he loves little Bella and has become a great "Daddy" for her. She will sit up on the sofa by him for hours and sleep, or he pets her. She doesn't seem to have a fear of women, so this makes me happy as she interacts with me as her "Grandma."

Bella is spoiled in some ways. With her sleeping almost all the time, we have four doggy beds scattered throughout the house, so whenever she wants to sleep she has a choice. At night she sleeps in her bed placed upon my bed and likes being close by me at night. Mark moves a lot in his sleep and this scares Bella, so she doesn't sleep with him at night. Maybe in time she will feel more comfortable sleeping with him.

Her little five-inch legs do not allow her to jump up on beds, sofas, or chairs, so we help by lifting her up. She is brave enough to jump down on the floor if she isn't too high up. Mark has been looking for a doggy stepladder that you can set by the bed, so a pet can get up and down when it wants to. If we find a ladder, we will see if she trusts herself to use it.

It has been a good thing that we brought little Bella into our home, as it was very quiet with just Mark and me. She does have some cute traits. She loves to give you kisses, and she seldom barks with a yip, but may howl from a loud siren. Also, she loves her Whimzees, a dog chewie that's good for her teeth.

Bella is a special little pet for us, and we hope she is happy living in our home.

Childhood on the Ranch

— Ruth Gray

IF MY CHILDHOOD WAS TOUCHED by loneliness, it was imbued by beauty of place. Such was the magic of the Hood River Valley and the tiny town of Parkdale nestled just two miles from the snow line of majestic Mt. Hood. Two rivers flowed from the mountain: the East Fork with its icy waters tumbling over light gray boulders which flowed through the edge of our property, and the West Fork of the Hood River on the other side of the valley, both rivers meeting in confluence before rushing out to the mighty Columbia, then eventually the sea.

The modest green-shingled home where my parents often visited became a haven for me when I came to live with my great aunt May. I awoke to a rooster shrieking every morning just as light broke the night, then the sound of many birds in the air and trees, the bawling of a calf or sheep, the bark of dogs and clucking of chickens. Aunt May would be up as I made my way into the kitchen for my oatmeal porridge. Often she would step outside the kitchen door a few feet into the well-house, where she would return with thick fresh cream for my bowl, and butter for my bread. The well-house was cool and dark with running water from an underground pool and where milk from our cow, as well as potatoes, onions, and turnips were stored. If an Indian fisherman had come by the night before, there might be a whole salmon on a slab for our noontime dinner that day. A block of ice was delivered every week during the summer warm weather and placed on the solid granite bench where it melted and dripped into the cistern.

After breakfast, Aunt May would have many chores. Her foreman was the first to appear at our kitchen door with a pail of fresh morning milk from the Jersey cow. Auntie was an imposing woman, even in her faded cotton house dress; she oozed New England authority with her tall erect posture, direct questions and orders.

After he left, she would straighten up the house as I made my bed and brought my dirty clothes into the outer enclosed porch with the ringer washer. She would always find light activity for me, perhaps drying dishes, sorting clothes or putting away the flatware. I would hear her singing as she worked. She would start preparing the noon dinner which was always the main meal of the day. Mouth-watering smells of roast beef with vegetables — sometimes venison, elk, ham, or salmon — home-canned relishes and pickles, Boston brown bread, and puddings of all kinds, brought me to hang around the kitchen so I could lick the bowls of sauces and batters. Our night meal was called supper, and usually consisted of soup or stew made from leftovers, and served with cheeses and her home-made bread.

Some mornings she would announce a trip to McIsaac's grocery store in Parkdale, to the post office, or to her friends in town. Once a week we would make the special trip to Hood River in the lower valley with its wondrous hardware store, Carnegie Library, churches with bells ringing the hour, cafés, hotels, dry goods stores. And sometimes we would go along the gorge of the Columbia River to George and Gladys Struck's vacation home on the peninsula. There I would sit on the bank with Dan and Jim, their sons, who would show me how to sift the sand through strainers to discover bright beads of many colors left behind by the Native Indians.

I loved the ordinary days that we stayed at home on the ranch. I had an amazing run of not only Aunt May's 40 acres but each of my relatives' properties. Aunt May had about 20 acres under cultivation, mostly pears, with a few cherry and apple trees. On the other end of our orchard was the foreman's home where his wife and family resided, a barn where the tractor and other farm equipment were stored and boxes for the fruit were made. A vast pasture for horses, the family cow, and sheep was surrounded by a barbed-wire fence. The rest of the 20 acres were in old growth Douglas fir which ended at the East Fork of the Hood River. Aunt May's niece (Aunt Barbara) flanked her property to the east, her brother (Uncle Harry Allen) was on the west. All in all, I had 160 acres to roam at will, much of it in woods and meadows. The ranch in those days was called Allen Orchards.

Yet, I knew no boundaries. One day, the wife of the ranger for the Mt. Hood Forestry Service called Aunt May to come get me. I had wandered over a mile away to the Forestry Service! The ranger's wife found me by the goldfish pool talking to fairies and my imaginary playmates. I told her I lived in the woods under the mushrooms. I believe I was three or four years old. She gave me cookies and was finally able to ascertain to whom I truly belonged.

After this experience, I was forbidden to go beyond Allen Road or any other public road. But I was not prevented from exploring the orchards or the woods with my five cousins or on my own. My cousin Allen and my grandfather "Oppa" from Portland taught me to fish by the time I was seven, and I spent many hours catching trout in the irrigation ditches and brooks on the ranch. Once, down at the creek toward evening, a beautiful beaver passed in front of me just three feet from where I was standing with my fishing pole. I was enthralled! Other wild animals I tried to make as friends, and a chipmunk I had captured bit me on the finger. My feelings were hurt more than my bleeding finger!

But most of all I remember enjoying the farm animals. My uncle Glen and aunt Barbara had a great A-frame chicken house with an inside track for the fowl to move up to the second tier of nesting boxes. There was a short ladder for me to climb to the second tier to gather the eggs after they had been laid. One day, I decided on my own to see if chickens could fly. I started throwing them off the large opening on this second tier. To my delight they did flap their wings to glide down to the ground with a soft landing. But as my experiment became more vigorous, I sent one unfortunate fowl downward with too much force, and she landed on her neck flapping wildly on her back until dead. This time I got into trouble!

I had a wild imagination as a youngster and carried on extensive conversations with my pet lamb and collie dog who roamed the land with me. I must have had dolls but do not remember them, and suspect that the animal life around me, including the barn kittens, were more interesting to me than toys. At any rate, my mother, who visited us on occasion, was troubled by my lively imaginary life, but I was not aware of her distress until years later.

Aunt May never spanked me but talked to me seriously about manners and morals. The morning of one Valentine's Day left a lasting lesson. She brought in a fancy heart-shaped box to my bed and told me I could open it. When I did, there was a single little cinnamon candy rattling around inside with dark brown crumbs.

"Dear Ruthie," she explained, "We purchased this Valentine for you which was filled with a big candy chocolate heart. But last night, when you told us a lie, it broke our hearts. So we broke the chocolate into pieces and gave it away so you would remember when you don't tell the truth, it hurts other people as well as yourself. You cannot be as sweet like chocolate when you lie. But the little cinnamon candy we hope will remind you that we love you and want you to become a truthful child." I remember breaking into tears. Thus, I learned by such lessons to differentiate truth from imagination.

When I was six, I began attending school in Portland, since there had been no kindergarten in Parkdale. I enjoyed the teacher, because she let me help the younger children. The Montavilla Grade School was just a few blocks from my great-grandmother Reed's home where we lived, and I was soon promoted to first grade, as I read well. There the teacher had us beat our hands with a ruler if we talked too much or did something wrong. She would stand over me and say, "Harder, harder," until my hands were smarting and pink. I was not the only child singled out, but I hated going to school.

I may have regressed to a "innovative" mind again at this time, as I found life with my mother difficult. She may have had problems of her own which may be why she slapped or whipped me often, sometimes with a leather shaving strap that belonged to my uncle Jim who lived in the same home. I know I was a handful as I would get into trouble with my "creativity." One time I gathered all the free advertisements and post office mailings I found around the house and went door-to-door in my neighborhood selling each piece for a penny. People were solicitous and generous. This kept me in candy money which I spent at the corner grocery store. Yet I am amazed today to think I wandered one or two blocks from my grandmother's home unsupervised, was often invited into people's living rooms, and yet remained safe.

There was a school for the blind in our Montavilla neighborhood, and I was fascinated by the men and women who passed by. One day, I took one of my grandmother's canes and a pair of dark glasses. An hour or so later my uncle Jim, on his way to the grocery store, was mortified to see me on the corner where I was pleading, "Please kind sir, would you help me across the street?" He angrily reported this to my mother which resulted in another good thrashing.

Soon I was returned to Parkdale and the beauty of life on the ranch. There I remained until I was ten, and we took the fateful drive to Downey, California with my aunt May.

Christine

—Irene Knudsen

SAHARA IS THE NAME OF MY CAR, a nice-looking, sand-colored Honda Accord. She was assembled in the city of Suyama, Japan. We have had a happy relationship for almost nine years, and she is still running great, for which I often give her praise. I also spoil her with gifts. Recently, I got her four "extra" good tires (she is worth that "extra") and on her last oil change, I presented her with four new floor mats. I am especially generous on her adoption day, which is the 11th of May. Last year she got a "spa treatment," a thorough detailing, that is. On her next anniversary, I will surprise her with her 65,000 mile check-up. She will like that! She likes getting pampered.

My car prior to Sahara was also a Honda Accord. It had a shiny silver body, so I named her Silvia. She was my companion for eight years, and we had a lot of good times together. My son took her over after I let Sahara into my life, and when he in turn sold her, he made sure, on my insistence, to relate her name to the new owner, who happened to be female and liked the idea of having a car with a girl's name.

I have owned many cars over the years, all second or multi-owned cars, none of them having names. Then, a car was just a transportation tool taking me from one point to another. When I finally bought my first brand new car in 1986, I did not name it either, at first.

I had no specific brand in mind, but I knew I wanted a station wagon, very popular at that time. It also had to be American. I was a believer in supporting American-made cars. With my husband and two daughters in tow, I visited several car dealers and finally found the perfect one—well almost the perfect one—at the Ford dealer. It was a Mercury Sable station wagon. The girls especially liked the extra two fold-up, rear-facing seats. Yes, it was perfect, except for the color. It was brown, not a nice chocolate or taupe, but a very ugly and unappealing brown—to be blunt, a shitty brown; and mistakenly, I voiced my dissatisfaction loud and clear in front of the car, not even suspecting the harm I had done. As this was the only car they had in stock of its kind, and it would take days to get another one, and I did not want to face another pushy car dealer, I decided to take it home, convincing myself I would get used to the color; it was just a car, transportation from point A to B. Was I mistaken!

After a few months, I had a feeling the car had taken on a female persona. I still was not happy with the color, and it seemed she (yes, I started thinking of her as a "she") could read my thoughts. To get back to me, she started getting moody and rebelled by taking her time to get started in the early mornings. After we sold our house and moved into a rental, in wait for our new house to be ready, she had to stay outside in the driveway in the cold and rain, which did not suit her at all. One especially gloomy December morning, driving the girls to school, she gave up with a screeching stop. She suddenly wanted a new transmission—I am sure, to get back to me somehow, and show she was the boss. This way she got out of staying in the cold and get lots of attention in the covered repair shop. She was in her "terrible twos." That means only two years old, and we just barely made the warranty.

After the move to our new home, she got her own space in the brand new garage, and she perked up and was pleased until I started working, and she again had to get going early in the mornings, five days a week. She became demanding, wanting new windshield wipers, new headlights and let loose the rear back mirror, breaking it in half, so it, too, had to be replaced. It was other small things falling off or getting loose, and every time I cursed her. Finally, one day she let her muffler down making a glowing trail on the freeway. The lady had a flair for attention. At work, my co-workers were more interested in hearing about my car than about my family.

It was around that time I read the book *Christine* by Stephen King, a horror story about a 1958 Plymouth, setting out to kill everyone who stood against her. That was the time my car named herself. Every time driving her, the name Christine popped up in my mind as if she wanted me to know she liked that name. In an especially weak moment, I gave in and named her Christine as a peace offering. She then wanted new tires to celebrate and started picking up stray nails. New shiny black designer "running shoes" are important to a lady with a famous name. I told her then, even if she scratched herself up, really bad, I promised to never, never give in and give her a new "coat" of paint. She pretended not to hear, and a few months later I could feel something else was brewing. I found her jumpy and unsteady at times as if she had a mind of her own. Something definitely had shifted. I did not seem to be in charge anymore.

One day, on the freeway, she started acting up again, and I had a hard time controlling her. Of course, she chose places with an audience and when people driving by tried to get my attention by pointing to my car, to warn me of danger, she was pleased to be the center of attention. I drove off the freeway and parked. Stepping out, I saw smoke coming from the undercarriage— not smoke as from a fire, but smoke from too much grinding, and she smelled, too. In the repair shop, which for her, by now, became a vacation destination, I was told the rod connected to the wheel mysteriously had a serious crack, a most unusual incident, and I had been in real danger of losing the whole wheel while driving, and who knows what could have happened? Was she that desperate to get a new coat of color, or had Christine taken over the dark side of her namesake?

At this point, I started getting leery of driving her. Did she have more sinister events in store? I seriously started thinking about replacing her with something more dependable and good-natured. We had struggled together for eight long and costly years.

When my husband told me about the good deals his union was having with the Honda dealers, I was ready to take a chance on a foreign car. On our way to the dealer, I assured Christine we were just going to have a look. I did not want to upset her. While trying out the Silver Accord, I fell in love with the car at once, color and all, and I felt it was mutual, and the car became mine.

Driving out from the lot, I glanced over at Christine. She seemed to be sulking and lost with all the nice new cars around. For a second, just for a second, I felt I had deceived her and felt sorry for leaving her like this. But pity was not for Christine, and when I looked back once more, she became her own self, mean and revengeful, and I felt a big relief letting her go.

A month later, one of my coworkers, the one who especially missed hearing about all the bad news about Christine, showed me an advertisement in the *Diablo Dealer,* a magazine with cars for sale. There was Christine in the middle of page 25. How appropriate for her to turn up in a magazine called the *Devil Dealer.* Although she was the oldest on the page, she competed well with the other cars, looking good and fresh, with a price tag of $4,999, and to my surprise, advertised as "runs great." I don't know what she put into the heads of those dealers. Obviously, she was trying to appeal to a kinder owner who would take care of her every whim. At least we could not hurt each other anymore.

Dinner at Grandma's

— Larry Ballard

MY MOM AND I WERE VISITING Grandma and Grandpa Fern. Even better: we were staying for dinner.

I can still smell the comforting aroma of the untreated wood in the old farmhouse. Years of cooking smells slowly released a faint, mellow air wick of forgotten meals and slow living. Comforting to a four-year-old. My ears soaked up the sound of the hand pump in the kitchen, squealing in agony under the considerable weight of my grandmother. And the wonderful comfort of her huge thighs formed from untold pounds of pork fat and biscuits.

I felt secure in those tender arms holding me in the saddle as her old rocker creaked with each stride of that great mount. Stories of the old west boomed out of Grandpa. His eyes gleaming in the semi-darkness of coal oil lamps.

It all changed after the massacre. I was suddenly alone. No comforting arms. No sweet smiles. Just a ring of giant people looking down at me. Evidence of my crime scattered around the farm yard. Six chicks, heads twisted on broken necks, bodies still warm, quivering. Not all quite dead.

My grandfather dispassionately relieved the little yellow bodies of their futile struggles.

My words, pushed past half paralyzed lips, not heard.

"They are for supper."

I turned and ran for the cover of forty acres of ripening corn that covered over half the Fern farm.

I was alone, standing in the soft dirt with stalks of corn towering over my head. Lost, cold and afraid of the darkness coloring what little I could see of the sky. The forest of corn started to whip around in the wind. I sat at the feet of corn trees, huddling against the deepening cold. I wanted to call out to those others, but feared those cold, peering eyes.

I sat there shivering and crying until my mother found me and carried me back to the farmhouse.

Dual Citizenship

—Jean Giunta Denning

BETWEEN MY FIRST AND SECOND TRIP to Modica, Sicily, I happened to attend one of our Italian genealogy club meetings in San Diego where the guest speaker gave a lecture on dual citizenship. I had never thought of this before and was shocked to learn that I was eligible because my father had not yet become a naturalized citizen when I was born (by a mere two months). I decided to apply, more as a full-circle tribute to my parents than for any other reason. Had I known about this earlier in my life, I might have gone to school in Italy, and/or worked and lived there as a citizen for a period of my life.

The closest Italian Consulate was in Los Angeles, a three-hour drive from the desert. The dual citizenship process required three frustrating trips to the Consulate and a lot of time and a bit of expense securing the necessary documents. It took a little over a year to accomplish this.

I was really lucky, however. It could have taken much longer, as when I first queried the State of California regarding copies of the marriage certificates I needed, their first reply was, "Due to budgetary constraints, our processing time can take up to two to three *years*." How frustrating is that? Fortunately, I was able to get my documents at the county level from various County Recorders' offices.

For those of you who are interested in pursuing your dual Italian citizenship, I feel I should include here what I had to submit. Others can just skip to the next page. An original plus one copy of the following documents were required:

- Notarized "Application for Italian Citizenship Jure Sanguinis."
- Italian Passport-size photograph.
- Certified copy of my father's birth certificate (from Italy).
- Certified copy of my mother's birth certificate (from Italy).
- Certified copy of my parents' marriage certificate, with Apostille* + notarized copy of "Letter to Accompany Parent's Marriage Certificate. (This was required because there were some discrepancies.)
- Copy of my father's Certificate of Naturalization. (Fortunately, I had the original, and they accepted a copy.)
- Certified copy of my U.S. birth certificate, with Apostille.
- Notarized copy of "Declaration of Applicant," which included the declaration that I have never renounced Italian citizenship before any Italian authority, a list of places of my residence since the age of eighteen, and copies of my current American passport and my California driver's license.
- Certified copy of my father's death certificate, with Apostille.
- Certified copy of my marriage certificate, with Apostille.
- Certified copy of my husband's birth certificate, with Apostille.
- Notarized copy of "Declaration of Deceased Italian Ascendant." (This was required because my father was deceased ... I had to list the places of *his* residency since *his* age of eighteen ... which was probably the hardest research job for me, because he lived in four different cities before I was even born.)

It was interesting to learn about Apostilles ... a term I had never heard before. In short, an "Apostille" is a form of authentication issued to documents for use in a foreign country. Mine were issued by the United States State Department, and turned out to be certification that my already certified copies were authentic. It seemed like an unnecessary duplication of work to me, and just another way for the government to make money; however, I had no choice but to comply.

In addition, <u>all</u> of the above documents—except for the Apostilles and my father's Naturalization Certificate—were required to be translated into Italian by a translator chosen from a list provided by the Italian Consulate (at a cost of $50 per page). Apparently, this is not a requirement everywhere, and was not a requirement in Los Angeles a few years back.

When I finally had everything ready, I tried to make an appointment with the Italian Consulate in Los Angeles to bring in all my documents. Mailing them was not an option. More frustration ensued, as the Consulate's phone number had a recorded message and was never answered by anyone in person. Three weeks passed, and no one had returned a single phone call, nor had anyone replied to my emails (which I had written in Italian) requesting an appointment. I mentioned this to one of my Italian genealogy club friends who had recently secured his dual citizenship and who had been encouraging me with mine. He said he had just met the new Consulate General and would mention my plight to him. Long story, short—I got a phone call the next day and was given an appointment. Thank you, Alessandro!

On appointment day the first week of February my husband Vaughn and I drove into Los Angeles, and I submitted all the information. They checked over my documents and confirmed they had everything they needed to proceed.

About ten days later I was surprised to receive a letter saying my citizenship had been approved. I thought it would take much longer, and even had been warned it might take another six months to a year. I was elated, and so was Vaughn. This was right around my birthday, and all I could think of was: *what a great birthday present!*

The approval letter included another form I needed to complete and return, called an AIRE form (<u>A</u>nagrafe degli <u>I</u>taliani <u>R</u>esidenti all'<u>E</u>stero), which deals with the registration of

Italians residing abroad. This form basically asked for "Head of Household," "Personal Information," "Family in Household," and "AIRE Registration City" (the city of my parents' birth, where my citizenship was to be registered). The approval letter also stated that if I wished to apply for an Italian passport, I could do so *two months* from the date of the letter. How exciting was that!

Two months later Vaughn and I again drove to the Consulate where I applied for my passport. That day I learned that Italian passport photos are smaller in size than American passport photos, and they would not accept my photo. Fortunately, there was a photo shop a few blocks away, and we had just enough time to have my picture retaken and return to the Consulate before they closed. It was interesting to me that the photographer said I could not smile in my photo but that I needed to have a "serious" expression.

About three weeks after our last visit to the Consulate, I was ecstatic to receive my passport, which turned out to be a European Union passport, rather than an Italian passport, which was even better. Any benefits to which I might be entitled would now apply in all the European Union countries.

Although my husband was now also eligible for dual citizenship, the Consulate said it wasn't necessary. If we wanted to live in Italy, he could apply for a "Special Visa to Accompany Italian Citizen." I am not sure if that would have provided Vaughn with medical benefits, however, which would definitely be a huge advantage of dual citizenship. Now Vaughn and I started thinking about spending six months in Italy each year!

I cannot express what a thrill it was to receive my Italian citizenship and my EU passport. I couldn't wait to go back to Sicily to do more genealogical research, hoping my dual citizenship would open up some doors in helping secure information and documents. After all, how could they turn away one of their own!

Family History ... Family Mystery

— Jean Giunta Denning

IT'S ALL MY BROTHER-IN-LAW'S FAULT! One day while visiting my husband's oldest brother, Clyde, in San Diego, he asked me if I could help him record some of the Denning/ Elkington family history into a computer genealogy program called PAF (Personal Ancestral File). Being Mormon, much of his family history had already been researched. I learned that my husband's paternal and maternal lines had been traced back to the sixteenth century in Wales, and his more recent ancestors were among those followers of Joseph Smith who pushed hand carts across the country to the Great Salt Lake area. Clyde introduced me to the Family History Center Library, and I spent a few months researching and verifying data for him, and entering it into the PAF program.

Much to my surprise, my husband told me Clyde had never been that interested in his Mormon upbringing nor the family history. We concluded that this new interest was sparked by his being on "borrowed time" (having been diagnosed with terminal cancer), with some urging from his son who was a bishop in the Mormon church.

Clyde was ecstatic when I presented him with a copy of his ancestral chart. At the time, our printer used sheet-fed, continuous perforated paper. Unfolded, the printed ancestral chart stretched the entire length of his living room.

Then he suggested to me — "Why don't you trace *your* family history!" — and thus began an obsession which was to take over much of my spare time for years to come.

At that time of my life (well into my fifties), both my parents had died, as well as their siblings and my three siblings. I remembered that many years earlier, one of my cousins (Margie, a paternal second cousin) had written saying she was looking into our family history (she had married a Mormon) and had asked for any information I might have. All I had was a copy of a little booklet about my father that my oldest sister Emma (June) had supposedly written in 1944 entitled *The Making of an American Minister*, which I sent to her. (June told me many years after my father's death that he had actually written it.) Margie said she'd send me a copy of her recorded findings on our family history, but must have forgotten, and I guess I wasn't interested enough at the time to follow up.

When Clyde suggested to me to start my own research, I thought I had it made — because, after all, I had the small book my father had written, as well as some documents stashed away somewhere — his and my mother's marriage certificate, their naturalization papers, their Italian passports, and even a picture of my father's family crest — and a cousin who might have done some research already.

First, I tracked down my cousin Margie, who was living in Salt Lake City, and I asked how far she had gotten with tracing our family history. Unfortunately, she had stopped at her maternal grandfather (my father's brother Santo), and had not gotten any further than the information I had sent her. She did have a little bit of information on Santo's descendants and sent that information to me.

Since the first step in researching one's family history is to record what you already know, I started with our immediate family, my knowledge of my parents' siblings, and my father's booklet. My dad's booklet said that his family settled in Sicily via Spain and before that, France. Since both my husband and I *love* traveling in Europe, I said to him, "This is great ... we can combine our vacations with my family history and visit all the places we uncover, wherever they may be!" I couldn't wait to get started ... I thought about all the traveling we would be doing in Italy, Spain and France — and that was just on my father's side of the family!

One of the most significant things I learned early on from the Family History Center was how important sources are. Information gained through hearsay and family stories needs to be substantiated by actual documentation (civil, church, military records, etc). So, I started ordering microfilm from Salt Lake City via the local Family History Library.

And here began my adventure.

From my trip to Sicily in 1965, I knew my mother's sisters who stayed in Italy (Carmela, Sebastiana and Nunziata), and the two who came to America (Angelina and Concettina). I remembered my father's siblings whom I had met growing up (Uncles Angelo, Santo, Amedeo, and my favorite — Uncle John). I had forgotten the names of my father's siblings who remained in Sicily, and I vaguely remembered his saying one sister had emigrated to South America.

My father's booklet described his grandfather as somewhat of a romantic ... Michael A. Junta, a young Spanish artist and musician, who had found his way from Madrid, Spain, to Piedmont, Italy, to join one of the legions of Giuseppe Garibaldi's army.

> *... But the war he had joined for Italian liberation did not end in the total emancipation of its people, nor was it consummated in the pre-announced goal of a republic. It did, however, unite the Italian people in a declaration of a free state and a free church. After the armies were disbanded, some men remained in the land they had defended. Some returned to their homelands without fanfare and without thanks. Some never could return. They had died in the cause of liberty.*
>
> *Mr. Junta, having met a charming Italian woman, Donna Cecilia Chiaramida, decided to stay in the land of his wife, Italianizing the name of "Junta" to "Giunta." From this union four sons and one daughter were born.*
>
> *Being a staunch protestant of the Waldensian faith (the oldest Protestant church in that part of Europe), the elder*

Giunta was instrumental in the erection and support of a Protestant church in the picturesque town of Pachino, Italy [Sicily], where he had finally settled and made his home. The family attended services regularly and sought to live strictly in adherence to the teachings of the Waldensian church.

The boys grew in "wisdom and in stature," all following the inclinations of their desires in law, medicine, music, and military science, distinguishing themselves in their various fields.

Joseph, the youngest of the brothers and a lawyer by profession ... met and married Emma Quartarone, the daughter of a wealthy landowner. Out of this union were born five sons and three daughters. Henry Conrad [my father] *was the youngest member of the family.*

There was nothing written about my mother's family. I did have some notes and photos I took when I visited Sicily in 1965. My mother had never known for sure if she was born on the third or the fifth of the month. We celebrated it on the third. She had always said she was born in 1900 (it was easier for her to remember)—but when it was time for her to collect social security, she admitted she was born in 1899.

The local Family History Center called when they received my first microfilm, and I rushed down to the Center to begin my research. The Center had only one reader that I was able to use because of the size of the microfilm of the Sicilian records. It made me a little dizzy at first trying to read the records until I learned to focus on one spot on the screen while turning the film. This helped a great deal.

My mother's civil birth record was the first record I found—I was so excited, I screamed out loud and about jumped off my chair, scaring everyone in the Family History Center. As fate would have it, another gentleman researching Italian records was present in the Center that day, and he helped me translate the document and gave me some hints about Italian records and the microfilm reader.

According to the Pachino, Sicily civil birth records, my mother was born on the fifth day of February, 1899. Since the names and ages of her parents were also on the record, I now had the years of their births.

Next I looked for and found my dad's birth record, and I was on my way!

Some of the years had indices, so I printed those and then marked all the Giuntas and Carrubbas to look for siblings of my parents, as well as cousins.

I found all my mother's siblings' birth records and noticed something interesting. The aunt I knew as Angelina, was really named Francesca. The aunt I knew as Concettina, was really named Carmela Concetta. I knew there had been another sister who died, and found her birth record. This sister, Paola, was born three years after my mother (and died at eight years of age). I then realized my cousin Paula had been named in her memory.

What I was shocked to learn was there was a boy born in 1890 (my grandparents' second child). Since I had *never* heard this mentioned by my mother or any of her siblings, I knew I had to look for a death record. So, for starters, I ordered the death record microfilm covering a ten-year period.

When I looked through the death records, I learned my maternal grandparents' only son, Angelo (named after his paternal grandfather following the Italian naming tradition), had lived only one year, dying two weeks before what would have been his first birthday. Since boys are revered in Italian households, it must have been devastating for them to have six more girls and never conceive another son.

The years of birth for my mother's siblings spanned from 1888 to 1906. The birth order was Carmela (named after her paternal grandmother), Angelo (named after his paternal grandfather), Francesca (named after her maternal grandfather), Carmela Concetta, Giuseppa (my mother), Paola, Sebastiana and Nunziata.

My mother's paternal grandfather has posed a problem for me. I have not been able to find a record of his birth, marriage or death, although I have the town of his birth (Avola), the approximate year of his birth (1818), and the year of his death (1878), which I got from another document. After reaching this stumbling block, I switched over to research my father's side of the family.

I found the records for my grandfather's birth, marriage and death—all in Pachino, Sicily, surprisingly. What was interesting to learn was that his father was recorded as having been born in Modica, Sicily, not Spain, as my father's booklet implied. Modica is about twenty-three miles northwest of Pachino in the hills. Although my great-grandfather was born in Modica (in 1831), he was married and died in Pachino (in 1852 and 1910, respectively). His son, my grandfather, died only one year later, leaving my father an orphan at age eight, since my grandmother had died one year earlier.

My grandfather had married a woman whose surname was Chiaramida, but her first name was Francesca, not Cecilia. She was also born in Pachino, not in Northern Italy. Is this the reason my great-grandfather left Modica—to marry my great-grandmother? Supposedly, this same great-grandfather was instrumental in establishing the protestant Waldensian church in Pachino. Could this be the reason my great-grandfather left Modica? Is this when the family broke away from the Catholic church? Or was there another reason? According to the historical record, there was a terrible flood in 1833. Could this be the reason the family left Modica? These are questions I have yet to answer.

Researching backwards a little more, I traced the Giunta line back another three generations—all in Modica, so far—to around the early 1700s. The Chiaramida line goes back to the mid 1700s—all in Pachino. In checking the history of that city, although there is evidence of some prehistoric settlements in the area, the modern town of Pachino was not founded until 1758 and populated by immigrants from the nearby island of Malta. So, for the Chiaramida line, there is more research to be done.

My father's mother's line, the Quartarones, who were landowners according to my father's booklet, date back to the mid-1700s — with Giovanni, my great-great-great-grandfather (born in 1741) from Spaccaforno (Ispica), Sicily, who married a Cicciarella from — guess where? Modica! My great-grandmother's name was Dimartino, whose family hails from Pachino as far back as I have been able to trace so far (circa 1815).

As you can see, there is yet much more work to be done, mysteries to solve, blanks to fill.

In the Blink of an Eye

—Gaye V. Borne

"IF YOU HAD WAITED just one day longer, you would have, in all certainty, gone blind." These words, spoken by my ophthalmologist, hit me like bullets of raindrops, exploding upon impact, dripping down a sheet of glass. I was behind the glass, dry and safe; but just a millimeter away, everything was wet and perilous. Just a millimeter away was blindness.... A whirlwind of activity ensued: signing surgical consent papers; a flurry of testing; cascading words describing "Laser Iridotomy"; having the surgery immediately; and trying to absorb verbal after-care instructions all the while not losing written prescriptions.

Colors! The lush, blended shades of green of a tree-shaded golf course. The vibrant purples, magentas and reds of bougainvilleas painted against a clear blue sky. The mesmerizing jewel tones of Christmas lights twinkling with promise. The wonder of seeing the heavens of God's House, ablaze with the fire of the setting sun, glowing against a color-streaked sky. The brilliant blue sea, kissed with diamonds of sunlight, versus the mixture of a moody midnight blue and cold, steel gray of an angry sea. I could go on and on. I have always loved color and have deeply appreciated the simple purity of it. Vision is only one of our senses. People have survived without it. And yet, the thought of losing it terrified me. Acute closed-angle glaucoma became a reality for me.

I am so glad I went to my annual eye appointment that day. I am grateful to have a doctor who saved my eyesight and for the medical technology that my doctor used. I am blessed to see the beautiful colors of the world and to be able to read. There, but for the grace of God, go I—I could have been blind—in the blink of an eye....

Is It My Time?

— Jean Giunta Denning

"WHEN WE GET HOME, let's go to the nursery and buy that fig tree you want."

"Good idea, hon," I reply. "If we pick it up today, the gardener can plant it for us when he comes tomorrow."

I'm sitting in the passenger seat of our Maxima on our way home from visiting our kids. It's about three in the afternoon on a typical clear and sunny Southern California day. Little do I realize that the next few minutes are about to change my life.

We are traveling east on Interstate 60 approaching Beaumont where the I-60 merges into the I-10. Both highways are busy with cars, recreation vehicles, campers, small pickups and large trucks—the trucks that are likely responsible for the uneven pavement and the rhythmic thump, thump, thump sounds emanating from our tires as they bump over the rippled surface of the road. Almost reading my mind, Vaughn says, "I wonder when they're going to get around to resurfacing this road—these trucks just beat up the road something awful."

As is customary, my husband is driving at the legal speed limit and slows down slightly as we round the curve approaching the point where the 60 meets the 10. There is no one in front of us, and our car eases into what becomes the right lane of the I-10. To my right I see a long freight train running parallel to the freeway and hear the sounds of the railroad cars clickety-clacking over the tracks.

All of a sudden an eerie silence overcomes me—I can no longer hear the sound of the railroad cars; I can no longer hear the thumping of the tires; I can no longer hear the radio. I don't feel the tap of the semi clipping our left rear wheel, causing our car to spin in front of the truck, nor do I feel the second bump which causes the car to spin like a top across all four lanes of the freeway. I feel us turning in complete circles and see the landscape change rapidly before my eyes as our car revolves round and round, again and again. I feel as though I'm in the spinning teacups at Disneyland—except it is all happening in slow motion.

Oh my God! So this is what it's like when you're about to die. It's just like being in a movie. Is this God's way of protecting me from the pain I should be feeling? There should be broken glass; there should be twisted metal; there should be broken bones; there should be blood; there should be pain. A strange calm and peaceful feeling comes over me. I can't talk, and I'm so calm that I'm barely aware of what is happening. I feel as though I am detached from my body and am looking down at the whole scene. *When I get to heaven, will my family be waiting for me?*

While I am in my calm, speechless state of euphoria, my husband knows enough to not touch the brakes and to turn the steering wheel in the direction of our spin; it's an automatic reflex action on his part from years of training as a test pilot. This saves us from flipping over.

In the next moment, the slow motion I am feeling ends. I have not moved an inch; my seatbelt is not even straining against me. We are stopped—in the center divider—just short of the westbound lanes of the freeway—with the car facing east. The whole incident has probably taken place in less than a minute. *How can that be?*

"Are you all right?" asks my worried husband, breaking the silence.

"Yes—I'm okay. Are you all right? What on earth happened? I never saw anything hit us."

"I'm all right. At least I don't feel or see anything wrong. I don't know what hit us either."

We both look at each other and can see no scratches, bruises or twisted limbs. Nothing hurts. The windshield is intact. Nothing in the car is displaced.

Was it really in slow motion? How could we possibly spin across all four lanes of the freeway without being hit by another car? What prevented us from crossing into the westbound traffic where we would have been easy targets for the oncoming traffic?

We sit there speechless, contemplating and picturing what could have happened.

Vaughn gets out of the car and looks it over ... Except for a small indentation in the left rear wheel and a small dent in the left rear passenger door, the car is untouched. The tires are all intact. There is no smoke coming from under the hood. He gets back in the car and moves it forward a few feet to see if it is drivable. Looking ahead and to the right, we see a large truck pulled over onto the right shoulder about twenty feet in front of an off-ramp. Its frantic driver is standing outside his door waving his arms and yelling across the freeway, "Are you all right? I didn't see you. You were in my blind spot. Oh my God, I hope you're all right. I'm so sorry. Do you need a tow truck? Is there anything I can do?"

"I think we're both all right, and the car appears to be drivable," we yell back. "Would you please follow us off the freeway and meet us at the top of the off-ramp to exchange information." *And file a police report.* We both pray that the truck driver will do that and not just drive off. We don't even have his license number.

I am still rather calm, much to my surprise. At the top of the off-ramp I spot a Chamber of Commerce building. "Vaughn, there's a Chamber of Commerce, and they have a good-sized parking lot. Let's go in and ask them to call the police for us."

There is hope for our society after all ... the truck driver follows us up the off-ramp and into the parking lot. He is in far worse shape than we are, again profusely apologizing, wringing his hands, and probably worrying about the accident being reported to his employer. My husband stays outside with him, gathering pertinent information. I enter the Chamber office.

"Can I help you?" the Chamber receptionist asks.

I step up to the counter. "Yes. Our car just got hit by a truck on the freeway. Could you please call the police for us. We need to file a report."

"Oh my God, are you all right? Do you want me to call the paramedics?"

"That's not necessary; we're both fine," I answer, but at that moment my words betray me. I start shaking all over, and my knees collapse, no longer supporting my legs ... I start to crumble. The receptionist runs around the counter and helps me to a chair.

"Are you sure you don't want me to call the paramedics? At least let me get you a drink of water."

"Thank you, a glass of water would be fine. Really, I'm okay. I think it's just a delayed reaction, and my body's now coming back to reality."

After calling the police, she brings a glass of water and a cool, wet paper towel which she places on my forehead. The police arrive, and we exchange all the necessary information. My shaking has stopped, we say our thanks and get back in the car for a very sobering drive the rest of the way home.

"Can you believe what just happened? That neither of us is hurt? How did we not see the truck? How did we avoid getting hit by the cars behind us? The drivers must have been terrified seeing us spinning across all four lanes of the freeway. How did we keep from flipping over? Did you notice how nervous and upset the truck driver was?" All I had were unanswered questions.

"I'm going to drive as slowly as I can in the right lane until we get home, just in case something goes wrong with the engine or the wheels. I'll take the car in tomorrow and get it checked out. We need to call USAA as soon as we get home to report the accident. By the way, thank you for acting so calm back there ... I would have expected you to start screaming, but I'm glad you didn't ... it helped me concentrate on trying to control the car. But I'm a little curious, why *didn't* you scream?"

"I don't know. I felt incredibly calm. I thought I was going to die, and I was at peace with that. Everything seemed to be in slow motion."

"That's odd you should say that ... it felt like slow motion to me, too."

When we pull into our garage, I feel like kissing the floor.

"You know, hon, we could be our kids opening the door to the house after being told their dad and step-mom were killed in a car accident ... I can just picture their coming in here, shaking their heads and wondering where to start and what to do first. I think it's time to put our affairs in order and leave some instructions for the kids in case something happens to us both at the same time."

"Good idea."

"I wonder why our lives were spared today. I think there is something you or I need to accomplish before our time is up. I'm going to try really hard to figure out what that *something* is."

Living in Stratford in the Early Seventies

— Marilyn McNeill

ARE WE GETTING SETTLED?

Everyone knows that we are newcomers and would kindly ask us if we are getting settled. It always made me smile. I loved the expression 'getting settled.' I remember my grandma would say to me not to bother the hens in the hen house because they need time to get settled.

When I was a little girl I would sit on the fence wearing my denim blue overalls, wait a few minutes and slowly go into the hen house and look to see if there were any more eggs. There were lots of hens, and I really think they got accustomed to my coming and going. I would find two or three eggs each time. My grandma gave me a basket to put them in. Keeping them in my pocket was not a great idea. I collected feathers, too. When I had a handful, my grandma would take some paper and make a band to fit around my head, and I would stick the feathers in the band. Maybe the chickens thought I was one of them.

Mrs. Reid lives next door, and she will always ask me if I am getting settled. She is a sprightly eighty-year-old. This makes me smile now when I write this because I am nearly her age, and I don't see myself as an old lady, but I am.

Every afternoon she walks into town for tea. She dresses up. Today she is wearing pale blue. Her hat is blue, her dress is blue, and she is wearing gloves and likely practical shoes, but I don't notice. This must be her favorite color because I have seen her wearing this before. I imagine that she meets some of her friends for tea, but I don't know for sure except she goes the same time every day. When I get to know her better I will ask her. She has not told me her first name, and I just call her Mrs. Reid.

Mrs. Reid lives in a large older Victorian home, and upstairs she has a suite which she rents to Richard. Richard is an actor. He often entertains in her beautiful manicured back garden. His table is set with white linen and silver candelabra; soft music plays in the background. He only entertains male friends.

Summers are very busy in this small Ontario town. Our population doubles, perhaps triples during the summer. Visitors love to come to the Shakespeare Festival (now called the Stratford Festival) and visit the art galleries and small antique shops. In the market square is a wonderful chocolate shop. It would be hard to leave without a box of these chocolate treats.

Summer is a time for garden parties. Many festival patrons give lavish garden parties in their beautiful gardens. The first one I attended was the most special, likely because it was my first.

The invitation had come in the mail, written on beautiful stationery. Mary Swerdfager had asked me to go with her for the afternoon. Her husband, Bruce, was the artistic director of the Festival, and Mary knew everyone who would be attending — actors, visitors and the locals.

I sighed and thought what would I wear. I needed to dress up. Stratford had a very beautiful dress shop. I decided that this would be just the store to find a suitable dress. I told the sales lady that I would be going to a garden party; she knew exactly what I should be wearing. The ladies would be wearing long dresses, she told me. I left with a long pale pink dress and a pink picture hat. This would be my favorite summertime dress, and I would wear it often that summer.

The sales lady had a small box of index cards and recorded my size and name. I didn't think this was necessary, but she seemed to think that I may be back to do more shopping in the future. She was right. I came to shop at her little boutique several times. She always knew what would be the most suitable for the occasion. When we lived in Toronto I had a little black dress that took me everywhere anytime.

The day of the garden party arrived. It was just a perfect summer day. Can you imagine seeing all these lovely ladies wearing beautiful long dresses and hats?

This was the seventies, and ladies wore long skirts and dresses when they were going to a party. The waiters were formally dressed. They wore white gloves serving us canapés on silver trays. I do not remember what we drank … perhaps iced tea.

Mary introduced me to many of her friends that afternoon. The only people that I recognized were the actors.

Little did I know that I would come to know them well, seeing them at many of the dinner parties throughout the winter.

Bill Hutt was always interested in exchanging recipes. He often called me Maid Marion because he thought that my name was Marion and would often speak in Elizabethan English with me. He had a good sense of humor, and I would respond in kind.

On one occasion I asked, "What happens if you forget your lines?" He could switch from one soliloquy to another, and I could not tell.

"My dear," he said, "you will never know." He was right. I did not know he had changed a line.

Autumn brought many changes to our city. The tourists went home; life returned to normal. The swans left the Avon River and returned to the barns, their winter home. We didn't have any more garden parties.

Soon it was winter. The winter weather was cold, and snow fell. Many times the roads were closed. No one traveled far in winter. Our actor friends had homes in Stratford, and we saw them often. Entertaining was a weekend tradition. Sometimes it was simple just getting together and enjoying homemade clam chowder. We often walked to our friends' homes carrying our shoes in a fancy shoe bag over our arm. My shoe bag was velvet. Some of the actors had the most fancy embroidered bags.

The evenings were not too late—especially if snow was falling. The most important part was finding two snow boots that matched and that fit!

Mean 2018

—Jane Ruona

YEAR 2018 STARTED OUT AS I PREDICTED: Rose Parade … check, happy guests … check, temperatures in the seventies starting right after Christmas … check. All my hopes for my eightieth year on track.

In February the bomb dropped! Joe Grillo, my daughter's husband and father to my two granddaughters, was hospitalized with yellow eyes and pneumonia. Joe didn't want to go to the hospital, but his daughters insisted. At fifty-six he struggled to breathe and was put on a respirator in Dominican Hospital ICU. His life went up and down like it was on a fragile spring branch in the wind. On Valentine's Day he told my daughter Heidi, "I guess I can't get you a Valentine, but maybe your present will be my move to the other side." Joe had been disabled for some time with a spinal cord tumor. He loved his "girls" and cooked dinner and did what he could to help Heidi who was teaching special education full time. Her principal was very stingy and would only give her minimum time off to be at Joe's bedside. Joe passed away March thirteenth after a month-long struggle in front of his daughters and wife. I went with my granddaughter Morréa to make hasty final arrangements.

Joe's "girls," Morréa, twenty-two, and Carli, fourteen, were without a dad. How could grandparents console? All we could do was reach into our souls and do our best to help with grieving. Hospice was a wonderful resource for Heidi, Morréa and Carli. Heidi found the strength to finish the semester of teaching. She was disgusted and disillusioned with her school and resigned. Carli continued with school and volleyball, and Morréa continued with her teaching and plans for grad school.

After a start like this, Bill and I tried to salvage our plans for this mean year. We did go to Cuba with friends. We really enjoyed the cultural contrast, especially dancing with Cuban grandparents. The Copacabana Nightclub was the highlight. It was a multifaceted show of dancing, singing, and acrobatics ranging from classical to current, including laser special effects. The show has continued since 1939 every night in an outdoor venue. They gave each table large bottles of rum and coke which we sipped until the show ended at 1:30 a.m.

The Cuban people were delightful and begged us to put in a word for opening up international relations with the U.S. Most had relatives in Florida ninety miles away. The scenery on this large island is beautiful. The cultural contrast goes back one hundred fifty years with farmers walking behind plows and oxen pulling carts.

The Cubans are not quite ready for tourism, but tourists are okay when they can return to a cruise ship each night.

Bill was intrigued by the 1950's U.S. cars and how the Cubans were able to improvise their own parts because they were not allowed to import due to the embargo. The owners of the cars drove us around the island and were very proud.

The only building in good repair was the Communist Plaza de la Revolución. There is little government money, and grocery shelves are very sparse. The people have to plant gardens. Health, school, and culture have priority. Children go to school six days a week, and Cuba produces a large proportion of international doctors and nurses.

In May Morréa and her boyfriend, Kevin, spruced up the backyard with flowers planted among the redwoods, and a memorial service was held outdoors for Joe. It was catered by the their favorite local Mexican restaurant. Joe was very social and had many friends. We heard many stories about fishing trips, Joe's band, and disc golf. Later a musical tribute with Joe's drums and other instruments was played by young and old. Joe listened from afar.

Heidi has had to tie all the legal papers together, and she has had the hardest time with grieving, even though she went to counseling. Carli couldn't understand what she would say to a counselor for fifty minutes each week, but she received great benefit and returned to her sunny self. Morréa had Kevin who has been a wonderful support, always ready to pitch in.

In June Bill and I drove Carli to Park City for my best friend, Marilyn's eightieth birthday party. Carli's friends were there. We continued on to the majestic Rockies to see my brother and sister-in-law and their three grandchildren under three. Carli was in her element ... very patient and intrigued with babies. Then it was on to Ouray and Durango via the million dollar highway. Carli's favorite stop was Four Corners where she could put each limb in a different state.

Next stop: Grand Canyon. Carli had been to one of our national parks before—Yosemite. On the way the thirteen-year-old questioned our wisdom asking, "Why are we going there?" When she had time to take in the voluptuous Yosemite Triple Falls, she said, "This was a good idea!"

As we neared the Grand Canyon we saw lots of parched brush in piles which looked like food for a hungry forest fire. All it needed was a careless or targeted match. The Grand Canyon takes my breath away each time I see it, and I am hoping this is not the last time. Luckily I got last-minute reservations for a cabin on the rim and the El Tovar for dinner.

In the morning we scampered down a short ways on the rim trail, but we had miles to go and didn't see the mule riders' weary return. We headed back to Bakersfield with 103 degree temperatures and then home.

Mean 2018 still held some magic. In July Bill and I flew to Hawaii's Big Island and stayed at Kolea where the giant sea turtles were waiting for us. We each decided to plan one day, most of which included another gorgeous swimming beach. Bill very patiently deferred golf and was our chauffeur. The night of my eightieth birthday we dined at the CanoeHouse, Mauna Lani with elegant music and a world-class sunset (no green flash). Bill couldn't help himself and stated, "This cost more than the down payment on our first house."

The last murky turn of mean 2018 was a sharp downturn of the stock market. It erased every bit of profit boasted by Trump in the last two years.

December brought a spike toward the positive when we stayed with Marilyn, Nadia (Marilyn's granddaughter), Carli, and Maddie (Carli's friend) in a Hilton suite on the thirty-eighth floor at Union Square in San Francisco. I saw my best sunset bar none. Next we took Lyft to the Waterfront Restaurant and watched the new Bay Bridge and the Salesforce Tower lights compete.

Still I was giving 2018 a good kick on New Year's Eve.

Medicine

— Corinne Lee Murphy

WE WENT TO SAN FRANCISCO on December 28 to meet again with the radiologist. A mold was made of Bob's neck and torso to create a mesh form to ensure that he would remain immobile during the radiation treatments to begin in the New Year. He would be pinned to the table. We then drove to Berry Street for the CT Scan that our radiologist would hopefully find more acceptable. He had dismissed the scan which had been taken in Sacramento as unreadable and of no use to him.

On December 29 we went to dinner with our dear friend Dick. Dick has a weekend home overlooking the San Francisco Bay. He had recently remodeled this home and filled it thoughtfully with new furniture and hand-picked original art. He had not stayed in the newly renovated home yet. Still, he offered it to us to use during the week while Bob was to be treated at UCSF. It was generous beyond measure.

The living room had a glass wall, and the view looked directly across to where the Golden Gate connects San Francisco with Marin County. To the left the Bay Bridge led from San Francisco to Alameda County. The scene was never static; the beauty was ever-changing. The sea varied from grey to cobalt to a startling turquoise with all the shades and variations between. The water moved, of course, with white caps mostly, but on rare occasion it could become almost glass like. And on the water there was constant movement too: there were sailboats large and small and commercial fleets; tankers would dock at refineries; and ferries were on schedules. Bob enjoyed pointing out the navy vessels. On clear nights, San Francisco appeared jeweled. Sunny days were lovely, but the weather could change suddenly. Fog would come close and curl around the house as we remained warm and protected inside. To gaze out the window was both mesmerizing and calming. It was medicine.

Dick had inherited this home from his beloved sister, Elizabeth, who had built the home on the hill with her husband, but she had been widowed for years before her death. A small photo of her in her youth was placed on the mantle. Each time we stayed in her lovely home I would say hello to her photograph and silently thank her.

[Excerpt from the book
Grace Fully: Making Peace with Cancer]

Miracle of Survival

— June Gaulding

IN LATE SPRING OF 1971, a lady in Kansas City, Missouri, heard a cat crying for about two weeks in the house next door. She called the police to find out what was happening. Upon entering the house, the police searched every room and did not find a cat. However, in one of the bedrooms they discovered a small child lying on her back and tied to a bed. She was a very thin little girl, so they assumed she had not had food or water for a long period of time. After untying her, they found all the hair worn off the back of her head. Her clothing and bedding were soiled. The neighbor told the police she thought there was a man and a pregnant woman with a boy about one year old who lived there. She hadn't seen them for two weeks. Also, they had lived there for a year, and she had never seen the little girl.

Once the police searched and found the family, the mother was questioned. She said, "The girl is an idiot, and I don't want her." She said that she couldn't talk. In looking back, the mother was the idiot. The little girl's name was Janet. Upon learning of the abuse of this child, the police turned the little girl over to the county Children's Services. If the mother had been in today's world, she would have faced prison time for abuse of a child. The man living with the mother was not the little girl's father, and the boy was a step-brother.

In late summer of 1971, Children's Services wanted to place Janet in a more permanent home. I am assuming the county didn't have an orphanage for her to go to, so they contacted the Catholic Family Service in Amarillo, Texas. A representative drove to Kansas City to pick Janet up and drove her back to the Catholic Orphanage Home in Amarillo. Janet spent the remainder of 1971 in the orphanage with her having had her third birthday on September 24th of that year. The new year of 1972 was approaching.

In the fall of 1971, my husband, Jack, and I lived in Lubbock and had a son, Mark, who was nine years old and in a remarkable coincidence, was a classmate of Skip Starkey. I was feeling the empty nest syndrome with no children around during the daytime. We had talked of adopting a child, a girl, and many of our friends had adopted infants, so we were familiar with the process. However, I didn't want an infant, and it didn't really matter to Jack, so we would focus on a little older child that could be a playmate for Mark. Mark was excited when he heard he might be getting a little sister. I contacted several adoption services, but all of their children were infants. There were three other adoption services with older children that I could contact. Since we weren't of their religious faith, two of the services wouldn't let us adopt. The last service was the Catholic Family Service of Amarillo, so I contacted them in October. We were not of the Catholic faith, but it didn't concern them, and they sent us a letter in November. In a couple of weeks, they contacted us. The process started by submitting forms with family history and the background of each one of us in the family.

It was now 1972. During the month of January, 1972, the Catholic Family Service wanted to place Janet for adoption. So, they contacted a caseworker, Bonnie Starkey, who lived in Lubbock, Texas, to come to their Amarillo office. They asked Bonnie to take Janet to Lubbock where she would live with her until a family became available for Janet's adoption.

Bonnie was married and had two boys and a little girl. When Janet arrived at her home, she was quiet and couldn't … or wouldn't … talk. She could only say "Mama." She was afraid of women, but she trusted Bonnie. Janet was not afraid of men and would hold onto them when they were leaving her. On the first night at Bonnie's house, Janet was given a bed, but soon crawled down to sleep on the floor. Bonnie's oldest boy, Skip, was ten, and he would get on the floor and sleep by her. In time, Janet began to sleep in her own bed.

During the month of February, a representative from the Amarillo office visited us. He said they were considering placing a three-year-old girl named Janet with us. This representative happened to be the Catholic priest who had picked Janet up in Kansas City. He wanted to share with us the time spent with little Janet on her trip to Amarillo. He said, "Janet was quiet and when we stopped to eat, she held the small hamburger gently in her hands." Also, he gave her half a piece of gum, and she daintily chewed it. He was amazed that after what this little girl had been through that she could be so peaceful. He said after a couple more interviews, we would be ready for the next step of the adoption with a visit in March from Bonnie, the local caseworker.

In the next three months we had several home visits with Bonnie. On the last visit, she said they wanted to place Janet with us. We were ecstatic! We had requested a girl from three to eight years old. Also, if the child had a handicap that we could help improve on, that would work for us. We wanted her to be able to blend into our family unit. Mark had blond hair and blue eyes. Bonnie said this little girl had minor handicaps and had blond hair and blue eyes. Perfect!

In late June it was time for us to meet Janet. We knew we would like her, but we wondered if she would like us. Bonnie had arranged for us to meet at a quiet restaurant at noon. It was Brittany's on College Avenue across from Texas Tech College, so that we could have hamburgers. That was Janet's favorite food. Upon meeting Janet, we noticed she was a cute, tiny little thing with a big smile. Enough time had passed for her blond hair to have grown on the back of her head, and she had gained some weight. We were told that she was still small for her age of almost four years old, but was equivalent to a two-year-old weighing twenty-five pounds. Bonnie introduced us to Janet as, "This is Mark, and Mark's mommy and daddy." She thought if I was introduced as a mother, Janet might be afraid of me. This was a fun and exciting experience meeting a new child to become a family member. Janet seemed comfortable with us that day. It was a wonderful visit!

After lunch, Bonnie said we would meet in a week on July 3rd, if that was okay with us. That day just happened to be my birthday. What a great present for me! We met at the same place for hamburgers and visited again. By this time, Janet seemed to be feeling very comfortable with us, especially with Mark. Since Bonnie's son, Skip, was Mark's age, Janet trusted him. After lunch and it was time to go, Bonnie said, "Would you like to take Janet for the afternoon?" Yes, of course we wanted to take her with us for a few hours.

Janet, in the first dress we bought her the first day she came to us, July 1972. Shirley Temple couldn't hold a candle to this little angel. Photo courtesy of LifeTouch Inc.

Arriving at our home, the three of us walked her through all the rooms and ended up in her bedroom that we had decorated for her. Mark introduced Janet to his miniature dachshund, named Heidi, that he would now be sharing with his sister. Finally we made a trip to the backyard where she would play. She was excited and ran all around the yard. She was confused with so many new things to see and do. I am sure she didn't understand what was going on that day. After showing her around our home, Jack went back to work. Mark and I took Janet shopping at a friend's children's clothing shop. She helped us find some cute clothes, shoes, a little purse, and toys for her. What fun we had!

Upon returning home from shopping, Mark took his sister to meet our neighbors. He was very proud of her and couldn't wait "to show her off." One of the neighbors had gotten a big Raggedy Ann doll as a gift for Janet. They couldn't wait to get home to show me the doll. It was as big as Janet. By this time she was getting tired, so Mark lay down with her for a short nap. We then called Bonnie to let her know how Janet was doing and that she was having a good time. I asked her when she would like to pick her up. She said, "I'm going to leave her with you for the night since she is doing so well." We talked with Bonnie the next morning. She told us that Janet should just stay with us since she was doing so well. This was a true moment of happiness for our family. She stayed with us from that day forward.

Now that Janet was in our family, she needed to have a name. We had discussed several names. However, when we found out that her name was Janet and that was all the little girl had ever known, we would keep that, but add a middle name. If her name had been Maude or Matilda we probably would have changed her name. We added the middle name of Michelle to give her the full name of Janet Michelle Gaulding. Of course, it would not be legal until we had a couple of home visits.

In the month of December we went before a judge to finalize the adoption. We all had to swear that we would take care of her for the rest of her life—a vow we all felt was sacred. She was now part of our family. What a great way to end the year of 1973.

Bonnie told us there were a few things that had to be done for Janet, so that she would adjust and hopefully live as normal a life as possible. We were told that while she was in Amarillo she had been examined for physical or psychological problems. She

Jack, June, Janet and Mark at Janet's adoption with judge on far right, January 1973.

165

had serious speech problems causing a lack of communication and underdeveloped large motor skills. In addition, we were told that she probably would never graduate from high school because her learning disabilities would be a handicap for her. Bonnie had already enrolled Janet in speech therapy and child psychology programs at Texas Tech Medical School in Lubbock in the spring before we met her.

As Janet became comfortable with us, she would communicate by saying, "Uh, uh, uh," when she wanted something. In time, Mark and I could understand what she wanted. This sound, and "Mama," were the only words she could say to communicate with us. It was now the second week of July, and Bonnie asked that I continue the scheduled therapies. The twice-a-week speech schedule was basic, with Janet learning to say an infant's first sounds and words. As months went by, she was able to say many words and short phrases. In a year, she could say longer sentences and was beginning to communicate with those around her. However, she continued in speech therapy through sixth grade, having learned to master almost perfect speech.

Mike was Janet's child psychology therapist at Texas Tech College Psychology Department. He was going to use her case for his doctorate degree in Children's Psychology Play Therapy. He said there was not much study done in this area, so he was excited to help Janet. She liked Mike and was excited to see him once a week for play therapy. He even visited our home twice and shared dinner with us to observe Janet with the family unit. Mike's play therapy continued through the fall and ended in December, 1972. This therapy would help Janet cope with many situations that she might be faced with in her daily life.

One day about a month after Janet came to our family, I had seated her at the small kitchen table for her lunch. I gave her a peanut butter and jelly sandwich on a plate, and I told her she could start eating. With a little smile she started eating. I was close by at the kitchen counter preparing my sandwich, and I heard Janet talking to someone to the left side of her. She had taken a piece of sandwich and offered it to the imaginary person. I let her continue for a couple of minutes, and I headed towards the table and sat down. When she heard me, she quickly stopped the conversation. I asked her if the sandwich was good, and she nodded her head. I started eating my sandwich, but asked myself, "Should I say something to her about whom she was talking with?" I decided not to say anything. I knew she didn't have the capability of voicing it to me. Her conversations went on for about a month when she was at the table by herself, and one day she just quit talking to her friend. She never did it again that I was aware of.

Our first family portrait with our sweet Janet, 1972.
Photo courtesy of LifeTouch Inc.

I have thought over the years about Janet's table conversations. It was my conclusion that she had created a little friend in her time of being all alone and tied to the bed. This was how she survived. However, I still wonder, how could a two-year-old do this? I have talked with Janet about this, and she said she remembers vaguely about talking with someone. She didn't know who it was or when she did it. Maybe someday she might pull it from her childhood memory. To this day, I firmly believe that little friend helped her survive.

I was able to get Janet enrolled in the special needs pre-kindergarten programs. Prior to Janet's attending class, I talked with the teachers about her background of speech difficulties and hyperactive actions. Thank goodness the teachers understood her needs at that time. With their help she learned to sit in her seat and participate in the education process. She continued speech therapy and went to a special needs study hall that ended after eighth grade. Janet had a full life with school, dance lessons, Campfire Girls, gymnastics, and overnight visits with friends. She was in the church choir and had the opportunity to go to Japan, Thailand and Germany. She enjoyed going to school and graduated from high school in 1987. So much for people telling us that Janet would never graduate from high school.

Janet, age 8, 1977.
Photo courtesy of LifeTouch Inc

We had always told Janet that we loved her from the moment we saw her and wanted her to be a part of our family. After graduation we were going to share with her more about her life before her adoption. However, tragedy struck our family three weeks before Janet's graduation. Jack died in an airplane crash on May 11, 1987. This was a sad time for our family. Mark was living in California and came home to be with us, as well as other members of the family who came to support us through this horrible time in our lives.

Janet, Senior portrait, 1987.
Photo courtesy of LifeTouch Inc

A few years later Mark and I did share Janet's early life with her. It was hard for her to hear, but she accepted it and moved on with her life.

In the fall after high school graduation, Janet started college at South Plains College at Levelland, Texas, thirty miles away, and lived in the dorm. She completed two years with studies in Child Development, as she was passionate about helping children.

During college she met Scott Frost stationed at the Air Force Base out of Lubbock. They married and moved to San Mateo, California upon his discharge from the service. He went to work with United Airlines Maintenance Department in San Francisco. About five years later, United moved the Maintenance Department to Indianapolis, so they moved there, too.

Janet went to work for KinderCare Day School as a teacher and is still with them after twenty-some years. She and Scott had two children, Jessica, now 20 years old, and Shane, now 17 years old.

Janet, Jessica, Shane, June, Mark
and our beloved, wonderful Grandma Faye,
whom we will never forget. She was such an
important part of our lives,
Indianapolis, 2005.
Photo courtesy of LifeTouch Inc.

After twenty-five years of marriage, Janet and Scott divorced in 2016. Scott passed away in November 2019 of a massive heart attack. Janet and the children are doing great with Jessie as a sophomore in college at Ball State, and Shane looking forward to being a senior in high school next year. My daughter has adjusted to life as a single mother and has moved on. She will be celebrating her fifty-second birthday. Janet is a miracle of survival!

Music in My Soul

— Ruth Gray

WHEN I WAS BORN, my mother composed a poem which later became a song that she sang to me. I do not remember all the lines, but it started like this: "Thirteen tulips on my table, tell of love in our stable ..."and referred to the thirteen tulips my father brought to her in the hospital room March 13, 1933, hours after my birth.

She sang many nursery rhymes to me those first four years before she became ill and I was sent to live with Aunt May on the ranch. The earliest were about a robin and two lost children. I remember both songs well and can still sing the tunes mournfully as she did.

The result of her singing these songs to me would be tears. Yet I would beg her every night to sing these songs to me before bedtime. I would be crying away and snuggling up to her, and I suspect she thought it was cute when through my tears I would plead, "Sing again to me, Mommy."

Aunt May sang also, though more to herself or with others. She suffered with three kinds of arthritis, and many mornings as I awoke I heard music from the kitchen as she was getting breakfast. Then at the breakfast table we sang Rebecca Weston's prayer together:

> Father, we thank you for the night,
> and for the pleasant morning light;
> for rest and food and loving care,
> and all that makes the day so fair.
>
> Help us to do the things we should,
> to be to others kind and good;
> in all we do, in work or play,
> to grow more loving every day.

I went to Quaker services with Aunt May in Portland, Prune Hill, or at the Quaker Camp in Twin Rocks, Oregon. I learned many other choruses such as "This Little Light of Mine," "All the Children of the World," "Let Me Be a Sunbeam," and of course, "Jesus Loves Me."

A few years later when I was living with my parents in White Plains and then Scarsdale, New York, my mother started searching for a violin teacher for me. I have her letters to music teachers about me, and her search was diligent and thorough. I was eleven years old when I began studying with a Mr. Green, and I remember him as a kindly Jewish man who had me sing before I learned a new piece. Because I learned quickly by his method I loved playing. My first instrument was a Hopf German violin that belonged to my grandfather Charles Reed. Mother also had played the violin, so we sometimes played duets together.

As Dad moved us around the east due to his work assignments as a government expediter, my teachers were short term, and some were jacks of all trades in music, and I knew more than they did about playing the violin. I did not learn very much until after the war when Dad purchased the ranch in the Hood River Valley in Oregon from Aunt May's estate. A wonderful teacher was found who had been brought to the USA by the American Red Cross when Viipuri, Finland had been evacuated during WWII.

His name was Boris Sirpo. He had studied under Sevcik and the composer Sibilious, and had been the founder and director of the Viipurin Conservatory.

By this time I was fourteen years old, and many of his younger students were far ahead of me. There were many Finnish families who lived in the valley, and their children had started string lessons with Mr. Sirpo from early years. I started practicing regularly, sometimes as long as four hours a day. By the time I was a high school senior, I was able to win a music scholarship to Whitworth College in Spokane, Washington.

At Whitworth I was expected to be a music ambassador of sorts, and almost every Sunday I was sent to various churches in and around Spokane with professors from the university who were speakers and student pianists or organists who played for the service and accompanied me. I played professionally in the Spokane Symphony and was paid $25 per concert; this was a lot of money in those days, and it paid for my textbooks and extra expenses! I was also concertmaster of our Whitworth orchestra and soloist twice, once for a Haydn concerto and once for a Mendelssohn concerto.

Before my junior year was finished, Mr. Sirpo asked me to return to Portland to be a part of an all-girl orchestra to tour Europe the following year. Thus I found myself in a most remarkable summer practice routine. We would arrive at his spacious home in Portland's Laurelhurst Park at 9 a.m. every morning and meet downstairs in the basement for a 1½-hour orchestra practice. By 10:30 we would break for breakfast. Mrs. Sirpo provided an amazing spread of breads, herring, sardines and cheese. After our break, we then went individually into various rooms of the home to practice our individual parts, while Mr. S. went from room to room, listening to us and correcting our playing. Finally we came together as an orchestra before going home at 1 p.m.

Mr. Sirpo placed pressure on my parents to purchase a better violin for me to play. He loaned me an Amati of his that was for sale, but it was way beyond what my parents could afford. I am very glad now my parents resisted, as it resulted in my own personal hunt and responsibility to find a violin which fit my temperament and ability. Later I discovered that many of my fellow players whose parents had purchased instruments from Mr. Sirpo had been duped.

I got caught up in the excitement of our future tour of Europe so decided to stay in Portland my junior year at Lewis and Clark College where Mr. Sirpo was a professor. This I did for one semester, but transferred to Reed College, as I was moving away from a vocational pursuit of music and into study toward the humanities.

I was also going through a personal crisis. My fiancé, Dick Gray, Whitworth student-body president, had been in a serious car accident driving to a leadership conference, and one of his best friends who had been riding with him had been instantly killed. Dick, in a heavy cast from a broken back, was also psychologically injured from guilt of the loss of his friend. Even though I made the trip to Spokane immediately, he was in shock and bereft and did not know what the future held for him. He broke our engagement.

Returning to Portland, I announced my plans to leave the all-girl orchestra. Mr. Sirpo was angry, and this resulted in an unpleasant parting. I returned to Whitworth for my senior year, but much had changed. My former fiancé had left for the University of Minnesota for graduate studies. I no longer had the responsibility as concertmaster of the Whitworth orchestra since a better violinist than I had taken my place. Dick's and my closest music friends had graduated and were no longer around. I felt myself in a social and spiritual vacuum. I left the Presbyterian and Quaker roots of my childhood and found solace at St. John's Episcopal Church where I was confirmed. Later, my dear former fiancé and I were reconciled.

After Dick and I were married, I played professionally in the St. Paul and Evanston Symphonies, and was a founder of a Baroque quartette in Bloomington, Indiana. But I stopped practicing diligently and was on to other pursuits.

But music itself was deeply instilled within me. Mother had taken me to see *Mignon* in New York when I was eleven years old, and I have held season opera tickets many years since. I am forever grateful to my parents who sacrificed so much for me in time, money and effort as I was growing up. When I think of my father driving to Portland round trip from the upper Hood River Valley, at times weekly, I am amazed. Thinking of my mother sitting through my many lessons, playing her violin along with me, accompanying me on the piano and singing with me, brings tears to my eyes. What a legacy it left me. And though I did not "grasp the ring" they may have hoped, music has given me its greatest pleasures and given me other transferable skills I would later use. I have sung in church choirs in Portland, Oregon; Palm

Desert and Carmel, California; and Bloomington, Indiana. I have played in many town orchestras including the Coachella Valley Symphony. I self-taught myself to play the mandolin, dulcimer and ukulele over the years, and as my ability to play the violin wanes as I grow older, I enjoy playing folk music in bluegrass bands. And today, I never miss a good concert or opera if I can go!

My Bermuda Triangle

—June Gaulding

MY HUSBAND, JACK, LOVED AIRPLANES from the time he was a child. He said he would lie out on the grass and look up at the sky and see planes flying and was fascinated as to how they could stay up there. Several years after we were married he wanted to take flying lessons and satisfy that fascination. After his first lesson he was hooked and continued until he had his private pilot's license for small aircraft. He started renting a small plane, but in time he found it possible to purchase an airplane, a Beechcraft Bonanza, to fulfill his dream: to pilot his own airplane.

Since Jack had an airplane, he did a lot of traveling for business. He was a conscientious and safe pilot. The kids and I would go with him on many trips. It was fun, and we enjoyed our travels. We had been to many places in the U.S. and a trip to Mexico, so I was very excited when he asked me if I would like to fly to the Caribbean Islands.

A couple, Bob and Helen Anderson, who lived in Dallas, had flown their airplane to St. Maarten Island a few years before and wanted us to fly with them again. We would fly from Lubbock, Texas to Phillipsburg, St. Maarten Island. The south part of the island is owned by the Dutch (St. Maarten), and the French own the north part of the island (St. Martin). We talked more about the trip with them, and I learned that we would both fly our own airplanes, as they wanted to stay longer. I decided it would be an adventure for me, so I said, "Yes." I was excited and a little scared, since I didn't know what to expect flying over water in a small airplane.

After making plans we flew out of Lubbock in June, 1976, to Ft. Lauderdale, Florida. We arrived in the afternoon to meet

Bob and Helen and to find out more about our eight-hour ocean flight. The fixed-base operator at the airport had a representative who would instruct us how to use the overseas equipment that we were to take with us. We had oxygen masks on our plane, but they supplied us with heavier oxygen equipment that we were to wear at high altitudes. Other equipment included life vests that we wore all the time and an inflatable life raft. The life raft had emergency equipment, such as flares, flashlights, and a small supply of food and water. I listened carefully during the instructions for operating all the life-saving equipment if we had to use it.

We met Bob and Helen for dinner that night where I was to hear more about their flight to St. Maarten Island a few years earlier. Their flight had gone well, but the subject of the Bermuda Triangle came up, as we would be in that area. I had read the No. 1 selling book, *The Bermuda Triangle* a few years before.

According to Google, the Bermuda Triangle is in the western part of the North Atlantic Ocean with Bermuda, Miami, Florida, and San Juan, Puerto Rico as its vertices, and Bimini Island on the Florida-Puerto Rico segment of the triangle. A number of aircraft and ships are said to have disappeared under mysterious circumstances in the Bermuda Triangle. The U.S. Navy and U.S. Board on Geographic Names says it does not exist, but popular thought is that the disappearances are paranormal or activity by extraterrestrial beings.

The earliest writings of the unusual disappearance in the Bermuda area, the northern part of the triangle, appeared in a September 17, 1950 article published in *The Miami Herald*. Two years later, *Fate* magazine published the article "Sea Mystery at Our Back Door," about the loss of several planes and ships, including the loss of Flight 19, a group of five U.S. Navy TBM Avenger bombers on a training mission. They were never found. It has been argued that these disappearances could be from an undersea earthquake or magnetic interference with the airplane or ship compasses.

The next morning we left Ft. Lauderdale as planned. I was a little leery about the flight after the reminder of the Bermuda Triangle. Everything was going well, and we were enjoying the flight. There were blue skies all around and blue water below with some white caps. Occasionally we would see a ship.

However, in the back of my mind, I would think about getting out of the plane with the raft and putting it in the water. I couldn't stop thinking: *if I couldn't get into the raft, what would happen?* I knew there were sharks, and if one caught me, I just wanted it to eat me up quickly so I wouldn't suffer. I tried not to think about that and listened to Jack as he chatted by radio throughout the morning with Bob and Helen. All was well with them. Midway on our trip we arrived at Bimini Island for gasoline and a lunch break. Then it was time to take off for the last half of our flight.

Again in the air, flying was "smooth sailing" for us for the next couple of hours. We received a call from our flying companions saying they could see our plane and all looked well, and asked if we could see them. Jack started maneuvering the airplane in different directions to see if we could see them. They were supposed to be flying above us. We just could not see their airplane anywhere, and now I was beginning to think we're in the Bermuda Triangle, and somebody has disappeared. I was trying not to be scared since we were communicating with them. This went on for about one and one-half hours. We were close to the arrival time at St. Maarten Island when we finally could see them. What a relief! We never did understand why we couldn't see them anywhere.

We finally arrived at Phillipsburg, St. Maarten Island, where English was spoken to make it easier for tourists. Since it was summer, the island was in the dry season, and there were few green plants and flowers blooming. That didn't stop us from enjoying our week at the hotel resort. We had the run of the place, as it was their off season, and just a few people were there. The young couple who managed the resort were good friends with Bob and Helen, so we dined as a family at night with them in the dining room.

During the week Jack and I explored the area by motorbike with me hanging on behind him. We enjoyed the beach, the pool, shopping and taking a nap most days. Midweek we all decided to fly to Martinique Island, a French Island, an hour's flight farther south of St. Maarten. We stayed for the day enjoying the island and then flew back to our island.

Our week was over, and it was time to start back home. The Andersons were going to spend another week, so Jack and I were on our own. We said goodbye to our friends and took off for Bimini Island, our midway stop. Everything went fine and no disappearances ... so the remainder of our trip back to Lubbock with a stopover night in Florida was rather boring after the scare of "my Bermuda Triangle" experience on our flight down.

My First Gardener

— Irene Knudsen

I HAVE NEVER BEEN INTERESTED in gardening, although I enjoy a well-tended garden. That duty fell on my husband. He was a natural, growing up on a farm. He could transform any backyard into an oasis with lush vegetation and even found space for fruit trees and vegetables. At one time we had a hen house, but as it attracted a family of vicious raccoons depleting our stock, we gave the survivors away in hope of giving them a less stressful life.

When my husband died and I moved to a smaller house, I had to look for a gardener. I had inherited a nice backyard, and I wanted to keep it that way. I went to Esther, my all-knowing neighbor living two houses down from me. She was not too happy with her present gardener — she changed gardeners atregular intervals — but I took a chance on Juan.

He came every Wednesday, around nine in the morning. He was an energetic fellow, and it did not take long until the place turned into a modest copy of the garden of Versailles. He used his hedge trimmer and shears with great enthusiasm. My hedges looked like well-trimmed squares, and my bushes took on round sculptured edges. Even my seventeen rose bushes got a more unison look. Sometimes his son, a shy little boy around five, came along. He sat quietly on the patio playing with my grandson's cars.

At this time my son, Olaf, was living with me. He was a great help with the move to my new house and in selling my husband's two El Caminos. We got along great, and it helped in sharing our grief. He got a temporary job at the gas company.

One Sunday evening watching the news together, I saw the name Juan Vieras in large letters across the screen. This Juan was wanted for attempted murder.

"That's my gardener," I said, turning to Olaf.

"No Mom, that is a very common name. Relax."

But I couldn't, and I waited patiently for Wednesday to come. No Juan showed up. I gave him one more week, just in case he decided to give himself a short vacation, but no Juan was in sight.

I had to find out for sure if it was he, so I drove down to the police station in Cathedral City where the incident had occurred. Maybe they had a picture of him there.

I went up to the female officer at the desk.

"Can I help you," she said, looking up.

"Yes, I saw on TV that you are looking for somebody named Juan Vieras. I want to know what happened to him."

"I can't give out any information of unsolved cases."

"Do you have a picture of him?"

She looked me over with a cloud of doubt.

"You are not a relative?" she said in a question that sounded more like a confirmation.

"No, no, I think he could be my gardener. He has not shown up for two weeks, and I hope he is not in any trouble."

She tried holding back a smile. "Stay here. I will be back."

It took a while until she returned, and I was hoping for good news.

"As I said, I can not give out any information," and lowering her tone leaning closer to me she added, "I strongly suggest you get yourself a new gardener."

Two days later two Mexicans came to my door to collect Juan's last paycheck. He had gone to Mexico for a while they said, but assured me the money was going to Juan's wife and son. I believed them, and thought about the shy little boy playing on my patio.

I got a new gardener, and my hedges and bushes took on their original form. Somehow I missed that French touch. I did not think about Juan again until I one day ran into Esther.

"Did you hear about Juan?"

"I heard he went back to Mexico."

"He had to. He got caught up in a road-rage incident, and almost killed the other guy. Never liked him. He mutilated my bushes."

Esther had obviously not been to Versailles or any other garden in France.

Then I got this picture in my mind of Juan rushing out of his car with his hedge trimmer in his hand, giving the other guy a very, very close crew cut.

I have had a few gardeners since then, but none as memorable as my first gardener, Juan Vieras Scissorhand.

My Swim Suit

— Marilyn McNeill

I LOVE COMING TO CALIFORNIA in November. The Pacific Northwest is cool and wet now. Not long ago, I loved when it rained in the city. That meant snow in the mountains, and we were a family of skiers. Now I am a grey-haired snowbird. I love the warm weather and the sunshine. I love to swim. This is my exercise and my fitness. Each day my friend Jane and I meet and swim for an hour.

Chlorine does a number on your bathing suit. My son and wife are coming for a week this month. Suddenly my plain practical polyester suit looks sad and baggy. I need a new one.

Nothing can ruin your day like the thought of going to look for a new swim suit. Today is shopping day.

The store is a beautiful store with many swim suits displayed. The salesgirl is about a size six. I discuss with her the fit … and that I would like something flattering. We do not discuss the price.

I wiggle into the suit she has suggested. She calls it the Miracle Suit. It will take care of all the sags and bulges. It is guaranteed to make me look ten pounds lighter. I take a peek at the price. When did bathing suits get to be so expensive? Two hundred dollars? I swallow and decide I perhaps should look around at some others.

I find four others and carry them into the changing room. I am seventy-five plus, and when I stand in front of a large mirror surrounded by bright lights, every bulge, sag, and wrinkle is magnified. Every suit reveals a seventy-five-year-old grandma who would like to look twenty-five. Why should I care? I don't use Botox or have implants. I am not looking for a new husband. I have been happily married for over fifty years.

When my grandma was seventy-five she didn't try to look twenty-five. She sewed and made me a flannel nightgown every Christmas. I wonder how far women have come in the last two generations. Straining after youth doesn't seem like progress.

I try on the other suits that I have brought into the changing room. There are prints and plains — all different colours. The salesgirl hears me moan. She asks if I would like to try the Miracle Suit one more time. She passes it under the door. I wiggle into it and turn sideways. It suddenly looks better.

Fifteen minutes later I walk out of the shop with a beautiful bag stuffed with multicoloured tissue and a Miracle Suit. I have been shopping most of the morning, and it is lunchtime. I was wondering if I should skip lunch, but tell myself that I have the perfect suit. It will make me look ten pounds lighter.

Swimming the next day I don't think anyone notices my skinniness … this body without so many sags and bulges. I don't really care!

Nurse Jane Fuzzy Fuzzy

—Jane Ruona

I WOKE UP IN A COLD SWEAT. Maybe it was just a hot flash, but it felt like something else, almost impending doom! Was it the cardinal symptom I had seen so many times when my patient was experiencing a heart attack? I felt my pulse ... 66 (regular). I was sweating, but no pain or nausea. The tape played deep inside my brain: deep breaths, relax, think positive.

My life seemed okay ... even too good. As a professional worrywart, I was waiting for the next shoe to drop. Was it my turn? Worry always caused me stress, but it also made me consider options and consult others. It almost felt protective, like the pain of hot water making me pull my finger back. Worry pushed me to evaluate a situation, use common sense, and often take the road less traveled.

I needed to know more about my family history. Had I accomplished enough? Where was I going? It was my forty-fifth year. Halfway? My beloved dad, Arthur Charles Tharp, had just died suddenly at seventy-three. He arrested six hours after an angiogram which showed a blocked left main coronary artery (the widow maker). In Palo Alto at the veterans hospital where I worked, he would have been treated differently from Denver where Dad lived.

The doctors took Dad off his aspirin and waited two weeks to schedule an angiogram. Even under my brother's watchful eyes and expertise as a specialized physician, they waited too long. Dad arrested and died at midnight seven hours before his scheduled coronary bypass surgery. Dad had written us all goodbye letters that night just in case.

The doctors said Dad was a perfect candidate for a bypass. He ate well, exercised, and had quit his five-pack-a-day Chicago smoking habit. He still loved his red wine.

I was at the Palo Alto Veterans Hospital working as night supervisor when I received the phone call. The staff came to my rescue and expedited my going home to cry and grieve.

The timing was impossible, as we had been planning a fantastic 50th wedding anniversary for my parents in the northern woods of Wisconsin. We'd spent many fishing vacations at Erler's Lodge (now called Sun Peaks Lodge). My sister, Nancy, and I had made easy summer money hypnotizing and catching frogs. We sold them to the fishermen: five cents for brown ones and ten cents for green ones.

Instead of an anniversary, we planned a funeral. The funeral was a tribute to Dad's life and career. He had been a regional manager for Uniroyal, which meant lots of free Keds. Dad loved his job and missed VP by a hair. He was fantastic at sales and never missed a chance to mentor.

We all got up and spoke at the funeral. Mom even wore the pompom outfit at the reception she had planned for the anniversary. Mom, Alice Covell Tharp, said, "My life is over, but I am going on to my new life." And she did.

One Man's Treasure

— Linda Hennrick

THE JAPANESE PUBLIC IS FICKLE — quick to follow the latest trend, but quick to tire of it when a new one comes along. This week's treasure is next week's trash.

In the 1970s, when I first arrived in the land of the rising sun, this was great for *gaijin* (foreigners) like me who planned to live in Japan for only a year or so who needed to furnish their apartments quickly and cheaply. Trash in Tokyo isn't picked up door to door but at designated neighborhood collection sites, so if their timing was right, *gaijin* could find gently used sofas, TVs, stereo equipment, tables, chairs, or lamps sitting out on the street at these sites the evening before pick-up. No one cared if anything was taken from the pile, and there were terrific bargains for those who weren't choosy about color or style.

But times changed, and when scattered waste became a problem in overcrowded Tokyo — household trash was put out in plastic bags that crows could easily tear into — the city made a new rule: trash could only be put out the morning of collection, not the evening before. Later, recycling was introduced, and trash had to be separated. By 2010, unlike the days when *gaijin* could furnish an apartment with castoffs they found on the street, getting rid of unwanted household items in Japan was hard work. My Japanese husband, Miki, and I discovered just how hard.

I'd met Miki in a recording studio in Tokyo where, after a career as a professional musician, he worked as a recording engineer. I was a singer who had turned to the more lucrative occupation of lyricist and wrote English lyrics for Japanese anime, movie and television theme songs, TV commercials, and recording artists. When we married in early 1985, Miki moved into the apartment I was renting on the outskirts of Tokyo convenient to downtown. But we soon found that it was too small for the both of us and began to search for a house nearby.

The house we found in Kugayama three stations away was the third one we looked at, one of two houses being built side-by-side on a large lot where a single dwelling had once stood. At the time, the house was only a framework, the skeleton of a promise, but we loved it and its surroundings immediately.

Our eight-hundred square foot two-story house—my dad called it a dollhouse—was located next to the Tamagawa Jyõsui, an historic manmade canal built to bring water to Tokyo, then called Edo, four hundred years earlier when Japan's capital was moved from Kyoto. The canal was lined by cherry trees that bloomed each spring in clouds of pale pink, and the unpaved road beside it was closed to through traffic—an ideal place for dog walkers and hikers. On one side of our property sat a pocket park where neighborhood children came to play.

With all the greenery around us, we often forgot we lived in the most densely populated city in the world, and yet we were only a ten-minute walk from Kugayama Station and an easy commute to downtown Tokyo. Perhaps that's why, instead of being the starter home as we'd planned, the house become our forever home.

But in 2009, our home was condemned to make way for a road that had been in the planning since the Allied Occupation of Japan following World War II. Reluctant to leave our beloved home, we watched as other houses in the neighborhood were vacated and then destroyed until ours was only one of two houses left standing on the block. According to the contract we signed with the Tokyo city government in December that year, some of our compensation—to be paid in three parts—was to go toward paying for the demolition of our house. We wouldn't receive the final payment until the house was gone and we had photos of the vacant lot to prove it. Once the contract was signed, we had a year to vacate and move elsewhere.

It was hard enough to leave the house where we'd lived together all the years of our married life, much less arrange to destroy it ourselves, but we steeled ourselves to the inevitable. *Shikata ga nai* as they stoically say in Japan—nothing can be done.

A frustrating six months of house hunting later, when we still hadn't found anything in Tokyo that could compare to our charming house or its unique environment, we wondered if we ever would. After carefully weighing our options and obtaining a green card for Miki, we decided to relocate to the U.S. and live in the vacation home we'd purchased in 1987 in Bermuda Dunes, California.

Other decisions soon followed as we began to dismantle our life in Japan. What should we take with us to our new life? As we sifted through closets and drawers full of personal belongings, we were amazed by how much we'd collected in almost twenty-five years, the longest either of us had ever lived in one place: Japanese dishes; computers; cameras and photographs (I spent months putting loose photos into albums; books, LPs, CDs, and DVDs); my files of contracts and published lyrical works; Miki's trumpets from his career as a musician; stereo and recording equipment; clothes, shoes, and accessories; knickknacks and wall art; and memorabilia. We couldn't take much with us on the airplane; most would have to be shipped.

Then came the hard part: what to leave behind. Our home in Bermuda Dunes was fully furnished, so besides the few things we'd use at the apartment we'd rent for the two months while our house in Tokyo was being demolished, we no longer needed most of our household goods, furniture, or appliances. How to dispose of it all?

Following the Suginami Ward pages-long printed guide for sorting trash and trying to figure out the schedule of pick-up days in our neighborhood practically required a degree in sanitation engineering. Mondays and Thursdays were for *moeru gomi*—combustible waste; Tuesdays for recycling PET (polyethylene terephthalate) bottles and paper; Saturdays for recycling glass bottles, other plastics, and cans; and every other Tuesday for *moenai gomi* — incombustible waste — broken glass, dishes, pots and pans, umbrellas, etc. Suginami Ward even had rules about what trash bags to use. Forty-five liter (approx. twelve-gallon) white translucent bags made especially to burn easily in the old Suginami Ward trash furnaces were sold locally.

I'd carried bags of trash to the collection site around the corner and down the block from where we lived early on the mornings of the specified days — it seemed like every day. But with no place inside our tiny house to keep trash, and very little space outside either, I was glad the garbage trucks came by as often as they did. The trucks themselves were much smaller than U.S. garbage trucks to be able to navigate the narrow streets — more like alleys — of our neighborhood. In some places in Japan, trash trucks play a melody as they make their rounds — *gaijin* are often fooled into thinking they hear an ice cream truck.

Small items that fit in the Suginami Ward trash bags could be thrown away on the regular pick-up days listed above, but larger items, like furniture or appliances (called *sodai gomi* or oversized trash), would only be picked up by the ward office by appointment for a fee. The amounts of the fees depended on the category or size of the item. Not all the fees were listed in the Suginami Ward booklet of trash rules, which required Miki to make several phone calls to the ward office to ask about specific items we wanted to dispose of. Once the price of the fee and day of pick-up were determined, we were given a reservation number. We bought special stickers at a local convenience shop that carried them and wrote the reservation number on them. The items for pick-up were placed out in front of our house on the predetermined day with the stickers attached. But we soon realized that having several individual items picked up this way could get expensive.

Most of our household items were in good condition — I hated the thought of just stuffing them into trash bags and throwing them away when they could still be used. Unfortunately, I didn't know of any needy *gaijin* to give them to, and charitable organizations in Japan don't collect cast-offs for resale as they do in the U.S. Some churches held annual rummage sales but wouldn't store goods beforehand. The Suginami Ward recycle center, already overstocked with unwanted goods, wouldn't take any more.

We looked for other ways to dispose of our belongings. I sold some books to a used-book store for a pittance, and donated others to the local library. Trying to figure out what a local recycle shop would and wouldn't buy from us proved too complicated and time consuming and we soon gave up. We spoke with relatives and friends and managed to find homes for a Singer sewing machine, desk, worktable, two nightstands, two coffee tables, small stereo set, bicycle, propane BBQ set, folding kitchen table and chairs, full-length mirror, wine glasses and rack, and Dyson canister vacuum cleaner. Our former next-door neighbor, Mrs. Yamamoto—already living in another house nearby—was happy to take a full-length mirror and small writing desk, but that still left us with several large pieces.

Around that time, Miki met with his life insurance agent. When he mentioned that we had furniture to give away, the agent was more than happy to help. She took several items herself, and through her we found homes for Miki's large office desk and chair, three-piece living room sofa and end tables, entertainment center, and large refrigerator. Our washing machine was promised to a couple that would pick it up the day we left Japan.

But we couldn't find any takers for our queen-size mattress, bed frame, and headboard—a bed that size was an unheard of luxury in Japan—a large chest of drawers, and two armoires. The demolition company agent, upon hearing of our quandary, told us not to worry; he'd get rid of anything left in the house at no extra charge. He also promised to come by our apartment the day we left Japan to pick up and dispose of anything else we weren't taking with us to the U.S.

We still had to find homes for many small household items too, but we were running out of time. Early on we tried holding yard sales but soon discovered that people weren't interested in buying used goods no matter how much we marked them down. A neighbor told me that when her mother died and left her with a houseful of belongings she couldn't use or didn't have room for, and a yard sale didn't produce any buyers, she put a sign out with the goods that said *jiyū ni dōzo* — free. It didn't take long for everything to disappear.

We tried the "free" way ourselves. Almost from the minute we began putting out folding tables covered with goods marked "free," the goods indeed began to disappear — and in the end so did the tables. Our last weekend in the house, as we emptied closets and cupboards, we'd take armloads of items outside to place on the tables, go back into the house for more, and come out again to find empty spaces. Dishes, glassware, pots and pans, kitchen gadgets, office supplies, lamps, rugs, sofa cushions, linens, towels — everything gone like magic. Now you see it, now you don't.

A group of seniors hiking along the canal in front of our house stopped to look at some extension cords, and happily stuffed them into backpacks before walking on. A passing bicyclist, a self-proclaimed stereo buff, noticed a pair of speaker parts on the table, something most people wouldn't be interested in, and stopped to take a better look. After confirming that we were giving the parts away, he was delighted to take them off our hands. Another man came back several times and loaded his bicycle basket as full as he could each time. On one of his many visits, he said, "*Tasukaru*" — this helps, and I realized from his shabby appearance, and the ragamuffin kids of all sizes who tagged along with him, that he probably didn't have any money to spare. "This helps us too," I answered, teary-eyed yet happy to see so many things going to new homes and, hopefully, become someone else's treasures.

During the afternoon, I noticed a sweet young couple admiring a hot air balloon wind toy. Newlyweds? Perhaps in need of a chest of drawers or an armoire? Miki and I invited them upstairs to look at the three big pieces. The couple was interested but lived in a small place themselves and didn't know if any of the pieces would even fit inside their apartment. We gave them some measurements, and they came back later that evening to take the chest of drawers — the smallest of the lot — off our hands. Miki helped them move it to their apartment nearby and said it barely fit up the stairs to their second-floor unit. We kept in touch with the couple until we left Kugayama and later convinced them to also take some of the things we used in the apartment: two chairs, a lamp, some towels, a set of silverware, ironing board, and iron. If they hadn't, those items would only have been carted off to the dump the day we left Kugayama.

I sometimes wonder if we should have worried less about the cost of shipping and brought more things with us. Even now, eight years later, I find myself looking through my U.S. kitchen for a particular bamboo spoon only to realize it's one of the things I didn't think I'd need in my new life — I can still remember exactly which drawer I kept it in my kitchen in Kugayama. Miki misses some of the tools he gave away thinking he already had the same tools on the other side of the ocean, finding later he didn't.

But I like to think that whenever someone turns on a small lamp, or uses an extension cord, or listens to a pair of speakers built from parts, folds clothes to put away in a dresser, or uses one of the cups or dishes picked up "free" a part of our house — a part of us — is still living in Japan.

[Second Place Winner in a Palm Springs
Writers Guild Memoir Writing Challenge]

Pinkie, Our Pet Fish

— June Gaulding

FIVE YEARS AGO IN 2014, our little dog, Chips, was very sick, and we had to have the vet end his life. He was twelve years old and had been a happy pet sharing the sofa with Wallis who was sixteen years old. They sat on either side of Mark every chance they had. There is such sadness in our home upon not seeing that little face every day. Chips had come to the family as a stray dog and was a joy from the day he arrived. He was a mixture but appeared more a dachshund with a gentle and loving personality.

After losing Chips, Wallis enjoyed getting all of Mark's attention for another two years. In June, 2016, Wallis was eighteen years old, and she became very sick. We took her to see the vet, and he said there wasn't anything he could do for her. So, at that time, we asked the vet to end her life. She was a Jack Russell Terrier and was such a happy, charming, and lovable pet to have had in our home. There was never a dull day with her jumping and running everywhere. Again, we felt that sad and lonely feeling upon losing another pet.

Shortly after Chips passed away in 2014, Mark and I had gone to Petco to get dog food for Wallis. On those trips we loved to look at the pets they had for sale, as well as the fish aquariums. This particular day, they had pint-size plastic containers with colorful tropical fish for sale. We thought it would be fun watching them, so we bought two fish. They were Beta tropical fish. One was a pinkish color with a dark red tail called a Half-moon Double Tail fish. The other one was a two-tone, bluish-red Dragon Scale fish.

Of course, we bought the plastic aquarium the sales person suggested that we get for the two of them. The fish were two males. They would hurt each other if they were together. In the aquarium there was a divider with small holes for water to circulate so each fish would have its own space. The aquarium was seven and one-half inches in length, four and one-half inches wide, and six and one-half inches deep. *Not much room,* I thought, but that is what they told us we needed. Other items were fish food, a small bottle of dechlorinated drops to add to water when it was changed, and a long-handled small net to move the fish to another bowl when the water needed to be changed. To add color, we added two small green bushes, one plastic and the other fabric, as well as small rocks for the bottom of the container. They said the fish would hide in the bushes when they wanted privacy.

Upon getting them home, we placed the aquarium on the top level of the kitchen counter bar. They wouldn't be in direct sunlight, and we could enjoy seeing them. Of course, the two new pets had to have names. So, the pinkish-red fish I named Pinkie, even though it sounded like a girl's name. I thought, he wouldn't know the difference, since he couldn't hear his name being called. From that time on, I always thought of him as a girl. Oh dear, I just made him a transgender fish. Mark named the other bluish-red fish Blue. We now had two new pets, Pinkie and Blue.

Mark and I shared taking care of the fish when it was needed. However, after six months, Blue stopped eating, and within a week he passed away and was floating on the water. Back in the day when my kid's goldfish died, they were flushed down the toilet. The kids never asked where they went, and we never told them either. So, that was what we did with Blue. It was a sad experience, but we still had Pinkie. I took out the divider, and she had the entire aquarium to herself. Within a month, I felt she was really becoming a pet and not just a cold fish in a bowl. She must have been lonely, as she started watching me every time I walked into the kitchen. I would stop and talk to her, and she would look at me like she understood what I was saying. I couldn't believe I was conversing with a fish. However, I knew she enjoyed my attention.

July 3, 2015 was coming up, and I was going to have my eightieth birthday. My friend Joan Slocum, who lived in Scottsdale, Arizona, invited us to drive over for my birthday celebration. I was concerned about leaving Pinkie at home, since she had to be fed every day, and my neighbors were gone for the summer. We left on a Friday morning, and, of course, Pinkie went with us. I poured out half of the water in the aquarium and placed it in a large cake pan. Since I was sitting in the front passenger seat, I put the pan on the floor by my feet. The cool air coming in by my feet kept the water cool for her. She traveled just fine. Upon arriving at the hotel, I placed her on the desk in our room, and then I added water to her aquarium and fed her. I often wondered if the maids thought some kid brought their fish along for the trip. Pinkie did just fine with my feeding and talking to her daily.

The next morning was July 3rd, and my birthday. Unbeknownst to me, Mark wanted to give me a big surprise, so he flew my daughter, Janet, in from Indianapolis to help me celebrate this big birthday. What a surprise! Of course I introduced her to Pinkie. She had a big laugh that I brought my fish along for the weekend. Needless to say, it was a wonderful weekend celebrating my birthday. That Saturday night we went to The Melting Pot and enjoyed dining on fondue. Sunday we gave Janet a tour of Phoenix and the area, as she had never been there before. She left that afternoon to fly back to Indianapolis. What a fun weekend we had. We drove back to Palm Desert on Monday, and Pinkie made the drive back just fine.

After another year had gone by, and it was July 3, 2016, my eighty-first birthday, Joan wanted us to come and stay with her for the holiday. So, we made the trip again to Scottsdale. Of course, Pinkie went with us. Joan wanted us to put Pinkie on the kitchen-counter bar where she could see us. We all settled in. I had hoped for another surprise, but Janet didn't get to come this time. I did talk with her by phone on my birthday, and we reminisced about the year before. We did have a wonderful weekend celebrating my birthday and visiting with Joan. When it was over, we loaded up the car with Pinkie and headed back home … another successful trip for Pinkie.

Pinkie really enjoyed having the aquarium to herself and watching the action in the kitchen from the counter top. She was always busy watching whatever was happening in the kitchen. I was sure that she was exhausted by the end of the day and slept well, as she didn't seem to sleep during the day. I guess she was afraid she might miss out on the action in the kitchen. Over the months, she seemed to have difficulty eating, so I started crushing her small pellets of food into even smaller pieces for her to eat.

It was now November, 2016. Mark's friend Steve lived in Tucson, and he wanted us to drive over for a visit with him over Thanksgiving. So, off we go again with Pinkie. However, it would be a longer distance for us to drive. It was five hours to Phoenix, but to Steve's home it would be a total of eight hours. I wasn't sure how Pinkie would do bouncing around in the water for that period of time. However, she did just fine on the long drive, and we finally arrived at Steve's house. Of course, Steve had a big laugh when he saw Pinkie in her aquarium, and heard my explanation on why I couldn't leave her at my home. I kept her in my bathroom off the private bedroom where I slept. There was a skylight in the room, so she had natural light. She was always ready to see me when I entered the bathroom and was very active during her feeding time.

We had a great Thanksgiving visiting Steve and enjoying his new home. I had never been to Tucson and didn't know what to expect. I found it was lonely and desolate looking compared to the Coachella Valley desert where we live. The area there reminded me of the locations of the old western movies that I used to watch as a kid. We did enjoy the holiday with Steve, but on Tuesday morning, it was time to start back home. It was another successful trip for Pinkie.

It was now late January, 2017, and Pinkie was showing signs of becoming a senior fish. She wasn't swimming as much; therefore, her air bubbles weren't breaking up on top of the water. I started scooping the bubbles out and swirling the water every day to keep it fresh for her. By now she wasn't eating much from the top of the water when I put it in. So, I would gently blow on the food, and it would start falling. She would see it and catch hold of it with her mouth. I do think she was partially blind. Pinkie had started leaning on the bushes or rocks at the bottom of the water to rest or sleep. In a few days I noticed that her body was in a crooked position and not straight as before. I told Mark during the middle of February that I didn't think Pinkie had much more time with us.

It was now Friday, March 10th, and Pinkie had stopped eating and was leaning on the bushes. She was almost folded in half, as she was caught on a branch. I took the spoon that I had used to scoop bubbles out and moved the branch so that she would unfold straight again. She was still alive, but I felt that she wouldn't be in the morning.

The next morning she was still in the same position. I wasn't sure she was still alive, so I left her for a few more hours, and then I knew it was time to take her out of the water. What was I going to do with her? I didn't want to flush her down the toilet, as we did with Blue. No, I just couldn't do this with Pinkie. She was a pet, and I couldn't dispose of her like that.

I had a large flower pot on the back patio by the door. The plant had died, and I had just left the pot there to plant another flower. I would use that for Pinkie's burial place. Mark found some dry leaves that had blown in on the patio, and he dug a little hole in the dirt to place Pinkie. We laid her on leaves and then covered her with more leaves and dirt. I am not sure what I will do when I have to get rid of the flower pot, but for now this is her resting place. I couldn't help it, but I did shed tears over losing this little pet. She was with us for almost three years, and I was glad that she outlived her life expectancy of a few months. As of now, I don't think we will replace her with another fish.

Polio and Me

— Larry Kueneman

BY THE TIME I WAS SIXTEEN YEARS OLD I was invincible at stop lights. On my bicycle, I would tear out when the light turned green, and when I took off, no car ever beat me crossing the street. That was fun. The next year was quite different. My family visited Crystal Lake in the Angeles National Forest, where we splashed in the water, but did not swim because the bottom of the entirety of the lake bed was covered with weeds a foot deep just below the water surface, and it both smelled and simply didn't look clean. We weren't the only ones — there were several other families there as well while we were there.

Shortly after that visit all four of us kids got sick. I was the oldest, then George, Mary, and the youngest, Joe. Our doctor thought we might have contracted polio, so he had my folks take us to the main hospital in L.A. where we were all given spinal taps which determined we all had contracted polio. As it turned out, George was hit the hardest, then me. The two youngest were hit like the flu, and it shortly passed over them.

Historically, people individually, had gotten polio for centuries, even when the large polio outbreaks didn't happen. Franklin Delano Roosevelt was struck with polio at age thirty-nine in 1921.

George and I were taken to Kabat-Kaiser Institute, a hospital in Santa Monica. This had been a fairly fancy hotel Henry Kaiser bought to convert to a polio hospital just one year before our stay. His son had been struck with polio a few years earlier.

There was one floor of the hospital entirely dedicated to iron lungs. These were basically a six-foot section of steel pipe about two feet in diameter mounted horizontally on a frame for access. There was a solid piece on one end and a place for the head of the patient to stick out on the other end. The round section was split down the middle with hinges on one side, so it was easy to install or remove a patient from the unit. When closed, a controlled air pressure system encouraged patients to get air both in and out of their lungs for those had been weakened. Neither George nor I were ever in one, but they were scary.

It was found that several other patients in the hospital had been to Crystal Lake as well, so the County put a steel fence around the lake and kept it there for forty years. Even after the removal of the fence around 1990, people cannot swim in Crystal Lake.

Because the primary symptom of polio causes muscle shrinkage, we were treated with stretching exercises and covered with steaming hot blankets, with the intention to soften tightened muscles each day. These blankets were heated to 114° for this purpose because it had been discovered that any temperature above 114° would cause skin burns. This was a process called the Kenny treatment, named for an Australian nurse, Sister Elizabeth Kenny, who had developed the procedure. (In this case "Sister" refers to her being head nurse.)

The staff were mostly world-famous doctors collected by Henry Kaiser for this purpose. Now, I'm going to digress here for a moment, but shortly you will see the reason.

Starting around 1834 a few doctors had made public their thinking that prior to either delivering a baby or performing surgery, all doctors should wash their hands. This when doctors washing their hands had never been a practice in the past. And it wasn't until a meeting of the American Medical Association in 1910 that a dictate was issued that henceforth, all doctors preparing to deliver a baby or perform surgery were mandated to wash their hands. Very interesting, but what does it have to do with polio? We are shortly going to see.

The polio virus multiplies, and leaves the body in feces. Centuries ago, far more so than today, feces were to be found in soil, almost all of which contained the polio virus. Prior to the AMA declaration of 1910, almost all children who played in the dirt (don't they all?) got polio. It actually wasn't a problem for babies, as this had been the pattern for centuries. Their mother's milk contained an antidote for the disease, because about twenty years earlier, the new mothers had been the babies playing in the same dirt. For centuries, mother's milk protecting kids when they were exposed to the polio virus was the norm.

This meant large outbreaks of polio simply hadn't happened in the past.

This new doctor hand-washing dictate meant that at some point, babies playing in the dirt would not have access to that antidote as before. This is precisely what happened in 1930 — exactly one generation after the AMA declaration — when the first really big polio outbreak happened. The bodies of young mothers that had themselves been babies in 1910 no longer produced and carried the antidote for polio.

A second condition added to the problem. Starting about 1904 companies began advertising their artificial bottled milk for babies, initially for women who could not produce food for little ones. The product was cow's milk and contained no protection for polio. This meant children who were fed with this new product were no longer protected.

These large polio outbreaks occurred periodically from 1930 until 1954, when the Salk injectable polio vaccine was released. Within three years, Dr. Sabin's sugar cubes containing an ingestible form of the prevention was made available.

I was at Kabat-Kaiser for two years both as an in-patient and an out-patient. At age nineteen I was released, and with Korea hot and heavy, I joined the Marines. With these war conditions, if you were warm and willing, you were in. They knew I had been a polio patient, so I never went overseas, but I was sent to a special school at Quantico, Virginia to learn how to repair 105 howitzers, guns that fired a shell about five and one-half inches in diameter — big explosion. I arrived just after another student had attempted to fill an equilibrator (similar to a shock absorber) on one of the big guns with oxygen instead of the recommended gas. Just before I arrived there had been an explosion, killing the student, destroying the gun, and blowing the side out of the brick building. A little scary.

Back at Camp Pendleton, near San Diego, I was assigned to the Third Marine Division until it was scheduled to go overseas. Then I was transferred to another group. As a mechanic I either had a wrench in my hand or a cup of coffee, and not being one to do things in moderation, I drank between eighteen and twenty-five cups a day. This resulted in my developing hypoglycemia, which I had until I married my wife in 1986. She put me on a sugar-free diet, and within a couple of years eliminated the problem.

I had not had any severe problems resulting from having had polio, but that changed in 1996. I had always been a semi-professional singer, and enjoyed that. My last effort was singing with the Idyllwild Master Chorale for twelve years. Post-polio sequelae (PPS) hit me that year. It weakened my diaphragm and flattened my vocal folds, such that I could no longer hold a long note while singing. Within a couple of years I had to quit singing with the Master Chorale. The PPS also destroyed the muscle that can lift my left foot called the anterior tibialis. So I walked oddly until a doctor at the VA one day saw me walking down the hall and set me up to have a brace made for my left leg that holds my foot from dragging.

While in the service, as an armorer, I worked right alongside the gun crew who all wore hearing protection. The government somehow never thought to provide the armorers with that same protection, so the main reason I started going to the VA was my hearing loss. Ain't this fun?

Remembering Alice

—Gaye V. Borne

HER EYES WERE LARGE and gave an all-knowing gaze. She had gorgeous skin, the color of a rich, burnished tan. Long graceful fingers with tapered nails complemented her young, svelte body. We became instant friends....

My grandmother, grandfather and I were on one of our month-long road trips that we would take during the summertime. This summer, we had taken the southern route across the U.S., from Santa Monica, California traveling through the Deep South, all the way to Florida. We were hit by torrential rain going through Louisiana and Mississippi. I worried when the windshield wipers could not keep up with the deluge from the sky, but my grandfather was skillful in navigating our car towards the state known for its oranges. We arrived in St. Petersburg, Florida and stayed for a while to visit with my grandmother's cousins. I remember seeing giant, exotic bugs skittering across the ceiling and walls at night.

The nights were hot and humid; the days were hotter and more humid. We said adieu and headed southeast.

As the junior co-pilot, I was given the privilege of looking at the state road maps and the hotel/motel tour guide book from the AAA (Automobile Club of Southern California). My grandparents were savvy and knew that if we stayed at a motel with a pool, they could have some quiet time while I happily splashed away. I made friends easily wherever we stayed—yet, during the long periods on the road, I sometimes got lonely. We ended up at the Everglades National Park—I was in paradise. Lush greenery surrounded us; exotic birds sang.

Of course, there was an alligator exhibit with which I was fascinated. They writhed and snapped their jaws in the pools which were bordered by fences and wood catwalks around the perimeter. My grandmother was glad the exhibit tour ended, although much to her dismay, on the way out of the park there stood the obligatory gift shop. As you know, all eight-to-nine-year-old kids love trinket/gift shops. I went inside and was in awe over the many postcards, key chains, jewelry items, tee-shirts, bumper stickers, etc. My wanderings eventually came to a screeching halt. There, on the display table, were REAL baby alligators—only they were stuffed! This was in 1958–1959, long before restrictions were place on alligator/crocodile products. I immediately spied the one I wanted and I begged to have it. Again, being savvy, my grandparents relented and granted my wish, knowing that I would be kept busy in the car while we were on the road.

I promptly decided my new acquaintance was a she. After I had proudly stated that her name was Alice, we became inseparable—much to my grandmother's unease, as the images of the adult alligators from the exhibit were still in her mind's eye. Alice stayed with me for the rest of the trip. She became my "roommate" at home in Santa Monica. I had her for many years—until somewhere along the line, she disappeared. I have a suspicion that she fell victim to a spring housecleaning engineered by my grandmother.

The years have come and gone, but I still remember Alice. She and I were best friends—and yes, she was an alligator!

Running on Empty

—Gaye V. Borne

"KEEP GOING—COME ON—JUST A BIT FARTHER." These words describe the highlight of our first trip from Simi Valley to Big Sur and Carmel in California. It all began innocently enough—we were the proud new owners of a brand new tent trailer. This was in 1979; I was 29, Robbie was 32, and Michelle was 4 years old. We had taken a few trips with it to Pine Flat Lake in Central California for waterskiing, and now we were ready for a big trip for a whole week.

Our destination was the Big Sur Campground and Cabins located just off Highway 1, which was nestled in the midst of towering pine trees right next to the Big Sur River. We could hear the river, which flowed lazily beside our campsite. The distant sounds of clanking horseshoes being tossed, mixed with the whispering of the pine trees and the scents of sage, pine and drifting campfire smoke, added to the ambiance. Rubber inner tubes were rented out by the campground's General Store, and happy campers, both children and adults, floated dreamily down the river meandering in and out of shady leafed tree canopies and into the sun-kissed open areas of the water. Variegated degrees of the most luscious green colors dominated the landscape amid the chattering of the woodland birds.

Robbie enjoyed playing basketball in the afternoons, and our evening campfire was an event after dinner. Robbie always made sure his many clothing outfits matched in coloration to the nth degree. Needless to say, we did not travel lightly—we brought everything, including the blender—all crammed into the tent trailer!

It was decided that we would drive the car up to Carmel, several miles north of the campground. At the time, my car—which was a 1974 red Cadillac Coupe de Ville with a white landau top and a rip-roaring 500 cubic inch V-8 engine—was our towing vehicle for the tent trailer. Off we went, ready to see the sights of quaint Carmel, luxurious Pebble Beach and the famous scenic 17-Mile Drive, oohing and aahing over the grand houses along the way. Little did we know...

Robbie has a penchant for extracting the very last vapor from the gas tank until it is as bone dry as the Sahara Desert. *Of course*, he thought there was plenty of fuel in the tank to get to a gas station. *Of course*, the gas gauge needle was way past empty. *Of course*, we ran out of gas, deader than a doornail right at the bottom of what seemed to be the biggest hill on the 17-Mile Drive. Way before cell phones were invented, we had no choice but to literally wait on the road right in the middle of this very ritzy neighborhood. There were no houses on the particular stretch of road that we were on, so we waited and then tried the ignition again.

Thank God! The engine sputtered to life on its last dying gasp; we finally made it to the top of the hill. The descending slope took effect just as the engine gave up. We literally coasted all the way down this hill and barely managed to creep into a gas station at the bottom. What a spectacle we were! The car was not easy to miss; its passengers—a puzzled little girl and the two frazzled young adults, one daringly adventurous and the other really angry. You can guess who was who—we were the talk of the area for quite a while, I am sure.

Over the 42 years that we were married, we have coasted into more gas stations than I care to admit. Every time has been due to the need for 'optimal gas mileage' to be gleaned from the car. Robbie is proud of the mileage calculations he makes regarding the gas tank.

To this day, Robbie 'runs on empty,' tempting fate. Me? I fill up promptly when it is time.

Now, if I could *just* figure out how far I can go in the golf cart without recharging it too soon....

Sailing on Lake Huron

— Marilyn McNeill

BLUEBIRD ARRIVED AFTER THE BOAT SHOW to the marina in Bayfield. Our sailing days would have many beginnings. This was our first.

Bayfield is a small heritage village of little red brick houses with a population of 1,200 located on the sandy shores of Lake Huron about twenty-eight miles north of Stratford.

The marina is located on the south side of the Bayfield River close to the mouth of the river as it empties into Lake Huron.

My parents, when they were courting in the 1920s, would picnic at Bayfield or go to the beautiful sandy beach at Grand Bend. I can remember seeing a photo of my dad at the beach wearing his knee-length wool one-piece bathing suit, and my mother wearing one of those practical bathing suits popular in the 1920s.

We have spent the last two weeks shopping for boat charts, books all about sailing, boat shoes, and most importantly life jackets — and more books about sailing. I have spent many an hour reading these books. These would be the only lessons I will get.

Cameron is three, and I will have a long safety line on his life jacket at all times, one clipped to his jacket, and the other to the boat. His teacher at preschool told me that he said "I won't fall off because my mom will tie me to the boat." It was not quite like that, but close.

The most popular area for cruising is the area from Killarney going west, running north of Manitoulin Island. There are many islands and coves to anchor off in this area. Killarney, Baie Finn, and Portage Cove are must places to see. We cruised the east coast of Lake Huron by going through the 30,000 islands known as the Inside Passage.

We had an amusing incident when we were close to Killarney. A man in another sailboat came toward us and asked if we knew where we were. He came alongside and handed us a map. It was a road map! We had a supply of boat charts. Stuart gave him several and showed him how to use them. This must have been his first time sailing. Quite scary when you are out in open water and you don't know where you are. There are no Esso stations along the way to stop and ask for directions.

In the late afternoon we would find a sheltered cove, put down our anchor, wait half an hour to see if it set, and just relax. The water was always warm in the cove, and it was time for a swim. Time for a nice bath—and please make sure you take the right cake of soap that will float.

Every few days it was time to do laundry. There was never any shortage of clotheslines—just find a tree with some nice low-hanging branches. We soon learned that hanging clothes on the boat while we were cruising was not a good decision because when the wind blew and the sails were set, it was goodbye to your favorite T-shirt.

The tiny galley was our onboard kitchen. I made frozen dinners ahead of time, wrapped them in plastic, then in newspapers, and placed the contents in our icebox. I hoped that our ice would not melt too soon. Meals that were closer to the top were eaten first.

There were lanterns onboard, and we each had our own reading spot during the evening. On one or two occasions we would encounter a windy night, and we could hear our anchor dragging. It was never much fun to dress, start the engine, move positions, set the anchor again, and hope that it didn't happen again.

Any small marina along the way would have a store, and we shopped for fresh supplies and ice. Killarney was our favorite. We would treat ourselves to an overnight stay, fresh hot showers and good home-cooked meals. Dessert was speciality homemade fruit pies. I would buy an extra pie to take along with us the following day; a fresh fruit pie was the best.

One incident is amusing now, but not at the time. We planned to leave early the following morning. The weather looked like it could change, and we wanted to get to a safe cove early. I had purchased fresh fruit, vegetables, ice, and a special berry pie. We were ready to go. Stuart had taken the boat to the gas dock and filled our tanks. The boat would leave the gas dock and come by the main dock to pick us and the supplies up for our trip back home. We would not take time to tie our boat, just move quickly ... and all aboard.

We scrambled aboard, pushed away from the dock, and were on our way. I turned to look back at the Killarney Inn and saw a boy waving a red and blue towel — a red and blue towel just like ours. That towel belonged to us. That boy waving the towel belonged to us, as well!

Shoes Have Souls

— Marilyn McNeill

MY SHOES WERE BROWN LEATHER flat oxfords with flat soles. I wore these begrudgingly over brown, ribbed cotton stockings. These were my school shoes, and I wore these every day until I was in grade seven. My feet were so skinny that no other shoes would stay on my feet. When the soles wore out, my dad took them to the shoe repair, and these shoes were resoled.

Every September Mother and I would take the bus into Toronto to Eaton's Department Store. It was time to buy new shoes. The shoe department had an X-ray machine. This was a smallish wooden podium housing radioactive material for casual foot X-rays. The X-ray source was at the base and would fire upwards through your foot and shoe. It wouldn't stop there; the radiation would shoot up into your baby maker, clearly a perilous occurrence. It was fun to look at your tootsies in the machine. My feet looked green staring back at me. I tried on several pairs of shoes just so I could look through the machine.

Happy was the day when my feet grew slightly wider so that I could wear a pair of loafers. I would be going to a new school and wanted to wear what the other girls were wearing. I still wore brown leather shoes, but these were penny loafers. In the 1950s the wearer of loafers actually stuck pennies in the little slots on the strap.

I was proud of my shoes and shined my shoes every night — or rather my dad did. Dad sat on a small stool, which my grandfather had made, and shined his shoes. He kept them in a ruler-straight line in his closet. My mother's shoes were not so organized. In her closet were sensible shoes, slippers and her heels. There was a pair of satin shoes that she kept wrapped in tissue paper and stored in their original box. These were kept for special occasions. She would wear these at Christmas or New Years. I can remember her favorite dress was black with very pretty beading around the neckline. Her dress-up dresses always had some glitter. She wore chandelier earrings with them and looked lovely.

Shoes are a rite of passage, a marker of milestones and events. Mine were the first little white shoes I wore as a toddler; then those practical lace-up brown leather shoes; then the happy day when I could finally wear penny loafers; my favorite red sandals I wore even though they pinched my feet, but loved and tried not to notice; then there were the blue and white saddle shoes that I wore with bobby socks when I was in high school. As I got older, there were high heels. I owned the most perfect pair of high heels. These were black patent leather and went with everything in my closet. When I wore them I felt really dressed up.

When I was in my twenties I kept my special shoes in tissue, just as my mom had done when I was small. These special shoes were blue satin, and I had worn them to my best friend's wedding. My dress was royal blue, and my shoes were dyed to match as was the custom of the day. I kept them wrapped in tissue and in their original box. I knew that I would probably not wear them again, but they were so special. Later these shoes went into the "Dress-up Trunk." My little girls loved them, and delighted in the noise these shoes made as they clip-clopped along the kitchen floor.

My stilettos now are few, none to be exact. I marvel at my granddaughters wearing six-inch heels. I am enjoying flat shoes again. One of my granddaughters recently bought a pair of Birkenstocks the same as mine. "Cool," she says. She thinks I am really trendy at my age. I am not trendy. I just want comfort.

Shoes are memories—polished with care, worn with pride, kept sometimes because they are too precious to be abandoned.

Sign Language

— Linda Hennrick

LIVING IN JAPAN FOR ALMOST FORTY YEARS, I came across my share of "unique" signs in English. But when I spotted a sign on a vending machine at Sano Service Area in Tochigi Prefecture that said "Hot Men," I walked closer to take a better look.

Intriguing and often humorous signs and words printed in English are everywhere in Japan. Like the sign on my local butcher shop that said: "flesh meats" — I think they meant "fresh," but the Japanese do have a tendency to mix up their l's and r's. Or the sign we'd pass on our way to see Midori, my husband Miki's sister. Our route took us by an old building that was once a door-to-door milk delivery service. A sign still hung on the building that said "Homo" (Morinaga Homo Gyùnyù — gyùnyù is milk), but an English speaker's eye would inevitably stop on the word in the middle, an unfortunate abbreviation of "homogenized."

Speaking of unfortunate, a region of central Honshu — Japan's largest island — that includes the cities of Osaka, Kobe, and Kyoto is known as Kinki. A popular singing duo from the area called themselves by the alliterative name Kinki Kids. Their fans couldn't understand why they received such strange looks when they wore their Kinki Kids T-shirts, printed in the English alphabet, in the U.S. — until someone told them what "kinky" meant.

Kinki is also part of the name of many companies based in the region including a travel agency called Kinki Japan Tourist. The agency once gave out travel bags with the company name printed in English letters to all its customers who may have wondered why when they visited English-speaking countries they were given a wide berth.

Kinki University eventually announced that it was changing its name. Students must have been tired of the strange looks they received when they said they studied at Kinki University. Pity their teachers. And alumni.

Back in 1972, the first full summer I lived in Japan, I was invariably offered Calpis — say that fast a few times — whenever I'd visit someone's home. Calpis is a milky colored yoghurt-like drink made by the company of the same name — imagine telling someone you work for Calpis. The drink was originally sold as a concentrate, diluted with water and ice before drinking. Now there's something called Calpis Water that doesn't need to be diluted, as well as Calpis Soda, a carbonated beverage, on the market. It still doesn't sound very appetizing.

I personally wouldn't wear an item of clothing, like a T-shirt, if I couldn't read what was written on it. I won't even wear designer clothes with logo marks on them that I *can* read — I think I should be paid for advertising if I do. But the Japanese love to use English words on anything and everything. Who cares if the words might actually *mean* something. A Japanese graphic designer once told me that it wasn't the meaning of the words but how they *looked* that determined what's printed on a T-shirt or other article of clothing. I don't know how often on trains I saw someone sitting across from me wearing a T-shirt with the most nonsensical message written on it. I remember one worn by a teenage girl that said, "I am a boy." Though we may have laughed at what they said, Miki and I often shopped for T-shirts with "funny" English on them to give as gifts to our American nephews.

But easily, the strangest combination of English words I ever came across was printed on the skirt of a young woman standing beside me on a train. Black letters on a beige background said "Butterick" and "Cold Sores."

How often have I turned to the last page of a menu at a restaurant in Japan to see "Desert" printed in bold letters at the top. Obviously they meant "Dessert," but they lost an s. That's okay. It's tough enough for English speakers to keep desert (as in "arid land"), desert (as in "to abandon"), and dessert straight. But seeing it on a menu, I always wanted to make up new desert-desserts like Sahara Sundae, Gobi Pudding, or Mojave Sand Pie just for fun.

I sometimes shopped at the small food vendors in Shibuya Station. One place sold uncooked hamburger patties seasoned with various spices—garlic, onion, or curry—and marked thus in English on the wrapper. Unseasoned patties were also available. You'd recognize those right away. They were the ones marked "plane."

Displays of "idea" goods, small gizmos and gadgets that make life a little easier, were often set up in front of my local supermarket. One item being advertised turned out to be a compact paper shredder, but it sounded dangerous. The sign in English said: Hand Shredder.

On walks around my neighborhood, I'd pass a dry cleaning shop in nearby Mitakadai with a sign that said "Fashionabl & Grad Up." I'd often ponder the sign. Did they leave the e's off intentionally to save money, or did they just run out of room? I'll probably never know.

The e was also left off a sign in a temple garden in Nikko indicating a type of tree—the Japanese Umbrella Pine became a Japanese Umbrella Pin. But I found the missing e in another part of Nikko on a sign that said: "Off Limites." Maybe I should have told someone I'd spotted the runaway.

On our travels around Japan, we'd see some of the most interesting signs. When we stayed with my sister Melissa and her boys at the Kowakien Hotel in Hakone, a resort area south of Tokyo near Mt. Fuji, the mats on the floors of the elevators were changed each day with the greeting, "Have a Nice Day Monday," "Have a Nice Day Tuesday," etc. We loved this idea so much that we still use the phrase with Melissa and our nephews as a form of greeting.

We also loved the sign in front of an eating establishment in Hakone that proudly said "The Leading Restaurant in the World." I haven't visited enough restaurants around the world to know if their claim was true or not, but I suspect some hyperbole was at play. My all-time favorite sign was over a restaurant in Enoshima, a beach resort just south of Tokyo: We Serve People with "TASTY THINGS." That one could be taken quite a few ways.

Entering a famous temple, shrine, or garden in Japan, one pays a fee and is given a pamphlet printed in both Japanese and English that explains the history of the place. The English is directly translated from Japanese and can be quite stilted and on occasion tickle the funny bone, especially the typos. Our favorite typo was in a pamphlet for Myoryu-ji in Kanazawa, Ishikawa Prefecture, better known as the Ninja Temple, a fascinating place with hidden doors, rooms, and passageways designed as escape routes for the ruling family in case of an enemy attack. A list of rules on the pamphlet in English included this one: No amoking. It's obvious they meant "no smoking," but amoking should probably also be prohibited when viewing antiquities.

On our many trips to Nikko, we'd always drive by a derelict gas station that had long been out of business. Year after year the gas station remained, blasted by the sun and wind, rusted by the rain and snow, a little worse off each time we'd see it, but eternally, optimistically displaying its sign in white paint on the windows: Open.

Tobu World Square, a theme park near Nikko, features exquisitely made miniature buildings from around the world. With our niece, Jessa, we spotted this sign on a miniature double decker bus crossing a miniature London Bridge over a miniature Thames River in miniature London: Stake & Kidney Pie. Vampires beware.

One year we took nephew Zach and his friend Sean to Nikko Edomura (Nikko Edo Wonderland), a theme park with replicas of buildings of old Tokyo. Tourists buy passes at the ticket booth to enter the park. Zach and Sean were first to notice the sign in English that explained each of the passes along with their prices. The most expensive said, "THE BEST SATISFACTION ... A full of good memories." For a lower price you would receive "Just a little bit SATISFACTION ... A few memories." But for the least expensive you would get "NO SATISFACTION ... No good memories." Clearly, you'd get what you paid for.

Miki, my sister Melissa, and I once traveled to Tendo, a hot springs resort area in Yamagata Prefecture near Yamadera, a famous temple built on a mountainside. We enjoyed the hotel where we stayed so much that Miki and I went back again several years later. We got a kick out of the banner in front of the hotel advertising a nationwide contest being held in Tendo for the sexiest lips in Japan that said "Love Me Tendo" in English.

One time, returning from a kite competition in Kanazawa, Miki and I drove through scenic Hakusan (literally "white mountain") National Park. Our route took us into Gifu Prefecture and the village of Shirakawa-gō famous for its old wooden farmhouses with picturesque *gasshō-tsukuri* (hands in prayer) thatched roofs. In photos taken from a nearby overlook, with light spilling out of the farmhouse windows and the thatched roofs covered with winter snow, the charming village is a fairyland worthy of gracing a Christmas card.

When we first saw the town, Shirakawa-gō had just been nominated to become a World Heritage Site, and the city had posted several tourist-friendly signs in English near the public parking lot. One sign pointed the way to Mozen-ji Fork Museum. A fork museum here in the land of chopsticks? Mozen-ji turned out to be the local temple also made with a thatched roof, but there wasn't a *fork* to be seen. Instead we found a museum inside the temple that explained how the *folk* in the area had lived.

A few years later, we visited the area again with my sister Melissa. By then Shirakawa-gō had officially been designated a World Heritage Site, and the sign had been changed to correctly read *folk*. Ah, progress — at the price of a smile.

I thought of these other signs I'd seen as I pondered the new one — "Hot Men" — on a vending machine standing shoulder to shoulder with other vending machines along the walls inside the restaurant/convenience store at Sano Service Area where we'd often stop on our way to and from Nikko. Highways in Japan are toll roads, and "parking" areas are provided at convenient intervals to offer travelers refreshments and restrooms—a "service" area like Sano also includes a gas station.

Vending machines—*jidō hanbaiki*—are a common sight all over Japan, in front of liquor stores, supermarkets, and twenty-four hour convenience stores where customers could just as easily go inside to make a purchase for less than that charged outside. Some can be found on private property along streets in residential neighborhoods, complete with wastebaskets for empty cans. Surprisingly, even when they're in the most out-of-the-way places, vending machines aren't tampered with. We saw one in front of a café in Bandai, a mountainous resort area in Fukushima Prefecture. The café stood at the head of a trail that led into a scenic gorge, the only building for miles in either direction along the winding mountain road; the vending machine sat in perfect working order just outside, braving the elements, surrounded by sunflowers.

Seven-year-old nephew Zach, visiting Japan for the first time, was amazed by the number of vending machines that line the streets of Tokyo. He called them all "Coke machines," but his beverage of choice, when we could find it, was Fanta Grape.

But besides dispensing hot and cold drinks like soda, tea, coffee, energy drinks, and bottled water, vending machines may also sell cigarettes and alcoholic beverages like beer, sake, and whiskey. Others offer rice, ice cream, bouquets of flowers, eggs, bananas, magazines, books, and even underwear. I thought I'd seen them all.

But "Hot Men"?

On closer inspection, I found the vending machine in question was selling cups of instant noodles. *Men* in Japanese means noodles.

What a disappointment.

Simple Pleasures

—Gaye V. Borne

I'M EASY TO PLEASE. It probably comes from my upbringing, environment and my innate nature. As a child, I reveled in small joys: watching the cloud formations float by while lying on the front lawn; feeling the air beneath me as my bicycle leapt over the raised bumps in my neighborhood's alleys; jumping rope double Dutch; enjoying a "Bubble-Up" ice cream soda with my grandmother; flying down Twenty-Second Street hill at Mach speed on my home-constructed skateboard; spending bonding time with my Shetland Sheepdog, Raffy.

Midlife, those pleasures turned into learning through more shelties; watching my daughter's innocent smile; belly laughing at a good joke told by my husband; a cat leisurely bathing whilst on my lap; appreciating my half-acre home of equine paradise colored with verdant hues of lush green foliage; drinking in the intoxicating sweet smells of freshly stacked hay; the velvety smooth softness of my mare's muzzle; riding dressage seamlessly with my mare as one in thought, mind and body; mucking stalls and corrals while listening to contented chewing of hay and the sweet songs of the nearby birds.

Now, later in life, a joyous pleasure is wrought from watching the flotillas of avian life on the golf course and in its lakes—stately, elegant egrets focused on fishing; coots assembled in formations on the well-tended grass; flocks of impressive, dignified Canadian geese leisurely grazing; the buzzing hum of jewel-toned hummingbirds drinking at their colorful feeders; bird music interspersed with the rasp of an occasional roadrunner; the peaceful, soothing silence of an abode lived in without noisy upstairs neighbors; the comfortable camaraderie rendered from the companionship of dear friends.

And, oh my, the ever-important splendid colors emitted from prisms and crystal; sunlight dancing through varying shades of foliage; and, of course, the sparkling intense hues of Christmas lights; and the ocean — her many moods evidenced by varying hues of blue. I could go on and on.

Yes, I'm easy to please. You may call me a simple person for my pure enjoyment of simple pleasures. They bring me joy and contentment. Listen to your heart and soul — you, too, will find *your* simple pleasures.

Skinny-Dipping Through Life

—Gaye V. Borne

"IT'S SUCH A BEAUTIFUL EVENING—let's have some fun!" said Aunt Kathryn as she watched me gazing through her sliding glass window. My eyes sifted through the scenery: a patio adjacent to the house, with an assortment of wind chimes hanging languidly from the ceiling; a modest, yet worn, redwood furniture set tidily nestled in a group seating arrangement; and beyond the patio, a shimmering oval of liquid cobalt surrounded by a manicured lawn and shrubbery.

Flowering Meyer lemon trees along the yard's perimeter wall exuded an intoxicating perfume making the evening air feel mystical and free spirited. Carefully placed colorful flowering plants joined the setting, sharing their own visual delights from nature's artist palette.

"The pool is just right. Let's go swimming," she said.

Brought out of my reverie, I replied, "Great! I'll go put on my suit."

"You don't need a suit. Just come on in."

"Wwwell ..." I stammered, "you mean no bathing suit?"

"Yep, come on—I do it all the time. It's so freeing to skinny-dip; it's wonderful!"

That said, Aunt Kathryn turned around and disappeared into her bedroom.

"Have fun!" I remember those two words being said to me by Aunt Kathryn throughout my time spent with her. Always ready for a good time, up until the years when her knees ravaged her with pain, she loved fun.

Aunt Kathryn was a professional dancer in the 1930s. A free spirit with a dancer's legs, she also danced on stage with Ginger Rogers. She met and married my uncle Phil, a dashing WWII navigator who flew on many missions. They had a daughter, my cousin Trella. From the early 1940s they lived in a bungalow with seven other bungalows sharing a courtyard on Sixteenth Street in Santa Monica, California. As I was born in 1950, I missed out on those years of neighborly closeness. A tightly-knit group of friends, they leaned on one another throughout the war years, all the while having courtyard potlucks and parties. My grandmother and grandfather also lived in one of those bungalows close to their daughter Kathryn. When my grandparents moved away from the bungalows, they stayed in contact with these friends while they raised me through the late 1960s.

By 1949, my aunt Kathryn and her family had moved to Ojai, California, out in the country. When I was four, I remember going with her to a well-known bar adjacent to a boxing gym. I have forgotten the name of the boxer who owned both the gym and the bar, but I sure did feel grown up while she and he chatted. Aunt Kathryn moved to Ventura, California by 1954. Always ready for fun and company, she would welcome my grandparents and me for visits.

During those years, she worked as a Van de Kamp's lady. A friend and I would take the city bus from Aunt Kathryn's house to go downtown to see her and, of course, get a free cookie. Dressed in her uniform and always smiling, she gave out her free samples with a twinkle in her eye. She always made me feel welcome and special. She made me feel important, and going to see her at work was one of the highlights of my trips to Ventura. I treasured the visits I had with her and would continue going to see her well into my teens. I even drove to Ventura from Santa Monica on dates with my boyfriend to visit Aunt Kathryn and Uncle Phil, as they were to me the parents I never had. They moved again, for the last time, to Artesia, California when I was seventeen.

When I was in my twenties with a little family of my own, we would make the drive from Simi Valley to Artesia to visit many times then and thereafter. One such visit had Aunt Kathryn and me getting our ears pierced at the mall, and then she whooped and hollered while I rode the mechanical bull ride.

I continued to drive to Artesia by myself, or with family in tow, until the fateful day on June 26, 1989 when Uncle Phil called and told me to "sit down." Aunt Kathryn had had a massive cerebral stroke and was gone. Our worlds were shattered. My world was never the same, and I still miss her dearly every day.

Aunt Kathryn took the place of my mother even when my mother was around. She never neglected to tell me "I love you" and "Have fun."

Emerging from her bedroom, Aunt Kathryn went outside to the pool and dropped her towel onto the decking. "Ooohh, this is nice. The water's warm and the air's lovely," she said. Nervously, I too came outside and dropped my towel on the decking. Slipping into the embrace of the water, I felt more comfortable.

Before long, I was swimming around the pool with my aunt without a care in the world. Skinny-dipping was fun—especially since I was with Aunt Kathryn who had been having fun all her life.

So Necessary

— Corinne Lee Murphy

BOB AND I HAD DISCOVERED our mutual love for the North Coast in the first heady hours and days of dating when it seems that you are so in tune, see things so similarly, that finding each other must have been fated. We found that we had both spent part of our childhood in Eureka, he during WWII when the family relocated there so his father could work in the shipyards for the war effort, and I in the early sixties. Bob had attended a parochial school, St. Bernard's, which was just three blocks from the Cape Cod on William Street where my family had moved when I was eleven. I was happy the two years there. I no longer shared a room with my sister, and I had my own bedroom upstairs with my very own bathroom. I recall so often leaning out the window of my lavender room and finding the first star of the night to wish upon. So, the California coast from the Oregon border to Carmel called to us, and we came.

On this trip to Mendocino we chose a hotel with a fireplace for the cool evenings and a view of the sea. We wandered into town to see the galleries and shops. We spoke of the beauty of the sea, the town. How happy we were to be there. How lovely some of the art was to us. How creative the pieces of jewelry were. Bob and I admired an opal and amethyst necklace, and he bought it for me and placed it around my neck. We found a toy store with lovely and unique things. Bob's younger sister's daughter was pregnant with her first child, the first grandchild. I had already dutifully purchased several items from the young mother's wish list on Amazon, but here was this perfect rattle, so beautiful, so necessary. The handle was made in Germany of a rare wood which wrapped around to hold a perfect round ball of a pink semiprecious stone that spun. Bob was happy to see me so excited to buy it. We were resolutely upbeat and considerate of each other's wishes. And there was a weight that we carried on this trip, each in our own way and left unspoken. And every action took on heightened meaning.

[Excerpt from the book
Grace Fully: Making Peace with Cancer]

Spring Arrives in Stratford

— Marilyn McNeill

AFTER A LONG WINTER, Stratford's swans march towards the Avon River. Visitors take a road trip to our city to watch the swans come out of the barn and make their way back to the Avon as crowds cheer and the bagpipers pipe.

I have heard these pipers practice every Saturday morning. They assemble at the school and begin in earnest about ten o'clock. I have had a free concert in my backyard for weeks.

This unique parade has been a tradition for twenty-seven years. Stratford's history with swans dates back to 1918 when the first gift of swans was received. These white mute swans have been in the barn next to the area all winter. The Stratford Police Pipe and Drums pipe them ceremoniously to the river each spring. These are "the true stars of Stratford."

When I was young, spring arrived when I saw the first robin return to Cooksville, and the grass turned from brown to green.

Spring has arrived on Mornington Street, too. Our grass is turning green, and all our lilac bushes are in bloom. These are French lilacs, and they form a long row between our home and Mrs. Reid's. Nothing is as fragrant as a fresh bouquet of lilacs. This has always been my favorite spring blooming shrub. The fragrance brings back so many happy memories for me.

Spring has also brought a boat show to Toronto. Stuart and I are going with our friends Ginny and Stan Leete. Stan is an avid fisherman and has a boat which he docks in Bayfield on Lake Huron.

Ginny and I have decided that instead of looking at boats, we would rather look at shoes. Winter has been long, and we are tired of wearing our wooly socks and snow boots. Ginny and I are looking forward to a day in the big city. There are two shoe stores in Stratford, and we all seem to wear the same shoes. We are shoe shopping.

Mildred is babysitting for the day. What a treat that is.

Three hours have passed quickly, and we meet our husbands for an early dinner. We are surprised to learn that they had been shopping, as well. After we talk about our purchases, Stuart smiles and says he, too, has been shopping. He has indeed been shopping. He has bought a boat—a blue boat called Bluebird.

I have always thought how nice it would be to paddle along the Avon. The whole idea sounds very romantic. Just imagine paddling along the Avon watching the swans and clouds float by. I could make a picnic lunch—very gourmet, of course—to eat on the river bank.

Bluebird would not sail on the Avon, but on Lake Huron. This is a thirty-two-foot sailboat, and she will arrive next week after the boat show.

I get car sick ... Will I get seasick? I will soon find out!

Talking With Grandpa

—June Gaulding

TO BE CLAIRVOYANT is the "paramount ability to see persons or events that are distant in time or space." The French word for clear is *"clair"* and vision is *"voyance."* One who sees clearly is clairvoyant.

I am searching to learn the word for talking with spirits of the dead. Is it psychic, meaning a paranormal ability? Is it a "dreamlike" vision? I have heard of different terms for people with this ability (medium, seer, prophet). In the last few years there have been several television programs on communication with the dead. A current television program, *The Long Island Medium*, has been popular for a while; however, many say the medium, Theresa Caputo, is a fake, although others believe in her. Is she really talking with the dead? I am not going to make a claim either way, but I do enjoy watching her shows.

My great nephew Everitt Jaxson Ellis is three years old. His parents are Matthew and Courtney Ellis, and he has a nine-month-old sister named Avery Celeste. They live in King George, Virginia. Jaxson has been ahead of his normal age schedule since birth. His accomplishments are surprising to his parents and other family members. I guess most parents feel that way about their children. Indeed, he is a precocious child of confidence and intelligence.

In the last few weeks when Jaxson was in his room playing by himself, his mother passed by and heard him talking to someone and asked, "Who are you talking to?"

He answered, "It's a man."

She just let his answer go for the time being but shared it with Matthew. Then later Daddy heard him talking in his room, and he asked, "Who are you talking to?"

"I was talking with Grandpa, and he had a blue shirt on, and he has a dog." Jaxson jabbered on and told him the dog's name was Packy.

Courtney says if you ask him a question about who he is talking with he gets silly and says crazy things. They want to catch him in the process of "talking to himself" to get a clear picture of what might be happening.

In the next few days Jaxson visited his grandma. Courtney had talked with her about Jaxson's talks with a man that he calls Grandpa. Grandma suggested that she and Jaxson look at her old photograph album. While looking at the pictures, Jaxson saw a man and said, "That's the man I talked with."

Grandma told him the man was his great-grandpa. Then she asked, "What do you and Grandpa talk about?"

"He helps me fix my toys."

Jaxson didn't appear to be afraid of the man he talked with. I can understand that a small child wouldn't be afraid, as my daughter, Janet, at three years old, communicated with someone while I was there with her. She would quit talking when she was aware I was listening. I never found out who it was.

Great-Grandpa has been dead for many years. Jaxson had never seen a photograph of him or his dog. How did Jaxson know about the dog, Packy, if he hadn't seen him during his contact with Great-Grandpa? How would a three-year-old talk with spirits unless they came to him? Do we believe that Jaxson has some clairvoyant or paranormal abilities for his age? His parents and grandma are going to pose more questions to find out if there are other stories for him to share. This may give a clue if Jaxson has a special talent for communicating with spirits.

Ta-Ta, Tatalah

— Gaye V. Borne

"NOW, DON'T CRY, or you will blow the deal," Robbie admonished me. I remember the date very well—it was a beautiful Mother's Day weekend in May of 1987. Stone-faced, I kept my composure, as Robbie "wheeled and dealed" with the car salesman. Robbie had an "M. O." that he followed when he shopped for cars. If the salesman got frustrated and exasperated enough to throw Robbie out of the showroom, then Robbie had won the war AND the car. My job was to be invisible until it was time to sign the papers. And sign the papers we did....

Five years for the loan—the loan was for more than what we paid for our new house on one-half of an acre! Were we nuts? You would think so, but we were determined that we had made an excellent purchase of a quality product. Driving away from the dealership, the sun gleaming on the white paint of the brand new 1987 Mercedes Benz 560 SEC, we had no idea that our expectations would be exceeded ten-fold.

It is always fun getting a new car. Robbie's next task, after proudly showing it off to the neighbors, was to get personalized DMV plates for the car. He promptly decided upon "TATALAH," which means "little father" in Yiddish. Bubba, Robbie's paternal grandmother, had affectionately called him Tatalah all of his life. So, now, fellow M.O.T.s — members of the tribe—would honk or wave at Robbie on the freeway or wherever he was driving.

And driving he did ... 50 miles each way to and from work in Vernon back to Simi Valley each day for five days a week; then 170 miles each way to Palm Springs and back to Simi Valley on the weekends, for a total of a minimum of 600 miles per week. Diligent mechanical upkeep and recordkeeping went without saying, in addition to an almost maniacal approach to exterior upkeep—washing, waxing, wheel and tire dressings, etc.

All of the careful attention to detail and hard work paid off. The car performed faithfully through the years. All twenty-four years, in fact. We put 410,000 miles on that car, and the engine was still as good as new. A few things had worn out and had been repaired or replaced due to old age, but nothing of major significance other than wear and tear on the leather seats.

We had since retired and moved away from Simi Valley to the desert. The new house did not have room for three cars and a golf cart, so the SEC regretfully got retired and put up for sale.

A nice young man placed a bid on the SEC through eBay on the internet. Robbie lovingly gave the car a final beauty bath, and we parked it covered in front of the house.

Ben and his father drove all the way from Orange County to pick up the SEC today. Robbie uncovered his baby and proudly showed the fellows the car and insisted they take it for a spin. I went into the house and waited for Robbie to come back after the "test drive."

Eventually, I heard the garage door close. Robbie's footsteps were heavy, and I could tell he was upset. "It's gone," he said. "Twenty-four years, and it's gone." As tears were rolling down his face, I just said to him with a hug, "It's okay—cry. Go ahead and cry. It's okay."

The Four Wheels and a Spare

— June Gaulding

WHEN I WAS FIVE AND SIX years old, I sang with my sister while we were out playing on the farm. She had a pleasing soprano voice. When I sang along with her, my voice didn't sound like hers. Mine sounded a little lower. At that young age, I didn't realize that I had an alto voice. Then in junior high I tried out for the choir, and I was told that I had an alto voice. After singing with the alto group, I finally felt that I was in the right place.

I went to Salem High School in Salem, West Virginia. The two-story school was located on High Street at the end of town. The building housed 127 junior high students and 172 senior students. There were 14 teachers, 1 principal, and 1 janitor. This made a total of 315 bodies in the building. This was a small school compared to today's school population. I was lucky the school even offered a choir and a band for the students.

Miss Powell, the English teacher, was the pianist for the band and the choir. She asked my sister, Donna, and me to sing as a duet. I was a freshman, and Donna was a sophomore. We were The Golden Girls. This was perfect, as our last name was Golden. She took us to several places in Salem that wanted entertainment. We sang at a nursing home, a hospital, a Lion's Club, and churches. Miss Powell chose the songs that we were comfortable singing. It was a lot of fun.

I remember one Easter Sunrise Service in 1951 that Donna and I were going to sing. I woke up during the night, and I coughed until I was hoarse. We had to be at the church at eight o'clock in the morning. I told my sister I didn't know if I could sing or not because I coughed all night. Before I left the house that morning, I gargled with some salt water and hoped that would help. When we arrived, Miss Powell asked us to practice the song we were going to sing. I couldn't believe that a note came out of my throat, but it did. In fact, there was no sign of my coughing spell that I had endured during the night. When it was our time during the Easter service to sing, we stood and proudly sang. That coughing spell never happened to me again.

In January of 1952, I was a sophomore and Donna was a junior when Miss Powell suggested that we add two more voices and become a quartet. That sounded great. She chose a bass voice, George McMicken, and a tenor voice, Dallas (Sonny) Bailey, Jr., to make the quartet. Sonny was quite musically talented. He came from a musical family. In fact, when we lost our choir and band director, Sonny took over the job of directing the two groups. He did a great job for a couple of years and still sang in the quartet. Miss Powell felt like we needed a name for our group, and we became The Four Wheels. We had lots of programs booked to sing that year.

Then in September of 1953, Miss Powell suggested that we add another voice, a baritone, to the group. She said it would give the group a great sound. She asked Tom McMicken (George's younger brother), a baritone, to join us as the fifth voice. It was at that time we became The Four Wheels and a Spare. We were booked for many programs that year, and we enjoyed sharing our music. We sang popular songs, hymns, and old songs, such as "My Old Kentucky Home." In addition, the five of us were still singing in the choir and keeping up with our classes. This made a busy year for all of us.

In May of 1953, Donna graduated from high school, so we had to find a soprano to fill her space. A sophomore, Shelby Davis, was in the choir and had a beautiful soprano voice, so Miss Powell invited her to be a part of our singing group. She said yes. So, in September of 1953, we started practicing as The Four Wheels and a Spare again. Shelby fit in great with the group, and we gave many programs throughout the year.

George and I had met in the eighth grade. Since there was only one class for our grade, we saw a lot of each other every year. However, during my sophomore year, George and I started going together as a couple. We went together throughout high school. Before we knew it, May 1954 had arrived, and George and I were graduating from high school.

In June, I headed for Washington, D.C. and went to work as a stenographer for the Air Force at the Pentagon. George joined the Army and ended up in Germany. The three remaining singers in the group graduated the next year. I never heard if Miss Powell had continued the group. I hope she didn't. I always felt The Four Wheels and a Spare was our special singing group at that time of our lives.

The Gift

— Corinne Lee Murphy

IT WAS A BEAUTIFUL CALIFORNIA FALL DAY with the sun bathing the land from the valley to the coast. Bob and I were on our way to Mendocino, a place we always loved. We had spent part of our honeymoon on the North Coast some twenty-eight years before and returned many times. We were excited and looking forward to our getaway.

We decided to take back ways rather than the most direct route. We both loved the scenic narrow country roads that wind through the hills and valleys. Family "rides" had been a tradition in my childhood; we would explore rural byways with my father religiously stopping at every "historical" monument. Such aimless rides brought back happy memories to me, a sense of contentment.

Bob and I weren't in any hurry. We chose to go through the Capay Valley to approach the coastal range of mountains, which we had to cross to join Highway 1, the world famous roadway which hugs the spectacular coast. I was navigating. At one point I made an error, and we took a road that was even more circuitous than I had intended. But I thought, no matter, we will see new territory. We were relaxed and happy as we leisurely traveled through the coastal range, the light constantly changing as we followed the winding roadway through the shadows of the mountainsides and the redwoods. We saw few other cars. Then, as we came around just another curve of the narrow road, a loaded logging truck was approaching fast, coming directly toward us in our own lane.

It was a stunning sight. Bob slid our car as close as he could to the steep mountainside to our right and stopped. There was no room to move our car more than a few inches out of our lane.

Then we waited. And watched. The cab of the truck moved into the other lane, but the trailer could not move as quickly and stayed in our lane as the truck rapidly bore down on us. There was literally nothing we could do. We didn't speak. Time slowed.

It wasn't until the back end of the trailer slid by the front bumper of our car with less than six inches to spare that we knew that we would not be struck. The truck kept going. I turned to Bob and said simply, "Well, that was close." He nodded, and looking straight ahead, responded that the truck driver had been a good driver. He explained that if the truck driver had touched his brakes at that speed, the tractor/trailer rig would have jackknifed, and we would surely have been hit and, no doubt, killed. I had just been waiting to see if the trailer could possibly miss us, but Bob had had another calculus in his mind also as he realized the consequence of the driver braking.

After the truck was gone, Bob moved fully back into our lane, and we headed toward our destination, saying little. If our Lexus had not been in good working condition, had Bob not been an athlete in his youth, if he had not remained calm and moved smoothly and immediately to stop as close to the side of the steep mountain as possible, we would have been hit. It was literally a matter of inches and of milliseconds of reaction time. It was one of those moments in one's life when you know, you understand, that the rest of your life is a gift.

[Excerpt from the book
Grace Fully: Making Peace with Cancer]

The Great White Apes

— Larry Ballard

I CAN REMEMBER THE LITTLE THINGS of those crisp starlit nights when Jerry Rose and I lay on the scraps of planks and old boxes, pointing out perceived movement in those faint orbs. We were certain those movements were fleets of spaceships on their way from those ancient suns to land right here in our tangled, vine maple forest. The weight of those gleaming silver vessels would sink deeply into the soft river bottom loam under our secret tree house. The home of the Great White Apes. A tribe of two. Super intelligent simians that Edgar Rice Burroughs would be proud of.

Our daring adventures were legendary in the Valley. (Although some weren't as generous when describing our action-filled endeavors.) Our high-pitched Tarzan calls from voices not yet mellowed by puberty, were not always appreciated. That echoing call was magic to us. Only we understood the secret messages imbedded in the high pitched yodeling. It was the cement in our relationship. We were best friends.

"Wow," whispered Jerry. "That sure is a humongous fleet."

"Humongous," I breathed. "Very humongous."

The moon had crept over the top of Eel Hill. The blue light diminished all color except Jerry's softly rounded, rosy red face. His face was always red, be he excited, running or sleeping. Always bright red. He was a lot smaller than I, and his thin arms and legs held little strength.

"Whaddya think, Jerry?"

He half closed his eyes. "Whaddya mean, what do I think?"

We both knew what I meant, but neither wanted to pull himself away from the unfolding drama of a possible confrontation with the approaching alien fleet.

"Yea, I suppose it is time," he said. Suddenly he sprang to his feet, grabbed a knotted hemp rope hanging from a charred, stubby branch we had decided had been hit by lightning— although there was an alternate theory involving laser beams— and clumsily worked his way to the semi-soggy forest floor.

"Ha, and ha again," he shouted as he dashed toward the fringe of fragrant salal brush that encircled our encampment.

"No fair," I yelled after him as he disappeared into the small trees that separated our domain from the county blacktop.

The race was on. I could tell by his thrashing around in the brush Jerry hadn't crossed the trail yet, so I slowed down until I could hear the quiet shuffle of soft leaves under his feet.

"Ha, and ha again," he yelled in triumph.

When I caught Jerry he was standing, straddle legged, in the middle of a shiny black asphalt river, the moon awash on his upturned, ruddy face. He leaped and punched a single fist into the dark spaces between the stars. "Ha," he grinned, and danced a crazy out of sync, wobbly war dance in the middle of the road.

We sat on the cooling tar for a few minutes before grudgingly heading home, neither of us wanting to hear the off-pitch yodels our mothers had learned would bring their wayward charges to heel.

The Last Goodbye

— Elia Vasquez Fuller

IT WAS SUMMER, AUGUST 1961, when we left Harlingen, Texas, and headed out to California. All six of us, three brothers, two sisters, and I had grown up in Harlingen in the Rio Grande Valley of South Texas.

On the day we were leaving, our neighbors were sad. They watched us from their windows as we loaded our belongings into the rented U-Haul. We had lived on West Madison Street in the same neighborhood for about fifteen years. Mother had lived in South Texas all her life. At first, neighbors had been dubious that we would really move to California. But they started to believe that we might leave Texas when our house was sold, including Mother's attached beauty shop. Now, with the U-Haul half filled up, neighbors realized our departure was certain and impending. To our neighbors California was like another world. Some of them had a notion that California was a wild and wicked place "with loose women and no morals." They had no desire to ever leave Texas. Most of them planned to live in Harlingen and be buried in Harlingen.

I had just turned sixteen. When my girlfriends found out I was moving to California they warned me that California would transform me into "one of those mini-skirt girls who irons her long hair, wears knee high boots and white lipstick."

But in spite of everything, we were leaving Harlingen, where elementary students would start their school day by singing the Texas state song, "Texas, Our Texas," followed by the University of Texas Alma Mater, "The Eyes of Texas Are Upon You," and finally our favorite song, "Deep in the Heart of Texas." It was my favorite because we would get to clap in the middle of the song. During the clapping part, a few students would try to clap louder and faster, on purpose, which at times, brought a reprimand from the teacher, making it even more fun to look at one another and hold in our giggles.

All our elementary schools were named after Texas heroes. My school was Crockett Elementary School, named after Davy Crockett, who died at the Alamo. During the early fifties, Crockett School was a segregated school for Mexican American students. All the neighborhood children walked to school together with groups of friends and older brothers and sisters. Crockett School was adjacent to a city park known as the Fair Park. Therefore, our neighborhood was known as the Fair Park neighborhood. Sunday afternoons were spent leisurely at the park by families enjoying their day of rest. The park's name was later changed to Lon C. Hill Park, after the founder of Harlingen. But everyone in our neighborhood continued to call it the Fair Park.

African American children in Harlingen also attended a segregated school. It was located a few miles away, across the street from my grandmother's house. It was named The Booker T. Washington School. I spent many hours on my grandmother's porch watching the children and their teachers with curiosity as they played outside. Sadly, we were indoctrinated by rules that we were not supposed to socialize with them or they with us.

There was also a school for Anglo children named for Stephen F. Austin, the founder of Texas. It wasn't until I entered junior high school in the late fifties that Anglo, Mexican American and African American schools were integrated, but with much controversy in the school district and opposition to allow the three African American teachers to teach in the integrated schools. In the end, the three African American teachers moved out of Harlingen to obtain jobs elsewhere.

By the time schools were integrated, we students had been institutionalized with stereotype perceptions about other races. Years of imposed rules of punishing Mexican American students for speaking Spanish were not easy to erase from our psyche. We had grown up in a society that judged people as superior or inferior by the color of their skin. It took a while after leaving

Texas and living in California for changes in our subconscious to evolve.

Our father, Alfredo Vasquez, was well respected in the community. At that time, there were only three Mexican American teachers in Harlingen. He was one of the three, earning him his nickname, "Profe," as he was affectionately known in our neighborhood. If anyone needed legal advice, needed documents translated, or had questions about available community services, they knew he would help them. He was a World War II Navy veteran. During the war, he was on duty aboard a mine sweeping ship which was hit by a torpedo. A telegram was sent to my mother and to my father's mother declaring him M.I.A., missing in action. Both women spent weeks in prayer until another telegram arrived stating that he had been found, barely alive, on a raft in the middle of the ocean with no food or water. He was lucky because some of the other men on the raft had not survived. When the war ended, after he returned to Texas, he used the G.I. Bill to get his teaching credentials. However, in Harlingen, he was only permitted to teach in the segregated Mexican American schools. My father, having grown up in Oklahoma, had not experienced blatant discrimination like there was in Texas. He wanted to move out of Texas, but all of Mother's family, her mother, two sisters and her brother lived nearby. Mother would never leave them. So my father became politically active, advocating for the end of segregated schools and was a founding member of Harlingen's League of United Latin American Citizens, known today as LULAC. But he never gave up the idea of some day moving his family out of Texas.

Mother, Coleta Vasquez, attained her cosmetologist license while my father was getting his teaching degree. She helped him pay for books and tuition by working days and nights in her beauty shop. We watched her shampooing and cutting hair, giving perms, facials, manicures and pedicures; in general, making women feel beautiful. In front of our house was a big sign: "Colette's House of Beauty."

As kids, we would sit on our front porch to watch ladies arrive for their appointments, curious enough to wait around to see what they looked like when they left. We knew all her regular clients, housewives who made weekly hair appointments for Sunday mass and young ladies getting ready for Saturday night dances. Widows came in for makeovers, and mothers brought their children in to get haircuts.

Colette's House of Beauty was always buzzing with activity. Mother's outgoing good-humored personality drew a lot of customers into her shop. It was a neighborhood information center, as well as a gossip mill. Women confided in my mother. They trusted her. Mother was wise enough to never betray any of their secrets.

Mother kept up with the latest hairstyles in glamour magazines. Ladies sitting under dryers browsed through movie star magazines to keep up with the latest scandals. One much talked-about scandal in particular, at that time, was the story of Eddie Fisher divorcing Debbie Reynolds to marry Elizabeth Taylor. There was always something fun, exciting and new happening at Colette's House of Beauty.

The loading of the U-Haul was almost completed. Soon we would be leaving all our friends—the ones we had played tag with in our front yard, while all the parents sat on the front porch, happily laughing amongst themselves … the same parents, alongside our parents, who proudly watched their children make their first communion. It was a proud and happy occasion at the Immaculate Heart of Mary Catholic Church. There were many other happy occasions: welcoming newborns, birthday greetings, school carnivals, and graduations.

Like my parents, most of the neighbors worked hard to make ends meet, but we all helped out one another during adversity. In 1955, when I was ten, our house burned down. After the fire, our neighbors brought us baby bottles, diapers, clothing, food, and took up a collection of money for us. They did whatever they could to help us out. Luckily, Mother's beauty shop survived the fire intact. It was the only part left standing. Because Father was teaching and Mother continued working in her beauty shop, they were able to rebuild our house out of bricks, much bigger and better.

But six years later, here we were, our parents leaving behind the life they had worked so hard for. Neighbors wondered why would our parents, at the age of forty-five and forty-three, decide to leave everything behind and start all over again. Our parents had so much more to lose than most of them had: a beautiful home, profitable careers, and they were loved and highly respected in the community. Some would say it was fate. Perhaps. But there was also a connecting string of two events that brought them to this moment of saying goodbye to the only place I had ever known. One was Father's desire to leave Texas to escape social injustice to improve the future of his family. But it was Mother who suddenly wanted to move as far away from Texas as possible. Her change of mind happened after a heartbreaking incident with her older sister. So the cards were dealt, and my father gladly accepted a teaching job offer in California.

When the loading of the U-Haul was almost completed, neighbors started coming out of their houses. It started to sprinkle as my father finally locked the U-Haul door and we piled into the car. Mother sat in the front with the two babies, Sylvia and Gerald. The three older kids, Richard, Velma, and I sat in the back. Our oldest brother, Alfredo, Jr., did not make the trip to California with us because he was in the Marine Corps.

By now rain was coming down harder. With windshield wipers on and rain drops sliding down the windows, as we backed out of the driveway I saw the sign "Colette's House of Beauty" for the last time.

All of our neighbors were standing on the curb in front of their homes. They had lined both sides of the street, standing there in the pouring rain. My dad drove slowly down the street.

As we drove by their houses, he would stop as each one came up to our open windows to shake our hand, say goodbye and wish us well. *"Dios los bendiga,"* literally translated as "God bless you," but also meaning "God be with you," a South Texan saying used when a person was leaving.

It was like being in a parade with friends waving to us on both sides of the street. Yet remembering their wet faces in the rain, now I imagine some of them were also wet with tears. It was a bittersweet moment that I will remember forever.

I remember it was a long, slow drive to the end of the street where we waved our last goodbyes, as our father turned the corner to get on the main highway out of town. My brother Richard says he remembers that to him it felt like we were celebrities being honored in a parade. My sister Velma remembers Mother started crying, and she cried all the way to California.

The One and Only Most Beautiful Dress (I Ever Made)

— Ruth Gray

IT WAS THE SUMMER OF 1946. We had returned to the ranch after the war, and I was looking forward to my second summer and vacation since our return. It was my favorite time of the year with all the fairs and festivals in our Hood River Valley, and I had just had my thirteenth birthday.

The summer before I had nurtured a calf my father had given me, grooming and training it to 4-H specifications, and winning a red ribbon for my efforts at the county fair. I had enjoyed raising my calf and showing it, but I was one of the few girls in the calf project, and someone had labeled me "a tomboy."

This summer I no longer had a young animal to raise, but some of my friends were urging me to join another club in 4-H. It was called "Stitch and Sew," and the project was for each member to make a dress for herself. This excited me, as my mother did not sew. Nor did we have a sewing machine, so most of my dresses were hand-me-downs or clothes chosen for me by others. Besides, I was ready to do something "girlie" so that I would no longer be labeled a tomboy.

I was excited as Daddy drove me to town to look through the pattern books at the dry-goods store. The sophisticated watercolor drawings of swirling silks, batistes, velvets, crepes and voiles whetted my imagination. After careful consideration I chose the pattern style all by myself — something just gorgeous I thought Shirley Temple would wear going to her first dance. Next I purchased the brightest, most silky gossamer material I could find that was splashed by colorful big butterflies and flowers. My imagination aflame, I saw the finished garment swirling around me: a rainbow of color as I descended a grand stairway of some future ballroom.

That night I was so excited unfolding and smoothing out the tissue paper pattern, pinning it on the material purchased, and cutting the pieces. This operation took place on the grassy lawn of our front yard since there was no room to spread out inside our little farm home. It was getting dark by the time I was through. I did not notice the uneven borders and the unraveling threads, thinking it would not matter when the garment was sewn together.

The next few weeks and months I would take my pattern pieces to our club meetings so the teacher, the mother of one of our club members, could help me match the parts together. Piece-by-piece I would take it home and sew each section by hand until the entire dress was put together. The last step was to iron the dress so it would hang freshly on a hanger for display at the fair.

Finally the opening day of our Hood River County Fair arrived. I was chuffed with happy anticipation as we claimed our dresses from display and put them on in the dressing room. We were ready to model! We would be on stage in the main auditorium of the building in front of all the people. As we mounted the steps to the stage, I doubt if anyone was as proud as I was at that moment. This dress was my very own creation, my unique accomplishment, done by my own fingers with needle and thread, inch-by-inch!

All seven of us girls lined up in a row on stage. We took turns stepping forward, turning around slowly, curtsying, then stepping back as the audience clapped. Then the judges asked that we come forward as our names were called and come down the steps to accept the award and continue down the center aisle so the audience could appreciate our hard work.

"First Place, Blue Ribbons, are tied, go to Jeanette Howard, age 13, for her buttoned pink chambray dress and also to Shirley van Riper, age 12, for her plissé print dress. Congratulations, girls!" A huge burst of applause followed as the winners dismounted the stage and returned to their proud parents.

Now there were five of us left on stage. The judge went on to announce the red and white ribbon winners, and a special "Honorable Mention Certificate."

The announcing judge sat down as the last of the girl winners exited and the applause died down with two of us still standing on the stage. The other remaining contestant and I looked at each other, realizing there would be no prize or award for us. I was in shock. The two of us did not know what to do or how to exit the stage. I felt my face getting flushed as we searched for a break in the back curtain. We grabbed each other's hands as we disappeared from public sight, and no one but us saw our tears of humiliation and shame.

I wonder . . . what ever happened to the one and only most beautiful dress I ever made in my life?

The Path Toward Others

— Ruth Gray

HOPE HAS LIFTED ME TO POSSIBILITY, promise and purpose in life, but it was borne of humiliation and disappointment during my high school years. I had internalized the attitudes of parity and worth of all beings from my aunt May, and I had reveled in the heady eastern experiences with my parents until we returned to the ranch. But post-war Parkdale, Oregon seemed changed from the magic little town I had left four years before.

When I was eight or nine years old, like most farmer's children, we were encouraged to work in the crops during the summer. Aunt May had planted strawberries in between the young pear trees on her acreage. During strawberry harvest, I took my place many mornings on my knees between rows picking the fruit, along with many itinerant families doing the same. Usually the children picked together, as we were slow: we sampled much of what we picked, the sweet juices sliding down our chins and marking the corners of our mouths. I thought it was fun. When it was lunchtime we would take our sack lunches and sit under nearby fir trees, visiting while we ate, then playing marbles or tic-tac-toe with our fingers in the dust of the ground.

One afternoon when I returned to the house, my mother who was visiting us, discovered the leftovers of a tortilla in my lunch sack. I told her I had traded my tuna fish sandwich with my friend for her bean tortilla. I saw a strange look on her face, but she did not forbid me. But soon after that, Aunt May had me come home for my lunches. But that did not stop me from enjoying my playtime with my summer friends, mostly Mexican, Native American and poor white children of itinerant families.

In the Parkdale grade school, most of my friends were Caucasian or Japanese. There were no Mexican or Native Indian children present. Many of the finest orchards in the valley were headed by first-generation and second-generation Japanese who had immigrated to the Hood River Valley because the flora and rivers reminded them of their native country. The Japanese fruit growers were highly respected by other farmers for the quality of apple and pears they grew. It was natural for me to play with my Japanese mates since the Suzuki and Noji orchards flanked our family orchards. Yet I noticed that some white children stayed to themselves in cliques.

After Pearl Harbor, the memory of flashlights through the orchard and Japanese men meeting around our kitchen table at night with Aunt May, Uncle Harris, Uncle Glen and some Quaker men, I was aware that there was something unusual occurring, and that my relatives had different ideas about the planned Japanese relocation by the U.S. government than many of our neighbors who were caught up in the wartime fear and propaganda.

While our family was in the East, our Japanese friends and neighbors had been sent to relocation camps in California. They were forced to leave their well-manicured orchards with other owner growers in the valley. After the war, when the Japanese returned to their ranches, many found the ranchers they entrusted to take care of their property had pocketed the profits and had charged to them the debts. Thus their property was forfeited to the very ones they had trusted. Many of our finest Japanese ranchers lost everything and had to leave the valley to begin life elsewhere.

My uncle Glen and aunt Barbara had been a few of the exceptional growers who were scrupulously honest and returned to the Noji and Suzuki families both their orchards and profits intact. (The Suzukis still have their orchard today.)

I noticed another difference when we returned. Many new people had moved into the valley during and after the war. They were not welcomed by the older generation of growers who wanted the valley to remain exactly as it had been prior to the war. They wanted no new development, no new businesses or enterprises. They excluded newcomers socially, and resisted when they could.

As I entered my teens, I became even more sensitized to how people were treated and started supporting those who I thought were marginalized.

Thus I comforted my friend Blanche after I found her outside our classroom crying, who was told she had to leave school because she was pregnant. A dwarf boy in another class whom I loved became my "project." I gathered up those who were hurt and excluded, and we bound together in our own set of sufferers. To my parents' credit, they drove us to Youth for Christ in Hood River occasionally. One Christmas my father hitched up an old sleigh to our jeep, and a group of us went around the town and country singing carols to old people and shut-ins.

For some reason, unknown to me to this day, there were two teachers at the Parkdale High School who took a dislike to me and made my life miserable at times. They were married to each other. Phil was the math and science teacher, and Bonnie taught physical education. One day, another girl and I were a few minutes late coming up from the basement, as my basket with my gym clothes had been misplaced, and she had stayed behind to help me search for it. When we came upstairs to join the class, Mrs. Brown said, "We need to teach these two the importance of being on time!" She continued and barked, "Girls, form a line; we are giving them the spats!"

The two of us were told to get down on our hands and knees and ordered to slide through the long line of legs spread apart so as we passed through them, they could whack us on our behinds. When we emerged, our knees were scraped and bleeding from the rough and splintered hardwood floor. My parents reported this to the principal of the high school the next day, but it just made the situation worse. Mr. Brown announced to my math class the next day in a whiney, mocking voice that

"Ruth Higgins' parents" had come to school complaining that Ruth is not being treated fairly, so "be especially nice" to Ruth.

Mr. Brown flunked me in both classes, math and science, so I had to go to Portland for summer school at Multnomah College to make up the credits. There I took algebra and a biology class and got A's in both!

But even though some of my teachers in Parkdale were kind, those negative experiences compelled me to hope for a new beginning. I asked my parents if I could go live with an aunt and uncle in Dayton, Ohio so I could go to another school for a while.

The summer after my graduation from high school another incident of humiliation occurred at a group family summer camp. I had driven there to meet my parents and my sister Mary. After lunch one day we were on our own to rest, read, or enjoy a recreational activity. Another girl and I took bicycles to explore the island, and we got back late. A group of college girl counselors were waiting for us and drew us into a circle. They accused us of being lesbians and shamed us mercilessly but never explained what we did wrong. We both were mystified, but we knew we had broken some moral rule of the group. So I sought out my parents and asked them, "What is a lesbian?" They told me the girls were being ridiculous, but neither of them wanted to confront the leaders of the camp. I was disappointed in my parents and angry with the counselors, so early the next morning, I slipped out of the cabin into my car and escaped. Two hours later I called my parents to let them know I was safe, fearing their anger with me for leaving. My father, to my surprise, approved and said, "Keep going!"

I was chuffed and excited. I believe I came into my own true independence of mind that day. It was still a few weeks before I learned what being a lesbian was, but I knew on that trip, beyond a shadow of doubt, that singling out anyone for ridicule was wrong. I also knew I was strong and capable and realized in my heart I would always stand for the "outsider," whether it was racism, sexism, or classism. That summer before entering college, I began to pivot from impotence to strength. It has never left me.

There But for Fortune

— Linda Hennrick

THE PROPOSED ROAD INTO TOKYO from areas west of the city had been in the planning since after World War II under the occupation forces headed by Douglas MacArthur. By 2009, the Tokyo government had begun in earnest the process of buying up land to complete it. The road would go right through the house in Kugayama where my husband, Miki, and I had lived for the twenty-four years that we'd been married.

We loved the house and its location on the outskirts of Tokyo along the Tamagawa Jōsui, an historic manmade canal lined with cherry trees that had been built to bring fresh water into downtown Tokyo from the Tama River over 400 years earlier. Although we'd searched diligently for more than six months to find a new place to live, we weren't happy with any of our choices within the budget we were paid by the government to surrender our land. So when Miki, a Japanese citizen, was granted a green card to live and work in the U.S., we decided we'd be better off leaving Japan and relocating to the States.

Members of Miki's immediate family who lived in Tokyo already knew of our decision, but Miki thought he should tell his relatives living in other parts of Japan in person, not on the phone. In October 2010, a month before we were to leave Japan and move to the U.S., Miki and I paid a visit to the Satohs in Sakata, Yamagata Prefecture, to tell his mother's side of the family, followed by another trip to Namie, Fukushima Prefecture, to visit the Takamatsus on his father's side.

Fukushima Prefecture is a few hours' drive north of Tokyo on the Pacific Ocean. Miki and I had visited Namie, the city where most of his relatives lived, soon after we were married.

Back then we'd gone by train, but this time we drove along a newly opened highway that we heard would shorten our trip considerably. Our route took us directly past the Fukushima Nuclear Power Plant that would be in news headlines around the world less than five months later.

We arrived at the Ide residence with its attached liquor store in Namie in the early afternoon, the home of Ya-chan (his nickname) and his wife, Mikiko. Ya-chan's mother was Miki's father's older sister—Ya-chan and Miki were first cousins. We found Ya-chan in the store serving sake to locals who would drop in during the day to sit and enjoy a nip or two along with neighborly conversation. Looking at a Google map much later, I was surprised to see that the area where the liquor store and house were located is called Ide, and the Ide Liquor Store itself is marked prominently on the map along the banks of the Takase River.

We'd barely arrived, been served a cup of green tea, and explained why we'd come, when Ya-chan whisked us out of the house to visit other relatives who lived nearby leaving Mikiko to mind the store. In the shop's delivery van, we drove first through rice paddies and then west away from the city up a winding mountain road—only wide enough for one vehicle—that followed the Takase River upstream. Along the way, Ya-chan pointed out a large parking lot next to a steep gorge and told us that busloads of tourists came each year to view the colorful autumn leaves for which the gorge is famous. Unfortunately, we were too early in the season to see the acclaimed beauty of the area for ourselves.

A few houses clung to the side of the mountain along the road and we turned into the driveway of one, the house where Miki's father had been born and where a family of first cousins still lived. Miki had many fond memories of the house from when he was small and his father would bring him and his siblings to visit the homestead during vacations, but the old ramshackle house that he knew from younger years had since been rebuilt into a more modern home. I remembered the shed in front of the house where a cow had been in residence on our first visit, but the shed was now empty.

We took the cousins by surprise — Ya-chan hadn't told them we'd be coming. Still mid-afternoon, the men of the house were already a bit tipsy, a large bottle of sake open on the low table in the *tatami* mat room where the family of four was gathered watching TV, laundry hung to dry willy-nilly around the room. Recovering from their surprise at seeing us, they immediately offered us some sake as well, and since Ya-chan was driving, Miki accepted a small cup. When Miki explained the purpose of our visit, they all expressed their joy at our visit, and then their sadness to hear that we'd be leaving Japan. We stayed only long enough for Miki and his cousins to catch up on family news, but before we left, as is customary in Japan, we paid our respects at the family altar.

As we retraced our route down the mountain, hoping not to meet another vehicle coming up, the rain that had been threatening since our arrival in Namie earlier began to fall in earnest. The road grew wider, and we were again passing through rice paddies when we stopped to visit the first of several family graves scattered around the city, quite a few of them since Takamatsus had lived in the area for generations. Braving the rain with umbrellas Ya-chan provided, we said prayers and dutifully placed flowers and lit incense at each gravesite we visited. All the while, Ya-chan and Miki discussed each person and how they were related to that individual, but after a while, I couldn't keep all the relationships straight.

Before returning to Ya-chan's house, we made one last stop at Aunt Kiku's house. Kiku, now a widow, had been married to Hideo, Miki's father's younger brother. Aunt Kiku was a tiny woman who'd obviously been quite a beauty in her youth. One of her four daughters, Miki's first cousin Mineko, had married an American man and gone to live in the U.S. about the same time that I'd begun to live in Japan almost forty years earlier. Mineko and I had always thought it ironic that we'd ended up on opposite sides of the ocean. She'd soon be surprised to learn that her cousin Miki was living in the U.S. too.

Aunt Kiku offered us tea and showed us recent photos of Mineko and her husband, then led us to the family altar so that we could pay our respects. When I followed Miki's lead and lit incense and struck the *rin gong* or "singing bowl" twice with a metal mallet before putting my hands together in prayer, Aunt Kiku was surprised. "Mineko's husband has been here several times, but he never prays at the family altar," she said.

That night, Ya-chan and Mikiko treated us to dinner at their house. Mikiko brought out dish after dish of local delicacies while Ya-chan would run off occasionally to help customers at the liquor store. Mineko's sister Nagako, Aunt Kiku's youngest daughter and the only one of the four sisters who still lived in Namie, came by after dinner to visit and to drive us to our hotel so that Miki could enjoy some sake with dinner. We left our car at Ya-chan's overnight.

Breakfast at the hotel the next morning was a challenge for me, a simple buffet of Japanese fare—rice, miso soup, grilled fish, and pickles—but nothing I cared to eat. I watched Miki eat his breakfast and then he joined me in a walk down the street to a convenience store where I could buy a sandwich. I remember that as we walked toward the store, I could see the ocean only a short distance away.

Back at the hotel, we called Ya-chan to come and pick us up. By the time we checked out he'd arrived, but instead of going directly back to his house, he drove us around Namie to show us some of the landmarks, most of them already familiar to Miki from his many trips to Namie with his father as a boy. He and Miki talked about several mutual acquaintances and what they were doing while Ya-chan pointed out their houses as we drove by.

We stopped along the Takase River and got out of the van to see the barrier that had been built across the river to trap salmon. Salmon had all but disappeared from the polluted rivers of Japan, but thanks to a concerted cleanup effort, they were beginning to return to Namie each year. With them came the tourists—a restaurant to one side of the river advertised fresh-caught salmon lunches in large letters on its roof. We walked across a floating bridge to the middle of the river to watch up close as salmon swam frantically over the barrier on their way upriver to spawn. For me that was the highlight of our visit.

Back at the Ide house, we found that one of the cousins from the mountain had come to see us off, and she went with us to pay our respects at one last grave, Ya-chan's mother's grave, not far from the liquor store. The weather had cleared, and it was a bright autumn day—what a shame that we couldn't stay and enjoy it longer. But we had things to do in Tokyo, and a long drive to get there. It was hard to leave, but everyone was supportive and wished us well.

In the month before we left Japan in November 2010, we introduced Miki's brother Yoshihito and sister, Midori, to Skype. We knew it would be a good tool for us all to keep in touch when we moved to the U.S. Yoshihito, who'd seldom called us on the telephone in all the time we'd lived in Kugayama, loved Skype so much that he began to call us at all hours of the day.

Fast forward to March 2011.

In the four months since moving to the U.S., we used Skype almost daily to stay in touch with family and friends in Japan. Trying to figure out the best time to call turned out to be easy; an atomic clock we'd brought with us from Japan kept returning to Japan Time no matter how many times we tried to set it to Pacific Time. In the end, we gave up trying; having a clock set to Japan Time turned out to be a convenience.

Around ten o'clock p.m. Pacific Time on the evening of March 10, 2011, we received a Skype call from our friend Makoto Inoue in Hokkaido, the northernmost island of Japan. Makoto and his wife, Yukiko, had been good friends of ours in Tokyo, but when Makoto retired in 2010, he and Yukiko had decided to move to Sapporo to be near their son and his family. They left for Hokkaido only a few weeks before we left for the U.S.

But this wasn't a social call. A massive earthquake had hit the main island of Honshu, and Inoue excitedly pointed the camera on his computer at his TV set for us to watch the live scenes of a tsunami battering the coast of northern Honshu. It was hard to see the TV clearly, but what we could see was frightening. I turned on our own TV to see the same live feed being shown on CNN and other all-news channels as well. I soon realized this was a major disaster in the making. We were mesmerized by horror as the tsunami swept relentlessly inland and destroyed everything in its path.

It was the afternoon of March 11, 2011, in Japan. The earthquake and tsunami would later be known as the *Higashi Nihon Daishin-sai* or the Great East Japan Earthquake.

When we heard reports that the widespread earthquake in northern Honshu had been felt as far away as Tokyo, we called Miki's sister, Midori. When she didn't answer her land line, we Skyped Yoshihito at the barbershop where he worked. He answered right away. The camera revealed Yoshihito and his boss, Imai-san, crouched down near the floor as an aftershock shook the building. Yoshihito's eyes were wide as he told us about the intensity of the first earthquake and how the aftershocks were coming one right after another. We asked about Midori, but all he knew was that she'd gone out for the day. Maybe we could reach her on her cell phone.

Luckily, she answered. She was sitting on a train at Ikebukuro Station, about a twenty-minute ride from her home. She'd been out shopping when the earthquake hit and decided to cut her trip short, but she'd already been sitting on the train for half an hour and the trains weren't moving. Miki was able to fill her in on what we knew at that point, which was very little, but more than she knew. While we had her on the line, we heard an announcement over the PA system that train runs had been suspended indefinitely. Midori was only a twenty-minute walk from the neighborhood where Miki's family had lived when he was growing up, and Midori still had friends in the area. She said she'd go visit one of them until either the trains began to move again or she could find an alternate way home. Feeling relieved for the moment that she was okay and had a place to go, we hung up.

We Skyped Yoshihito again to let him know that Midori was on her way to a friend's house. He was happy to hear the news since he'd discovered that cell phone service was down in much of Japan and he couldn't reach her himself. We'd spoken to her just in time to let him know she was all right and where she'd be.

Midori didn't make it home that night. Like hundreds of thousands of other people in Japan, she was stuck where she was until train service began again the next morning. We later heard the many stories of people who walked home long distances that night, and many other stories of people like Midori who were lucky enough to find a place to stay. No one in Japan had much sleep. The aftershocks continued all night and for several months thereafter.

In California, as the horrors of the earthquake, the tsunami, and the aftermath became known to us and the rest of the world, we didn't get much sleep either. We were glued to the TV for news as it came in, watching over and over the scenes of the tsunami on its relentless path of destruction. The local Japanese-language cable channel began to broadcast free of charge so we were able to watch Japanese news reports over the next few weeks as they happened. Videos and news reports were posted all over the Internet as well.

We spoke with Midori and Yoshihito every day. They'd returned home to find belongings shaken down from shelves, but their house was structurally sound. In the ensuing weeks, they'd experience shortages in Tokyo. When gasoline became hard to find, Yoshihito gave up driving to work, using instead the electric bicycle I'd left in Japan with Midori — we often wondered if there were enough customers to keep the barbershop open or if he just didn't like staying home all day. Bottled drinking water became scarce at one point, and later there were shortages of yoghurt and other food products that were no longer coming out of the tsunami-hit zone. Like everyone else in Tokyo and the rest of Japan, Midori and Yoshihito managed to cope with each new situation.

The number of casualties continued to rise, but news reports soon began to center on damage to the nuclear reactors in Fukushima—the ones we'd passed on our visit to Namie—and fears of a meltdown. We were worried about Miki's relatives, whom we'd visited the previous autumn and lived near the reactors. None of them had Skype and the phone service was still down in some areas.

Yoshihito did his best to locate family members and let us know their whereabouts. A few days after the quake, we learned through him that Mikiko, cousin Ya-chan's wife, had been with a friend when their car was caught in the tsunami in Namie. Mikiko somehow managed to get out of the car and drag herself out of the raging water, but had to watch in helpless disbelief as the car and her friend were swept away. A kind stranger gave her a lift home where she found her husband unharmed but shaken, most of their house and adjoining liquor store destroyed by the quake. They spent an uncomfortable night in their delivery van. The next morning, they heard on the radio that the nearby nuclear reactors had been damaged in the quake and their area was being evacuated. Only taking what they were wearing, they drove their van inland to Ya-chan's sister's house in Fukushima City. When they rolled up in front of the house, the gas needle was on empty, but they were safe. Mikiko spent the next few weeks trying to locate her friend, fearing she was dead or missing. We were all relieved to hear her friend had been rescued and was in a hospital, nothing short of miraculous news. But the friend later died of her injuries. Still, Mikiko was thankful that her friend had been found at all and wasn't among the thousands still missing.

Relatives that lived in the house on the mountain in Namie where Miki's father was born were also accounted for. They had their own share of adventures trying to evacuate. When they found huge boulders blocked the only road down the mountain, they didn't sit around and wait to be rescued. These people were tough. They banded together and cleared the road themselves.

Miki's aunt Kiku with his cousin Nagako and her husband were also accounted for, safe in Tokyo with Nagako's sister Kyoko. Only one cousin, Sadamu, was still missing; no one knew his whereabouts, and they weren't able to reach him by phone. When the Red Cross began posting lists of names on the Internet of people at evacuation centers, Miki scoured the lists trying to find him. Finally, days later, his perseverance paid off. Sadamu's name appeared on a list of those evacuated to an elementary school near where he'd lived. Miki asked Yoshihito to call and find out for sure, but with telephone service still sketchy, Yoshihito was unable to get through. Miki tried calling the school from the U.S.—strangely enough, international calls still went through. It took a couple of tries and some long waits, but finally Miki was speaking to his cousin in person. Sadamu was at first surprised and then touched. He hadn't realized that he'd been "missing." Not long afterward, Sadamu and all the others from the shelter were also evacuated out of the area. By then the phones were working again, and Yoshihito was able to keep track of him.

The devastating earthquake and tidal wave that destroyed so much of the northern coast of the main island of Honshu, Japan, severely damaged the city of Namie. I thought about the convenience store near the ocean where I'd bought breakfast the morning we'd left Fukushima. That store and other buildings along the coast were undoubtedly gone, destroyed by the tsunami. The salmon run that had taken so many years to clean up was also ruined. The gorge along the Takase River with its beautiful autumn leaves would no longer be visited by busloads of tourists.

Worse still, one of the reactors at the nearby Fukushima Nuclear Power Plant had melted down. Miki's relatives, who'd lived in Namie all their lives, had been evacuated with the rest of the citizens of Namie and surrounding communities leaving them ghost towns.

Our relatives are all resettled now. The Red Cross has looked after them very well, and they don't want for creature comforts. But they will never be able to live in their hometown again. Visits to family homes and graves are allowed but closely monitored for radiation. The few belongings left behind that weren't destroyed by the earthquake or the elements can't be taken out as they too were radiated. The Takamatsu cousins lost everything, but are grateful for their lives.

Other family and friends living in Tokyo, who didn't lose their homes to the earthquake or the tsunami, may have also been radiated by the nuclear power plant meltdown. Some of them fled Tokyo for western Japan when news was first released concerning a "possible" meltdown at the nuclear reactor. But by then, it was already too late. We now know that radiation was released within minutes of the earthquake. It will be years before it's known to what extent their health may have been affected. The older of our acquaintances aren't worried; they're closer to the end of their lives than the beginning, and signs of radiation won't appear for several years. But what about their children? And grandchildren? How will the radiation affect them?

Like millions of people around the world, we'd felt helpless when we heard about the disaster. Even now we're amazed that we were able from a distance to help find members of Miki's family and relay messages to them when they were unable to do so themselves. We're thankful that we ourselves weren't in Japan to have to experience the quake and its aftermath. But if things had worked out differently in our lives, if we hadn't made the decision to leave Japan when we did, our story could have been much different.

Treasures in the Attic

— Marilyn McNeill

THE THIRD FLOOR — OR THE ATTIC — as Grandmother called it, was filled with many treasures. When I was a young girl I spent many summers at Grandma and Grandpa Roy's farm. The farm was two hundred fifty acres of some of the finest farm land in Canada. The farm was called Cloverdale.

A typical day at the farm began with chores in the barn. These chores consisted of milking a large dairy herd, feeding the horses, pigs, chickens and the rest of the farmyard animals. Grandpa and the hired men got up early to start their chores. I did mine later in the morning. I was in charge of the barn cats. Grandpa left milk in a small pail in a tiny cupboard for me to give to the barn cats. I would often want to bring them in the house, but Grandma said they would not be happy inside, and they should stay in the barn so they can find little mice. I don't think I could have caught one anyway because they were not all that friendly. Often I would find a new litter up in the hay mow. Hay was kept in the upper part of the barn. A small ladder led up to the upper floor, and hay was thrown down to feed the horses. Grandpa had eight draft horses. These were beautiful horses with lovely feathered feet. Grandpa had a black riding horse called Dixie. In the evening he would ride Dixie back to check on the cattle. Sometimes he would take me with him. I would ride in front and him behind. I can't remember if Dixie had a saddle or not.

After the barn chores the men came to the big house for a hearty breakfast, truly a big country breakfast. This was served in the summer kitchen. The long pine table was covered with oil cloth and would seat twenty easily. A big black stove sat in one corner near the back pantry. Grandma would bake bread and pies in that oven later in the morning. A hot fire was made in the stove and when the heat was just right, Grandma did the baking. I can't recall any burnt pies. She was an excellent cook.

After dinner I was to have some quiet time. I looked forward to this quiet time because I could go to a special place, the Third Floor. I would go up the back stairs, down the long hall to a third stairway that led to the third floor. This was not just an ordinary attic because the ceilings were high. Across the front were large windows also beautiful stained glass windows on one side. Near the window was a small bed made from willow branches and a table and a beautiful chest. On the back of the table were the markings "McL." These were on the beautiful chest, as well. In the drawers were some books and a doll with a china face.

After quiet time I joined Grandma for some tea and scones in her parlor. It did not take me long at all to get to the main floor because I came the front way and slid down the huge banister. Lucky for me there was a large wooden ball at the end, or I would have slid right onto the floor. I had a special teacup that I used each time; my tea was really warm milk with just a spot of tea. I guess Grandma didn't want me to leave with any bad habits. We would eat scones with fresh berries and whipped cream. Behind the smokehouse was a raspberry patch, and on the other side strawberries grew. It was my chore, too, to pick the berries. The first few days I would pick one, eat two, and tell Grandma that there just were not too many right now. She smiled and would always say, "Well maybe next time." I have many, many happy memories of my summers at the farm.

Time passes quickly. Thirty years later we were living in Stratford, Ontario where my husband began his orthopedic practice. Our home was about fifteen miles away from the farm and although my grandparents were no longer there, we visited my uncle Wilfred and my aunt Reta on the family farm.

One morning, I was having coffee with my neighbor and commented on her lovely dining room furniture. She told me she bought it when she bought the home. On the back was "McL," the same imprint as my treasures in the attic. My grandma was Agnes McLagan before she married, and my grandpa James Roy. Where did this furniture come from, and did the McL mean McLagan? There were many old stories about our family and the beautiful furniture. I wondered where all the furniture was made and if the McL was indeed our family.

Belonging to this writers' class I have become interested in looking into some of our family stories ... and I have found the secret of "McL" written on the back of the furniture.

Briefly, in the first half of the twentieth century, Stratford was home to Canada's largest furniture industry. It employed about one quarter of the city's workforce, the second only to the railway. During the 1920s, about one-sixth of the furniture made in Canada was made in Stratford.

George McLagan had spent a few years in the early 1880s as an apprentice in the furniture business in Grand Rapids. It was his dream to return to his hometown, and in 1900 he built the first of the large furniture factories in the east end of Stratford. This was to become the furniture district of Stratford. Some of the McL pieces were shipped as far away as California and East to Newfoundland. George McLagan was destined to become the leader of Stratford's furniture boom. The McLagan Furniture Company was the leading company until the 1930s.

I never knew what became of these attic treasures. I wish I had acquired some McL furniture. It turns out these *were* part of my family history, as I *am* related to all those McLagans who were my grandmother's cousins.

What Is He Doing!

— Corinne Lee Murphy

THE WOMAN WAS READING the local newspaper and saw a spectacular winter travel deal to London or Paris offered by Continental Airlines, which included a hotel and tours. There was a number to call, and she impulsively dialed it. The female operator said that, as this was a national promotion, there would be a wait of perhaps forty minutes, but that it would be a mistake to hang up because the dates and flights were filling up quickly. By the time an operator came back on the line, forty-five minutes later, the dates were limited. She chose December 30 to begin the trip for herself and her five-year-old son, who would only miss a few days of kindergarten.

And, so, off they went for their first adventure abroad together. The boy had received a Game Boy™ for Christmas, and the woman had purchased new games she did not give to him until they arrived at the airport. The boy was delighted and engrossed in his games for the hours of waiting and travel.

They arrived in London in the morning, having traveled all night, she with no sleep and he with less than he needed. They found their way to a charming little hotel, Victorian, with its wooden facade painted a pristine white. They walked into the lobby filled with overstuffed leather chairs and sofas and dark woods, decorated for the Christmas now passed. It was charming to their exhausted eyes. Their room was not ready and would not be for hours, but the clerk took pity on the woman and her small fellow traveler and provided a tiny staff room with a full-size bed where they slept for hours before moving to their room. By this time it was around 10 p.m., and there was no food service at the hotel. They were directed to a "sister hotel" down the street, two blocks.

So into the dark night, on an unfamiliar street, they ventured. The hotel was indeed a "sister" with its white portico and small faux balconies at each window. Inside it was warm and crowded with chattering people in a room with a long wooden bar, booths and tables. She asked if they might order food, and the staff said that the restaurant was closed, only the bar was open with olives and such. The boy was the only child in the room and kindness again prevailed. A woman cheerfully went into the kitchen and foraged for food for them. And they rang in the New Year in a room full of celebration, in warmth and with full stomachs.

The next day was for exploring. They walked down three blocks to the large street of Bayswater which bordered the north side of Hyde Park and Kensington Gardens, turning right to find Queensway where they would find the two tube stops, surprisingly close together but servicing different lines, the Central and the Circle. She showed the boy how she was reading the maps and signs and where to stand to wait for the train. And after a couple of missteps, he learned to hang on as the train lurched toward new stations.

As they walked the City, she explained that the cars came from different directions than at home, that there were even warnings at the curb to look to the right. And she noticed with amusement that her son felt the need to protect her for the first time in his young life; that at intersections his small arm would fling out straight in front of her as his head rapidly swung back and forth, watching for cars, preventing her from stepping into danger.

And then he asked what if something were to happen to her. What would happen to him, he asked urgently. She could see that it was a real fear; they were so far from home, so far from anyone or anything he knew. She knew it was not enough to say nothing would happen to her, that everything would be fine. She told him that in the unlikely event that something did happen, he should ask an adult to help find a policeman, and that they would take him to the American Embassy, and they would call his father, and his father would come to get him. He had a plan, a contingency, and that seemed to placate him.

266

She wanted the boy to like museums, to not associate them with drudgery or boredom, so they set off to the British Museum with the resolve that they not stay if he began to tire. They went straight to the Egyptian mummies which she thought, correctly, would interest a little boy. They also gazed at a leathery man, in a fetal position, that had been found preserved in the bogs in the north and now was preserved under a glass dome. Then she asked him what else he would like to look at, and she was surprised that he was fascinated by Ancient Greek and Roman statuary as she followed him from room to room.

But then there was enough. He was hungry. They stopped at the gift shop on the way out and purchased a small pencil box of metal in the shape of a sarcophagus, richly decorated both inside and out, for his kindergarten teacher. And they purchased a similar box for him. And she bought for herself a tiny metal Egyptian cat, deceptively heavy for its size. The cat was black and lean and sitting erect, its head straight up, watchful.

They wandered into the cold and found a roasted chestnut vendor with his wares steaming in the chill, and they shared their first chestnuts together as they searched for a restaurant that looked inviting for a proper meal.

It was hard for the boy to adapt to the new time zone, and he would awaken early, before daylight, so she would entertain him as quietly as possible to keep from bothering the other sleeping guests with his pent-up energy, only somewhat successfully. There was whiffle ball, the small plastic balls safe for indoor play and stories, but it was a challenge to keep the boy occupied until breakfast opened at 7 a.m. in the basement of the hotel, to her exhausted relief.

On the second morning, as they sat at their table eating breakfast, she noticed a woman, pregnant, and accompanied by the only other child in the room. She watched them carefully as they spoke between themselves a language that she did not recognize. She supposed it to be a tribal dialect because they appeared to be African, although their clothing was European. The boy seemed to be about her son's age. When the African woman spoke to the waitstaff it was in British English, so the woman knew she would be understood if she approached them. So, she walked to their table and spoke to the woman introducing her son and saying they were on holiday and wondering if they had plans or would they perhaps like to go to the playground in the park with her and her son that afternoon. The mother looked surprised at first but agreed that they would very much like to do that, that it would be lovely for her son to have someone with whom to play, and they arranged to meet later.

The mothers and their sons crossed Bayswater and walked to the far side of park, almost to its southern edge, rounding the Serpentine, the large but narrow body of water than snakes through Hyde Park. As they walked, the mothers talked. She was obviously from America with her pronounced American accent. The other mother was from South Africa, she said, and on holiday before her new baby would come, while her husband remained working. The woman knew of Apartheid, the separation between the races in South Africa, but she did not ask anything about the situation for the South African woman in her homeland. She thought to herself that her husband must have accommodated himself to the situation and made himself useful such that his wife could afford holidays in Britain.

The mothers talked about California and what they had been doing on their respective vacations. They talked about the new baby, a girl. They watched the boys recruit other boys on the playground to play soccer with the ball she had packed so that her son could have relief from museums. It was the crispest of days; the clouds had departed. It was one of those rare London winter days with the sun almost impossibly bright. But it was very, very cold, cold enough to snow if there had been moisture. But there was not. And all the children played soccer with abandon and delight in the winter sun.

The mothers sat together on the bench in their wool coats and gloves and scarves. Her son wore the jacket he had begged his grandmother for and so had received it even though it was a little large. It was brown synthetic leather and looked like a pilot's bomber jacket with patches of valor and a small American flag, as if there was any doubt that he was American. It was padded inside and provided warmth along with his gloves and knit cap.

It was so evident that the boys had such fun together that the mothers planned to get together again though the African family would be leaving in two days. The woman and her son were booked for a London tour the following day, and the African mother tried to book seats so they could all spend their last day in London together. But the seats were all booked, and they sat in the lobby saying their goodbyes.

Her son noticed that his new friend's shoe was untied and, anxious to show his skills, bent down and began to work. The African child looked astonished and said to his mother, "What is he doing!"

The mother straightened herself almost imperceptibly and said serenely, but with what appeared to be deep satisfaction, "He is tying your shoe."

What My Working Life Has Been About
— Larry Kueneman

THE MAJORITY OF MY WORKING LIFE, fully thirty-five years, was spent as a technical writer. Here, I worked with the explanations of parts designers, engineers, and often people with doctorates. These are folks who write and speak in languages I call academese*. My job was to rewrite their writings and instructions so the product user, the person I call "the guy on the street" could understand them. The end products were intended for use by mechanics and people in parts departments, as well as people who bought a product that came with instructions.

My last formal position in this field was as head of publications for the Parts Division of American Honda Motor Company. I came on board in mid-1971. Here, the job was to provide parts catalogs for products Honda sold, including vehicles. I was hired at the time the company mostly produced motorcycles, and was preparing to introduce their first real automobile, the 1973 Honda Civic. The parent company in Japan provided materials both in parts illustrations, which were well done as far as they went, along with a listing of those parts, mostly in English.

For a few years Honda had produced and sold two tiny, two-passenger cars in Japan, the N car and the Z car, that each had an air-cooled motorcycle engine. In accordance with their extensive motorcycle experience, Honda Japan had historically provided their printed materials for use by parts and service department usage in just two sections, a frame section and an engine section. I was expected to prepare these two for presentation to the Parts Departments of new Honda automobile dealerships.

It was here that old experience that I had gained working in the Parts Department of a Ford dealer before my technical writing experiences really came into play.

I went to the head of the division to explain that in America, a parts catalog for use by automobile dealers would need to be broken down into more than two sections. It would need to have that separate section each for engine and frame parts, but it would also need sections for engine cooling, electrical, steering, braking, upholstery, windshield washers, glass, door hardware, et cetera. I was told to proceed as I felt was in the best interest of the catalog users, so I assigned one writer to make the appropriate separation of data and parts illustrations for these multiple sections.

The conversion actually took about ten months, but resulted in the catalog design used by dealers today, almost fifty years later.

My life has continued as one who questions everything; not to deny something, but to see the truth in each subject I see, or think and write of. As a writer of nonfiction, I work to follow the guidance I found in a Rudyard Kipling poem published in 1902. I virtually use this poem as a guidance for my life, and encourage others to do so as well. I believe it to be a form of stability that will serve to guide mankind to the phase of humanity I call Civilization. That poem's first four lines are as follows:

> I keep six honest serving men
> (They taught me all I knew)
> Their names are What, and Why, and Where
> And How, and When, and Who.

* Academese refers to the terminology used by professionals within many endeavors. They use terminology used only by their particular industry. It makes life easy for them, but hearing their wording is often very confusing. For example, if someone is speaking to you who is employed as a designer of certain specific

electronic equipment, and they are talking about a product they designed, their conversation will include terminology no one outside their industry understands, and this can be a problem for clarity. Each and every industry uses its own terminology that is unique to them, using some words no one outside their industry understands. It is the role of a technical writer to transpose information provided by the product designer into terminology the buyer can readily understand. A problem exists today in that most corporations have gotten rid of technical writers, and have had the designers of the products provide instructions. This is almost disastrous, and the problem continues to get worse.

Willie McCool: A Homage
William C. McCool
(Commander, USN) ~ Nasa Astronaut

—Mark Gaulding

MUSIC HAS BEEN ONE of the most important aspects of my life. I sang in choirs the first chapters in life. Standing amongst a group of voices, chorally, is one of the most vibrant, life-affirming experiences that I've experienced. The collective voices create a vibration that transcends anything I've ever felt. It doesn't always occur, as many choir leaders could attest. But when it does, it is the sweetest of spots in life and music. All of the voices become simultaneously one harmonious wave of sound and energy. It is pure synchronicity. It is most sublime for those who are singing.

Many of my happiest early life memories were from my choir experiences.

In my mid-teens, during the late 1970s, I sang in my church choir for a few years. The choir was named the Wesley Singers. We were under the direction of a brilliant organist and musical conductor, Gordon McMillan, at the Lubbock, Texas First United Methodist Church.

I was then, and remained many years after, a tenor. I loved singing. But there was one other who was more passionate than all. We were seated next to each other in the early days by our music leader. It was a strategic placement because I was a younger neophyte to the choir, and I was seated next to the strongest singer.

His name was Willie McCool. He was a tall, blond young man, a couple of years older than I. He was a competitive high school swimmer, and I remember he often smelled freshly pristine of chlorine. And occasionally his blond hair had an otherworldly green glow. He was the most heavenly person I've ever met.

Willie McCool loved to sing. With every molecule in his body. He sang joyously. He was the most vociferous singer in our choir (in all fairness, there were a few others who sang with his gusto) … His beautiful face and head held high looking to the skies. And he sang with passion. I remember it was a remarkable experience to sit beside him. He sang and expressed himself in a way that would transcend our Lubbock church choir.

In 1978, the Wesley Singers went on a three-week "friendship ambassador" tour of then Soviet Union Russia and Poland. We shared our music in cities such as Moscow, Leningrad (now St. Petersburg), Warsaw, and Kiev, among others. It was a remarkable and transformative experience for a choir of young adults and our chaperones. For me, it truly influenced and guided my future, especially the visit to the most infamous of Nazi concentration camps — Auschwitz — in Poland.

In a couple of decades the USSR collapsed most spectacularly with the symbolic tearing down of the Berlin Wall culminating in 1990 which created worldwide celebration. And then, in the new 21st century, the world would witness yet another horrific global event like the Holocaust and the erection of the Berlin Wall … 9/11/01. These events impacted and monumentally changed the global landscape in just a few short decades since my first trip abroad in 1978.

Early in 2003 I was commuting from San Diego to Palm Springs. We were in the process of selling our home in San Diego and moving back to the desert. I had started my job at Eisenhower Medical Center in Rancho Mirage, and I was commuting back and forth for a few weeks until we closed on the purchase of our home in Palm Desert.

On February first I was driving home via my customary route on Highway 74, which is the back route to travel between Palm Desert and San Diego. In Temecula, Highway 74 runs into Interstate 5 and, traveling southbound, you end up in San Diego.

I was listening to NPR on the radio as I merged onto I-5. The radio was reporting that something had happened to NASA's Columbia space shuttle. Residents from a broad swath of Texas reported seeing something happen in the sky. Shuttle flights had become so routine that they weren't as widely reported. Inexplicably I had followed this particular shuttle flight a little more than usual because there had been some damage to the shuttle at liftoff.

As I headed to San Diego I continued to listen to the news reports. A short time later they announced that the Columbia had been destroyed upon re-entry. It occurred over the state of Texas.

I was horrified.

They started listing the Columbia's shuttle crew members. I heard "William McCool," and it struck me as familiar. But I just couldn't think of why. I kept thinking *McCool ... McCool ... that sounds so familiar.*

I had left Texas in 1985 and had lived in California for a couple of decades. As I drove further on the freeway, I continued to be confounded, because the name "William McCool" seemed so familiar. Suddenly it dawned on me that this was Willie McCool, my fellow tenor in the Wesley Singers—that sweet, tall, blond beautiful young man we traveled to Russia and Poland with in 1978. He was one of the purest souls I remember. And he always sang with such pride and joy.

I had to pull off the freeway when I finally realized that Willie McCool had become an astronaut (not surprising). I was in shock and very upset. I hadn't thought of Willie in decades. And suddenly I hear that he had just perished in the Colombia disaster.

This has been a very personal and painful experience in my life, as I am sure it has been with all my fellow Wesley Singers.

I hadn't even known he'd achieved such greatness as an astronaut, until I heard of his tragic demise. There wasn't anyone to share the shock and loss with. I had lived a very full and complicated life since I left Texas. How had my previous life become so compartmentalized from my current life? It upset me.

I was extremely troubled for weeks. It was the first time that I fully understood this concept that I deal with firsthand these days that whole parts of my life are nothing but a memory. And there is no one left to share the experience with.

Everyone in 1978 knew that Willie wanted to become an astronaut. And he did!

Since then I revisited and am mesmerized by the beautiful line from Walt Whitman in *Leaves of Grass*: "I sing the body electric." That personifies the Willie McCool I sang with in the Wesley Singers tenor section in 1978.

Poetry

A Consecrated Thing

—Richard A. Vasquez

There is a great divide
between where we hide
and that place
where we can find
the light that allows us to see
it is not a random choice
but more about a scared child's
inner voice
that tells us that it's not
the revealing of the truth
but rather
the hiding from it
that sets us free
the conscience is not
a consecrated thing
but instead something that must be trained
to remain inside us
the heights that we can reach
start from the bottom that we've found
there's a point past how far we can sink
places dark and terrifying
but there are no limits to what lies above
the blue heavens merging into a endless universe
and to such he rose
after teaching us
how love displaces the heaviness of hate
thus bringing light and
the breath of life
to all corners of the circle

A Mother's Ode

— Anita Sharf

We should have flown more, you and I
The busyness of living reduced our lives
And for that I apologize
There should have been more time
For fairy tales and nursery rhymes
We should have spun more real into dreams
Using scent and laugh and feel
I manacled you
With admonitions
While butterflies escaped cocoons
Free and beautiful
Flitting from blossom to bloom
Seeking honey from strange and wondrous vines
That trailed to Never-Never-Land
Now, I say follow the Monarch
Sip the clover and arc your wings
To dive and soar or hover
Over reflected rainbows on rings of dew
Go frolic, Tinkerbell, Peter and You

And Yet

— Anita Sharf

I did not know him well — this tall young man in blue
And yet — he was my kin — and when we met after years
We knew
That there was a deep feeling — a bond —
That neither miles
Nor years could break
He was so proud — so very straight and trim —
He loved
His country —
Today this to some this may sound trite and grim
I was there for his graduation from a training:
Hard — callous — cold — miserable — degrading — and yet
The best a man could have or get — for it trained his body
For war and hardships — and more —
And it trained 'esprit de corps'
Such camaraderie — a closeness — an undefinable love
My eyes were wet that day — the colors were on parade —
Un — sophisticated — and yet
He did not know how or why we were in this war —
But he knew
We were — that was enough —
So he went — this tall — handsome — young
Boy — no not a boy — a man — you can be sure
The telegram read — 'Fragments in head and body —
Shot by friendly fire' — and we ask
Why — God — why this young man — is there a purpose
We — do not — know — we — cannot understand

Continued ...

But we know there is a God — and He loved him — too — and I
Think — is it better to lose a child wrapped around a tree
In metal — or mentally lost by drugs or bugaboo
I look at my four-year-old man child — I — do not want to bring
Him up to be — 'shot by friendly fire' — and yet
Isn't that what kills us all — 'shot by friendly fire' —
When we least expect it —
And are so unaware
So — cheers — my dear young man in blue —
For you were so proud and true
And said — I do — I care

A Solitary Walk

— Richard A. Vasquez

Even though we walk
amongst many
we walk alone
the view from our eyes
is ours alone
the things we fight
the fears we face

we are born
with *goodness*
with *peace*
can we hold on to what
we were given
or do we
squander it
what will we do today
to change the greenness
   around us
the blueness of the sky
world peace
hunger
what holds us back
what is greater than
   our promise
lonely amongst many
we are one
can one make a difference

fight the monsters
we create
inside ourselves
wallow in our own
unanswered pain

can we reach out
touch the face of God
do you still believe
can you still believe

Beyond What We Realize

—Richard A. Vasquez

From the silos of tomorrow
comes the replenishing
of passion
inspiration
hope
and even when the days surrender
into remembrance
they remain the connecting points
of the infinite
the whole
when I reach out for your hand
I understand that I am reaching
to touch stardust that traveled
eons of time
unfathomable distances
past infinite possibilities
to be here on this planet
as you
as me
brought within reaching distance
by inscrutable serendipity
and when our fingers touch
flesh to flesh

Continued ...

the eventuality becomes far greater
than the explosions in stars
the immeasurable span of the universe
the immutable laws that govern
the circles of gravity
for that very moment
of lucidity
of consciousness
of choice
and the knowing of that feeling
surpasses
all the inanimate
unreasoning laws

and exists
as its own
endlessly
in the stream of time

Divergence

— Larry Ballard

I wake and start to write down a dream
This is not the place for dreams
Dreams are too real
too substantial for these pages

I yearn for the
reality of the dream
The overt conflict between warring parties
the crispness of the terrain
the directness of the antagonist
the clarity of direction

He is here with me now
a driving force in the waking hours
His emergence is subtle
He sells our sameness
with unworldly deftness

I throw him scraps
to keep his hunger down
Can't feed him what he wants
I give him bits of symbols to appease him

Today we are at odds
a trace of horses locked
in determined divergence
Trudging heads down
Foraging for the inconsequential
Rolling past and over the interesting
and events of consequence

Continued ...

Smashing them under the treads of monotony
Too tired to stop and examine
what is interesting
or complex
The joy of completion
not remembered
Each of us without drive
in different directions
Loss of hope about different things

The exhaustion of straining against his needs
and his mine
brings us to the ground
entangled in harness and strap

We gratefully slip
into sleepless dreams
away from the dogged yoke of unity
free from the bonds of reality
and the certainty of unrelenting
drudgery

His warm breath no longer
hisses profanities in my ear
My sense of him diminishes
as he moves to darker regions
where he can feed on the ghosts
of unresolved sins

Both dreading the coming dawn

Dust Walking on Dust

—Richard A. Vasquez

Yet we have entered this linear path
where time never retreats
alone and lost
deaf and mute of the language we have known before
only to come to learn what the demons speak
to learn what angels would never say
where is it from which we came
footprint in the dust moving one direction
only one direction
I in my lemming's chore proceed through the open door
one more horizon to reach
one more hill to climb
what is atop to find
the vanishing of the familiar path
the disappearing of the past
no way to look behind
dust walking on dust
moving in one direction
only in one direction
there are no causes
to both believe in
and disbelieve
that which we can
summon through
our inner strength
is not just
the willpower to succeed
but also that which
does not allow us to be defeated

Continued ...

faith in ourselves
faith in the power of
something greater than ourselves
lines drawn into the invisible
that we are dared not to cross
limits
barriers
apathy
ignorance
circled by the wagons of fear

I Am Invisible

— Richard A. Vasquez

I am the vessel of what I carry
that which makes me
me
as well as that
which I have left behind
because of the
chasms of challenges
and the bridges that couldn't be crossed

loneliness often comes from the knowing
of choices we cannot make
seeing the roads we cannot take
walking through places
where we cannot ask others to come
certain
they would not understand
also
the not wanting to take the risk
of being vulnerable
being misunderstood
of people thinking
we need someone to love
and someone to love us

fear comes from
a voice that does not answer
when you call it
the sun that does not come out
from behind the clouds

Continued ...

and the realization
that if the answer is not there
it is not there
so at some point
where or how we choose to hide
becomes irrelevant
because
you do not need to hide
what cannot be seen
and the conclusion then becomes
that the needing someone to love
is illusionary
because what gets left behind
are the best parts of ourselves
thus I am not me
I am invisible

Isolation

—Larry Ballard

Sweet, sweet child
So mild
For a thrill
will kill
any who come for him
leave him there
not aware
he's alone

Let him roam
through the loam
of empty fields
this sweet, sweet child
who simply smiled
when his mother left him alone

It's 119 Degrees in the Shade

— Elia Vasquez Fuller

no respite
heat June through September
baking oven car windows
door handles sizzle
plants scorched
flower pots empty
no patio paper reading or eating
abandoned evening walks
compressor jolts loud
their roaring constant
keeps napping babies
and grannies awake
drowning out hoots from owls
and other screeching fowls
at night looking for mates
electric bills that kill

swamp coolers mute
soaked in drenching humidity
neighbors don't stop to talk
in triple digits
oh relentless brutal
steaming
burning
heat
we envy those who escape—
snowbirds ... deserters
desert rats would have an
easier time in hell
after spending summer here
ahh ...
but we won't have to ...
we already served our time.

Kissing Frogs

—Larry Ballard

He sat patiently
waiting his turn

(snapping up an occasional fly)

as she skipped by

She turned and smiled at him
then bent and kissed his cousin on the chin

then another
and another

As he watched her
turn around the lake
bending and kissing a prince to make
he continued to sit in the sun and bask

she continued her awful task
bending and kissing
and wiping her lips
chasing down frogs
with hops and skips

Continued ...

When she passed near
where she could hear

he asked

"All the frogs in the pond you kiss so free
why is it you never kiss me?"

"Why I couldn't kiss you
it wouldn't make sense
I only kiss frogs
never a prince."

Long Dry Spell

— Larry Ballard

It's raining.
The well is dry.
Shallow water in here.

The voices and presences
are gone.
The dogged apathy of everyday life
swept away any dredges of the divine.

Sometimes the creative surge comes.
This place and that place
become tied together.
A fleeting engagement.

But maybe . . .
A little of that old curiosity.
A gentle probing.
A soft ripple of energy.
A small spark fanned into a roaring fire
that once warmed
and sometimes singed.
Maybe.

Mother's Day

— Richard A. Vasquez

Between earth and sky
we should not cry today
but instead
rejoice
and pass on what we have been given

there are those still left to save
as they saved us

from the day we were born
they drew us near
and we heard
the heartbeat we knew
since before they bore us
the heartbeat
we still hear
in the *clicks of time*
and in the rhythms
that define us
no matter where they are

on this terrestrial plane
or given to the heavens

we can always find them
because *they live on inside us*
of goodbyes said
or never said
it does not matter
Love is eternal
goodbyes

Music

—Elia Vasquez Fuller

you arrive song of
the morning dove
with love
and sunlit
windchimes playing

to rattling pots
in the kitchen
once my mother's domain
now unfamiliar terrain
to her

Music ... you restore the light
in her green eyes
and she sings once again
recalling moonlight serenades
sung to her
outside her window

until the lost look in her eyes
sinks her like
a sun going down
behind stormy clouds

Continued ...

a cold avalanche
swallows me up in darkness
I can't breathe

Music my savior
you lift me into sunlight
soaring above tropical shores
Jobim's soft samba in my ear

Music
Healer
Comforter
Hope
to hearts of all
ages tongues and strife

delight to those who delight
refuge to those who need it
tonight I drift off with Bocelli
the melody lingers in my dreams

My Gym Teacher

— Ruth Gray

In the middle of my senior year
whole, happy, healthy
I moved from a big city in Ohio
to a little country high school in Oregon.
my first day I couldn't find the wire basket
to change into my shorts.
Blanche stayed behind to help me search.
we were late for class.

In the auditorium
(which doubled as a gym when cleared of chairs)
our teacher, hands to hips, eyed us crossly
"We need to teach Ruth and Blanche a lesson.
Line up, girls, spread your legs and
give them what they deserve."

The punishment was called "The Spats"
but I did not know it until later
humbled and bent down on all fours
we crawled through the gauntlet
of slaps and spanks on our behinds
our knees bleeding from the splintered floor
scraped scabbed it really hurt
our eyes stung

Continued ...

"Don't bother feeling sorry for yourselves
nor whining to your parents," she sneered
her name was Bonnie
I don't remember if she introduced me
it doesn't matter if she did or not.

I hated high school I hated gym
and never since liked the name "Bonnie"

I wear long skirts to cover my scars.

Ode to Pumpkins

—Elia Vasquez Fuller

sister
of the orange harvest
moon
yellow flower
bloom
child of traveling
vine until
magic fairy dust turns
you
into Cinderella's carriage
Indian friend
to pilgrims introduced
many moons ago with
prayers of thanksgiving
your precious
gift
scooped out
saved
for planting next
winter's feast

while
our jack-o-lanterns glow
toothy grins for
ghoulish
wide-eyed
trick-or-treaters
you linger through
fall
to grace Thanksgiving Day
golden spun pumpkin
pies
bountiful
your roasted seeds
an extra treat
Calabasa Gloriosa reyna
I crown you
Queen of the season
in any language
Royal Majesty
Empress
of all autumn fruits

Painted Thunder

—Richard A. Vasquez

Storms brew
within you
outside you
nature
mimics your pain
the wind
sings
its brooding song
raindrops accompany
beating anxious percussive rhythms
the inside of dark grey clouds
show
the scowl
of angry light
changing the colors around them
bolting
jagged fingers
reach out
to touch earthly things
tearing them asunder
the fiery glow
momentarily awakens the darkness
making all things bright
then quickly
returning to darkness
the timid ground
shakes

Continued ...

with the sound of painted thunder
a reminder
we that play God
even as
we forget all about Him
are alive
are mortal

there are no places safe
nature's wrath
knows no limits
there are no places safe
the storms of life
are inescapable
there are no places safe
when anger-filled dark clouds
taint the glow of light
there are no places safe
when the
earthly things
we touch
we touch
with jagged fingers
there is no end
to the storms within
when
the enlightenment we find
we leave behind
as we retreat
into the darkness

Rehearsal in the Quad

— Anita Sharf

Multi-lingual pizzicato
Plinked out of mouths agitato
Rasp harsh as the crisp October day
Note-black strands swing in rhythm
To syncopated nods
While finger batons
Puncture the air, all maestros
Pulling forth staccato sounds
Deeper-than-brown eyes dance
The façade of comprehension
Supportive smiles weave like
Reeds of jazz greats
In and out and wrapped about
Consonance and assonance
Titters waft on the mild Santana
When piccolo tongues refuse to perform
Woodwind, brass, percussion, strings
Tune to produce the discordant
Orchestration of communication for
THE NEW AMERICAN SYMPHONY

Remembrance

— Larry Ballard

forgotten ancient chimes
whose rhythms were lost
in the chaos of troubled times.

remembered by a mote of
passed on flesh
to move and weave
through song and dreams,
and soft recognition in color
and form.

listen closely.
you will hear whispers
from a child not born,
unmuted
by the noise of misconception.

listen even closer
to the almost forgotten
song you used to sing.
still lovely
still waiting to be heard.

Reprise

— Ruth Gray

do you remember
the songs of the sparrows
and how perfectly white
the blossoms shone
on the pear trees that day?
how blue the sky that framed Mt. Hood?
the one cloud feathering over its point?
the grass shimmering green
as we stretched our bodies in the front yard
how soft the breezes
with scent of salvia trembling our hair
our babies tumbling about
us sun kissing faces

I still hear the music of that day clearly do you?
you could if you would

I wonder if you remember
how that perfect day
matched the beauty
closeness
the flowing melodies
between you and me

we have lost the harmony
I wonder
can we recapture
the shining bliss of that perfect day?

Stormswept

— Ruth Gray

Black chrome night in car
rain on rain
little sister sweats
fog on glass
tears on windows fall.
grey on grey
Leaving Great Aunt Mary

Black chrome morning dawns
rain on rain
chill on chill
little sister shivers
fever climbing high
cloud of fear surrounds:
breath on breath
Pray for Great Aunt Mary

Black chrome day of thunder
rain on rain
wind on wind
sighs and cries
through flood and flash
strike of lightening comes:
news of death.
grey on grey to black.
Pray to Great Aunt Mary

Continued ...

["Stormswept" is a childhood memoir of my experience with my family in a Model T car on our way to the Los Angeles General Hospital with my three-year-old sister Barbara, Mary and me in the backseat, my father and mother with baby Rachel in front. In memory of Mary Harris Allen, 1877-1942, my aunt May, with whom I lived on her Hood River, Oregon apple and pear ranch from 1936 to 1942 while I was three to nine years of age. RG]

Super Clucks

— Anita Sharf

Our beaks ever pecking
We stood in preening circles
Clicking, clacking, clucking
We were Super Clucks
Hovering, covering, smothering
Our perfect young
Black crepe dresses
Single strands of pearls
Camouflage for Clucks of chicks
Raised Dr. Spockily, Clockily, Rockily
Eyes beaded with parentinitis
No war or poverty penetrated our nests
We were busy hatching, scratching, latching
A sophisticated Rhode Island Red approached
Our circle clucked her in
Do you have chicks?
CHICKS ARE PREDATORY VULTURES
BREACHING, SCREECHING, LEACHING
She chipped, snipped, ripped
Feathers ruffled
Then drooped from possible truths
Stuck in our craws
Super Clucks molted to dull biddies
Choringly, boringly, snoringly

T𝒽e Last Walk

— Richard A. Vasquez

That I could measure the distance
between the poles of my life
from the darkness of the womb
to the darkness of the ground
a distance unknown
a distance
in the light
given to me to see
given to me to find
that which I both take with me
and
leave
behind
to know the time left for hope
would be profound

that I could map the intricate heart
like a cartographer lost in a wilderness
exploring the paths from here to its horizons
a picture drawn
to show the way
to all its mysterious places
so others would follow

Continued ...

that I could find the astral directions
the north star
the constellations
in your heart
that would navigate me
to its center
to become the only place
left for me to go
the last place for me to walk
the remaining distance
in the light

The Line in the Sand

—Richard A. Vasquez

There are things that
exist to us
that we're
convinced
we can see
it's maybe not
the image of a truth
or the story
told by eyes of reality
but rather *something*
defined
in the hazy shades
of need
of want
and even when surrounded
by many

we feel alone

we think
we're moving forth
yet we find ourselves traveling
backwards
but
backward
or forward

Continued ...

it doesn't seem to matter
the feeling is always the same

things have gone past
that line
that we've drawn in the sand

when the honest words
that we once found
escape the mind
elude us in the tides of time
we feel lost
unconsoled
unanchored
however remember this
there are some truths that will always be
doing good
just for the sake of *good*
will always be your best compass

Continued ...

the unloved
will keep wanting to be loved
timid hearts
will continue wanting
to be brave hunters
and *errant hearts*
will move on clueless
without a care in the world
so what is it that you *seek*

what is it that you've *found*
what is it that now points out the road to you
how do you measure
the miles left
the miles done
are you where you're meant to be
was it worth
the cost

The Long Arc

— Richard A. Vasquez

The drum beat you hear
may not suit
others
but perhaps
you know
a dream does not fly as the crow
nor does
the river reverse
its flow
for those wanting
of
a new direction
yet
the arrow travels in an arc
higher than its mark
brought down
by things we cannot see
to be
where
it was sent
to be
by the
wise
foresighted
archer

The Move

— Anita Sharf

FRAGILE
HANDLE WITH CARE
THIS SIDE UP
Cartons are designated
Room by room
With bated air
They wait to accept
Jigsaw pieces of lives
Save for last
The strongest carton
I must not shatter
Chip or crack
Label must read
PRESERVED FOR CONTINUITY
OPEN FIRST

Thoughts

— Larry Ballard

Write it down
before it goes away
Thoughts are ethereal
little creatures
who pass through
and reincarnate
before you can
reach for a pen

Time

— Larry Ballard

No time.
Can't stop to enjoy
cause it doesn't rhyme.

A little sip to get the flavor
no deep droughts
Smelling
roses on a chance breeze

No escape
from the room with no room
where I can't be

Unveiled

— Larry Ballard

It's easier to see now than then.
Not as much of what I'd like
what I'd need
Less of the old images
and desires
More of who it is which you are
and less of me intruding

I see you my love
More clearly than you
are aware
I see the softness between the
hard and th hard
less denied than before

The reaching less threatening
for each and both
as needs recede
and wants take force

The love
present and present,
untouched by lapses

Full and full
the love remains
For what I see
again and again
is you my love.

Waiting

— Elia Vasquez Fuller

A chattering flock of black birds welcome me
as I arrive back to my childhood town
They follow me swarming into a tree
where as a child I would run up your porch steps

Oh what a great big welcome you would give me
and what a sad goodbye each time I left
Through your brave waving smile
I could see the tears in your eyes

Fifty years have flown away since then
Standing here I breathe in deeply
a balmy breeze taking me back to yesterday
feeling the same sensation

The old abandoned house bids me a sad welcome
because you are no longer here to greet me
But the birds suddenly burst out of a tree
in a chorus of celebration

She's come back
She's here
After all this time
She's come back

Continued ...

I look up in disbelief
at the mystical black ring they form
flying around the faded yellow house
their birdsong piercing above me

She's come back
She's come back
She's here after all this time
She's come back

It's almost as if they too
have been waiting
Waiting here to welcome me
For you

Untitled

—Gaye V. Borne

Crystal blue sky ... meshed with cotton clouds ...

... wind dashing thru ...

TRY

TO

APPRECIATE

LIFE ...

do not always seek love —

LET LOVE SEEK YOU.

Meet the Authors

Larry Ballard

Gaye V. Borne

Jean Giunta Denning

Elia Vasquez Fuller

June Gaulding

Mark Gaulding

Ruth Gray

Linda Hennrick

Mary Kirk

Irene Knudsen

Larry Kueneman

Marilyn McNeill

Corinne Lee Murphy

Jane Ruona

Anita Sharf

Richard A. Vasquez

Author Biographies

Larry Ballard lives in Rancho Mirage, California. He served in the U.S. Navy for four years. After leaving the service he roamed up and down the West Coast working as a logger, steeple jack and factory worker. He got tired of the vagabond life and started school using the GI Bill. He received a B.A. at Humboldt State University and a M.A. in Clinical Psychology at Sonoma State University. Much of his writing is derived from his own life experiences and his work in the field of psychology.

Gaye V. Borne was born in Dallas, Texas in 1950 and raised by her grandparents in Santa Monica, California. Following her graduation from Saint Monica Catholic High School and a year at Santa Monica City College, she worked for General Telephone Company for two years, and then at Security Pacific Bank for five years. She and her husband, Robbie, were married in 1974. After living in North Hollywood, California for a year, they moved to Simi Valley, California, where they lived for thirty-five years. Their daughter, Michelle, now forty-four, is an educator and reading specialist. While living in Simi Valley, Gaye bred, raised, and trained her show and pleasure Arabian horses for twenty-nine years with a focus in Dressage and Halter Conformation. She has a certificate for Artificial Insemination and Horse Husbandry 1 & 2 from Moorpark College.

Gaye worked with her husband in their meat trading business from 1980 until late 2009 when they retired and moved to Indio in California's Coachella Valley. She still misses having her barn, tending to her horses, being greeted by neighs of "hello" and the sweet smell of freshly stacked hay. Gaye now has one cat and a sheltie, would love to take up golf again, enjoys taking her golf cart to the gym, belongs to a book club, makes award winning chili, and used to drive the 40′ diesel motor home which she and her husband traveled in. Divorced in 2019, Gaye now resides in Sun City Palm Desert, California.

Jean Giunta Denning was born in Rhode Island to Italian immigrants and currently holds dual American and Italian citizenship. She grew up in Ohio and moved to Southern California following high school graduation. Jean has an A.A. from Pasadena City College, a B.A. in Anthropology from Cal State University, Long Beach, and a Publishing Certificate from Stanford University. Jean was a technical writer for Blue Cross of Southern California and Pacific Life, and is currently editor of Occasional Papers for the Coachella Valley Archaeological Society. She has published her husband's autobiography of his military career titled *A Pilot First, Last and Always*, her own memoir titled *Growing Up Italian: a Family Tribute*, as well as about thirty books for various authors. Jean has taught self-publishing classes and currently continues to do free-lance editing and publishing. Before her editing and publishing pursuits, Jean spent many years as a community volunteer for Children's Hospital of Orange County, Bowers Museum in Orange County and Eisenhower Hospital in Rancho Mirage. Besides editing and writing, having given up tennis and golf, Jean continues to enjoy chorale singing, watercolor painting, genealogy, archaeology, and travel. Jean would like to thank Kurt Kaltschmidt for permission to use this DSC Class photo.

Elia Vasquez Fuller was born in Harlingen, Texas. In the early sixties her family left Texas and moved to Palm Desert, California. She worked at the College of the Desert Library while obtaining an A.A. degree, and received a B.A. degree from San Diego State University. Elia retired after working twenty-five years for the Coachella and Mecca Libraries as Branch Manager under the Riverside County Library System. She enjoys getting together with her three children, her granddaughter, her siblings and her friends. Planting flowers with her husband, Alfred, and watching them bloom, while sitting on her front porch swing, is her favorite hobby.

Elia has a brother, Richard, who is a writer in the same writing class. "Richard is the writer in the family. I am the family historian, writing down my grandmother's memories about the Mexican revolution and my own recollections about our family as we were growing up."

June Gaulding, aged 85, has been in the writing group for more than six years. She had always wanted to write her memoirs. This writing group has facilitated that wish. And she's expanded her writing to include fiction, as well.

June was born and raised in West Virginia. After graduation she moved to Washington, D.C. and worked at the Pentagon. She met a young soldier, Jack Gaulding, who was stationed at Ft. Belvoir, Virginia. She made her first flight on Lockheed Constellation TWA to Amarillo, Texas to marry. June and her husband settled in Lubbock, Texas where they raised their two children.

After she became widowed, June moved to Palm Desert to be nearer her children, Mark (57) and Janet (51), who both lived in California. She was a travel agent for ten years and enjoyed traveling to many exotic destinations. Many of these journeys have appeared in her writing. She had another career beginning in 2000 when she and her son and mother, Faye, owned and operated an internet-based book-selling business for ten years. Working closely with her now deceased mother was one of the great joys of her life.

June most enjoys her daughter's children, Jessica (20) and Shane (17), who live with their mother in Indianapolis.

Mark Gaulding, 58, was born and raised in Lubbock, Texas. At age 22, he did as country singer Mac Davis sang, "Lubbock Texas in your rear view mirror." Following college living in Dallas and Austin, he moved to Los Angeles and worked as a Flight Attendant for Western Airlines (and then Delta Airlines).

Living in California since 1985, Mark considers himself rather like a Southern California gypsy, having lived in Los Angeles, Long Beach and San Diego. He has resided in Palm Desert and the Coachella Valley for nearly thirty years.

Mark was a healthcare business professional having worked both as a consultant for many national firms and as an employee for Eisenhower Medical Center since 1990. He has a myriad array of hobbies and interests, including graphic design and reading. For ten years Mark owned and operated, with his mother, June, and Grandmother Faye, an internet-based book-selling business that specialized in British history, British royal family (particularly the Duke and Duchess of Windsor), architecture, interior design, cookbooks, art and lifestyle, coffee table books, to name just a few.

Mark enjoys spending his time with his small existing family, his mother, June (85); sister, Janet, (52); and her two children, Jessica (20) and Shane (17). His niece and nephew and their mother live in Indianapolis. Besides Jessica and Shane, the light of his life is his canine "daughter" Bella Bobble Head. She rescued Mark and his mother, and they are forever grateful and blessed.

 **Ruth Gray** was born in Portland, Oregon and inherited Puritan roots from her father and Pilgrim roots from her mother's ancestors. She won a scholarship to Whitworth College and played violin in the Spokane Symphony. She married the Whitworth student-body president and editor of *The Whitworthian*, and they lived in Minneapolis, Minnesota; Washington, D.C.; St. Louis, Missouri; Evanston, Illinois; and Madison, Wisconsin; and had two sons, Devin and Grant. When her husband was teaching at Northwestern University, Ruth worked for the Office of Economic Opportunity with families who had moved to Chicago from Appalachia. She founded the Middletown Child Development Center while she was in graduate school. When they moved to Bloomington, Indiana, and Richard became a dean, Ruth was appointed director of the Indiana University student YWCA, then subsequently the director of the Bloomington Hospital Medical Social Services.

After her husband died, Ruth returned to the Pacific Northwest to be near her mother. There she established the Stanwood Counseling Center and served as pastor to the Nooksack Native American congregation in Everson, Washington, later serving three large Methodist congregations as Associate Minister. Ruth has degrees from Whitworth University, the University of Wisconsin, and Christian Theological Seminary (Magna Cum Laude, 1986). She now lives near her son's family in Bloomington, Indiana.

 **Linda Hennrick**, from the time she was small, loved to read. "Why don't you write a book?" her mother once asked her. "But I don't have anything to write about!" she replied. Besides, her first passion was singing. As a member of a semi-professional singing group called the Young Americans (YAs) based in Southern California, she toured the U.S. performing at state fairs, on stage, and on TV. She also toured Australia and the Far East, but was particularly drawn to Japan. After leaving the YAs, she returned to Japan to live and work on her own. Later, she found work writing English lyrics for TV and movie theme songs, commercial ads, and individual Japanese artists, and enjoyed a career that spanned three decades. But as the years passed and the economic climate changed, jobs in the Japanese music business became fewer. So when she and her Japanese husband, Miki, lost their beloved home of twenty-five years on the outskirts of Tokyo to eminent domain, they decided to leave Japan and relocate to their second home in the Coachella Valley.

Semi-retired and wondering what to do with her abundant spare time, she began to write about her experiences in Japan and the music business there. Better yet, she found a group of writers with whom to share her stories. It was by listening to the stories of her fellow writers that she realized she had a lot to write about, and they had a lot to teach her. She was inspired. From writing her memoirs, she branched out to writing fiction. She's fond of saying, "I've finally found what I want to do when I grow up."

Mary Kirk is a native Californian, born and raised in the Bay Area. At the age of seventeen she left home for college at the University of Oregon, where she met and later married her husband of nearly sixty years, Dennis.

Her love of writing started in grade school where a favorite teacher would post the *Life Magazine* picture of the week at the front of the class. Each student had thirty minutes to write a story about the picture. "Often we had no idea what we were looking at — it could be as simple as a knot hole." Mary entered college as a journalism major, but graduated with a degree in education.

After being transferred to California, she got her real estate license and went to work for a firm buying, selling and syndicating apartment houses. In addition to her sales activities, Mary wrote monthly investment newsletters that were distributed to the firm's several thousand clients.

In 1985 following a move to the Temecula area, Mary purchased a Coldwell Banker office with a partner. The business grew to include two real estate offices, an escrow company and a property management firm. As broker/manager she trained new agents and wrote training manuals that are still used today.

As she approached fifty, Mary fulfilled a life long dream to go to law school. For the next four years, she attended law school in the afternoons and evenings in San Diego, while continuing to manage her real estate firms. Upon completion of her J.D. degree she returned to full time real estate, while teaching Real Estate Law and other classes at Riverside Community College in the evenings.

They sold the companies in 1998, and Mary and Dennis moved to the desert where they have retired and now spend a good portion of their time traveling the world. "I was delighted to learn about the writing class at The Joslyn Center, and am thoroughly enjoying returning to creative writing after a hiatus of more than half a century."

Irene Knudsen was born in Stockholm, Sweden. At the age of twenty-one, Irene was hired by Pan America Airways and brought to New York for training. Her first home base became Seattle and after a year and a half, she transferred to San Francisco, where she flew for another fifteen years. In 1968 she married a Dane, Jens, and moved to Palo Alto. They had three children, a boy and two girls, whereof one is adopted from Guatemala, after losing her parents in the strong earthquake of 1976. On the sideline, together with her husband, Irene started an antique business by joining an Antique Co-op, and imported antiques from Denmark and England. As a child Irene loved to draw and write stories, but did not grab the pen for writing again until the age of fifty-four, when she became inspired to try poetry and short stories and started a few chapters on a fiction novel. She gave it all up after moving to Palm Desert when her husband, Jens, retired. In 2002 Jens passed away. For six years she worked as a hostess showing model homes and sitting in open houses all around the valley. A few years ago Irene discovered Dr. Wade Maltais' Memoir Class at The Joslyn Center and started working on her memoirs, and still is.

Larry Kueneman, now eighty-eight years of age, spent thirty-five years in the field of technical writing, asking questions of highly trained and doctorate inventors to make certain the assembly instructions and operational guides he wrote were such that "the guy on the street could understand them."

Long after retirement he still asks questions to make certain he understands what is before him. You may have read some of his work if you bought a printer, or worked on a Honda automobile, or even if you were on an early space flight.

Marilyn McNeill was born in southern Ontario Canada. Growing up in a small rural town outside of Toronto, Marilyn attended a one-room school with her mother as the teacher until she was twelve years old. Marilyn received a B.A. in Social Science from McMaster University in Hamilton where she met her future husband, Stuart, a young medical student. Upon completion of Stuart's surgical training, they settled with their growing family in the renown Shakespearean town of Stratford, Ontario. Marilyn worked managing Stuart's growing orthopedic medical practice while raising their four children. Life's adventures took Marilyn and her family to the west coast, where she and Stuart currently reside as "snowbirds" dividing their time between Vancouver and Palm Desert. Marilyn enjoys an active life style and spending time with her grown children and many grandchildren. Marilyn's writing, imbued with a sense of humor, is inspired by memories of growing up in a rural community and family life.

Corinne Lee Murphy wrote for a living as a lawyer, serving as a Deputy Attorney General in Sacramento, California for most of her career. Even after retirement she took on projects for the Office of the Attorney General, investigations which essentially required pulling together facts and multiple viewpoints into an understandable "story." She did not write for other reasons until her late husband began his journey through cancer. He, many times, asked her to write about that journey, to tell their story. He said it might "help someone." She promised, and the promise nagged at her until she happened upon the writing classes at The Joslyn Center. With the encouragement of the teacher and other students, she worked until the book was completed. Since then she has attended the classes just for the joy of it. She described her work as ephemeral, written quickly simply for the pleasure of sharing in the classes, then never viewed again.

Jane Ruona, R.N. M.S., Geriatric Nurse Practitioner, was born in Milwaukee, Wisconsin. She attended the University of Colorado and San Jose State University. Jane worked as a Public Health Nurse, Nursing Supervisor and Geriatric Nurse Practitioner at the VA Hospital in Palo Alto thirty years and worked at Mission College Santa Clara thirty years.

Anita Sharf, born and raised in South Dakota, found out at a very young age that she loved words. Although she and her husband and later young family moved from place to place, she took that love of words with her wherever she went. An educator herself, she continued to take writing classes whenever she could. She and her husband now divide their time between the Coachella Valley and South Dakota. "To be able to fit words to thoughts and ideas I have is still a thrill. Sometimes the word or words I know I want get stuck in my brain. It takes much thought and patience to bring them back. When all goes well, it's as though my pen, pencil or computer has a mind of its own and flows freely with a panoply of words. Bless our writing group."

Richard A. Vasquez grew up in Harlingen Texas. His family moved to California when he was fourteen years old. He graduated from Indio High School in 1966. After high school Richard attended College of the Desert in Palm Desert, California and the University of California Riverside. Richard worked as an Intern Migrant teacher at Van Buren School in 1969. After his stint as a teacher he went to work for the Department of Labor as Job Developer and Educational Co-coordinator for the New Careers Training Program. Funded by the Economic Opportunity Act, this program provided entry level training for low income persons. He was also the owner of his own Home Property Management business for twenty-five years. Richard is now retired and lives in Palm Desert. He enjoys writing and visiting with his four adult children and many grandchildren. He has been involved with The Joslyn Center writers' group for about seven to eight years.

Index by Author